On Hollywood

On Hollywood

THE PLACE, THE INDUSTRY

Allen J. Scott

PRINCETON UNIVERSITY PRESS

PRINCETON AND OXFORD

Copyright © 2005 by Princeton University Press

Published by Princeton University Press, 41 William Street, Princeton,
New Jersey 08540

In the United Kingdom: Princeton University Press, 3 Market Place,
Woodstock, Oxfordshire OX20 1SY

LIBRARY OF CONGRESS CATALOGING-IN-PUBLICATION DATA

Scott, Allen John.
On Hollywood: the place, the industry/Allen J. Scott.
p. cm.
Includes bibliographical references and index.
ISBN 0-691-11683-0 (cl: alk. paper)
1. Motion picture industry—California—Los Angeles—History. I. Title.
PN1993.5.U65S35 2005
384'.8'0979494—dc22   2004044314

British Library Cataloging-in-Publication Data is available

This book has been composed in Gaillard

Printed on acid-free paper. ∞

pup.princeton.edu

Printed in the United States of America

10 9 8 7 6 5 4 3 2 1

Contents

Figures

Tables

Preface

THIS BOOK REPRESENTS the continuation of a long line of academic work in which I have tried to develop a comprehensive theoretical and empirical description of the geography of economic activity, with special reference to the dynamics of urban and regional production systems. As it happens, Los Angeles, and more broadly, Southern California, have figured prominently throughout this line of work as both research laboratories and exemplars. Here they crop up again, under the sign of Hollywood.

For the most part, this work has focused on attempts to show how the structure and dynamics of modern production systems give rise to massive agglomerations of capital and labor forming the basic building blocks of the large metropolis. I have also consistently maintained in this work that the causalities involved in this relationship do not come to a terminal point with the formation of urban centers, but always lead back recursively to the production system itself. In other words, cities certainly owe their genesis to basic economic processes, but they in turn play a critical role in the social reproduction of economic systems and are an essential element in the formation of competitive advantage. More recently, I have tried to deploy these same ideas in an effort to understand the recent rapid rise of cultural-products industries (in sectors such as motion pictures, television program production, music, architecture, fashion clothing, and so on), and the reasons for their dominant though not exclusive location in major global cities.

The present volume picks up on these themes and reexamines them in an extended essay on the economic geography of the motion picture industry of Hollywood. Along with Silicon Valley and the business and financial clusters of New York and the City of London, Hollywood must surely rank as one of the most highly developed agglomerations of productive activity anywhere, and a major urban phenomenon in its own right. That said, and despite the huge amounts of literature that have been written about Hollywood (in the form of business commentaries, film criticism, cultural analysis, exposés, hagiographies of celebrities and their assorted hangers-on, etc.), its development and functions as an operating industrial system, tightly bound up in both local and global relations of reciprocity and competition, are comparatively little understood.

In this account, I proceed on the basis of a conception of the Hollywood motion picture industry as an organized ecology of specialized but complementary production activities and labor tasks, and I show how it came into being, how it grew over the twentieth century, and how—for better or worse—it came to dominate global markets in entertainment. What is of special interest in the present instance is the circumstance that the outputs of Hollywood have both a *cultural* and an *economic* meaning. They are, in particular, artifacts that work powerfully on a broad cognitive register but that also have an important impact on the gross domestic product of the United States. As current processes of globalization run their course, the cultural and economic power of Hollywood is evoking a growing number of complex political responses in different parts of the world. At the same time, perhaps ironically, globalization is making it possible to raise a question that in the recent past has more or less been consigned to the dead letter category, namely, is it plausible to think that other centers of cinematographic production in other parts of the world might rise to challenge Hollywood's hegemony?

On Hollywood is centrally concerned with just such issues as these. It is thus not only a descriptive account of Hollywood as an industrial agglomeration in the narrow sense but also a theoretical inquiry into the wider problem of urban-*cum*-regional economic development in the context of intensifying globalization. Of equal importance, the book is concerned with the broad question of the commodification of culture, and with the ways in which basic physical conditions of production and the symbolic content of outputs are intertwined with one another in the modern economy. As a corollary, the book is also preoccupied with the phenomenon of *place* as a unit of social and economic organization and as a concentrated locus of conventionalized human practices whose characteristics leave deep traces on the form and cognitive meanings of products (and above all *cultural* products) as they emerge from localized systems of industrial activity.

The book will appeal, I hope, to a wide audience. It will in the first instance appeal to all who have a direct interest in Hollywood as a place where the actual creative and physical work of film and television program production is more intensely realized than anywhere else in the world. It will also appeal to the rapidly expanding group of economists, sociologists, geographers, urban planners, and others who have recently discovered (or rediscovered) issues of agglomeration and industrial districts and their relevance to questions about economic development and the routines of daily life and work in contemporary society. In addition, the book will be of special concern to those social scientists and culture theorists (including students of film) whose work is focused on the inner logic and meaning of the modern "economy of signs," as both a concrete system of production and a critical site of hermeneutic expression. The book will also be of relevance to all with an interest in the emergence of a vigorous globalized cultural economy over the last couple of decades and in the rise of Hollywood as the supreme source of worldwide popular entertainment.

.   .   .

This book is based on a core argument developed in three research papers originally published in *Regional Studies*, *Review of International Political Economy*, and *Media, Culture and Society*. I thank the publishers and editors of these journals for permission to reproduce material from these papers here. Previously published work incorporated into the present book has been extensively edited and rewritten, and the text has been considerably expanded by inclusion of a great deal of new descriptive, analytical, and statistical material. I wish to make special acknowledgment of the financial support provided by the National Science Foundation through grant number BCS-0091921, and without which none of the research underlying the book could have been accomplished. Supplementary research funding was generously supplied by the Haynes Foundation of Los Angeles. All maps and diagrams were drafted by Chase Langford, whom I thank for his promptitude and patient attention to detail. Finally, I thank Keiko Aimi, Romi Rosen, and Yixiu Ye for their invaluable assistance in helping me to carry out much of the research on which the book is based.

On Hollywood

CHAPTER ONE

Preliminary Arguments: Culture, Economy, and the City

ONE OF THE DEFINING FEATURES of contemporary society, at least in the high-income countries of the world, is the conspicuous convergence that is occurring between the domain of the economic on the one hand and the domain of the cultural on the other. Vast segments of the modern economy are inscribed with significant cultural content, while culture itself is increasingly being supplied in the form of goods and services produced by private firms for a profit under conditions of market exchange. These trends can be described variously in terms of the aestheticization of the economy and the commodification of culture (Lash and Urry 1994).

An especially dramatic case of this peculiar conjunction of culture and economics is presented by the motion picture industry of Hollywood. In purely geographic terms, Hollywood proper is a relatively small district lying just to the northwest of downtown Los Angeles (see figure 1.1). It was in this district that the motion picture industry was initially concentrated in pre-World War II days. Today, the motion picture industry and its appendages spill over well beyond this original core, stretching out to Santa Monica in the west and into the San Fernando Valley to the north and northwest. This geographic area is the stage over which the main features of Hollywood as a productive milieu are laid out. At the same time, greater Hollywood, the place, is not simply a passive receptacle of economic and cultural activity, but is a critical source of successful system performance. This recursive relationship between place and industrial performance is a recurrent feature throughout the space-economy of modern capitalism. It is evident, above all, in the propensity for viable production systems to emerge on the landscape as localized complexes forming a mosaic of industrial clusters scattered around the globe.

The primary objectives of the present book are to provide an empirical description of the genesis, changing fortunes, and current market reach of Hollywood, and to offer a number of general contributions to the economic geography of the cultural economy at large. On one side, the discussion can be represented as a sort of natural history or regional description of Hollywood and its various appendages. On the other side, it is an attempt to establish generalizations about Hollywood-like phenomena (i.e., localized articulations of cultural-products industries), and to decipher some of the basic processes in space and time that drive them forward. Above all, the

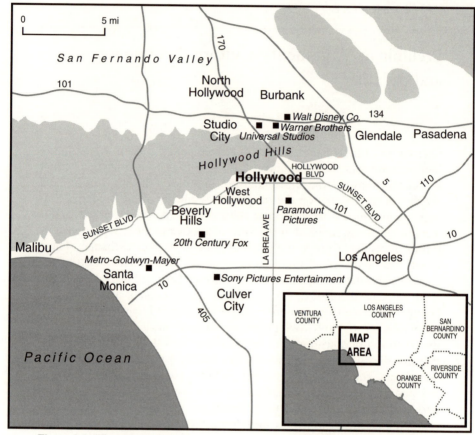

Figure 1.1. The geographic situation of Hollywood within Southern California. Selected place names and landmarks are indicated. Head offices of major studios are shown by black squares. Mountainous areas are shaded.

entire argument that follows is focused on the central question of how and why these localized articulations of economic activity are so frequently endowed with large measures of productive efficiency, innovative capacity, competitive advantage, and historical durability, and why it is that globalization, so far from dissolving away these features, actually tends to intensify them. Thus, the analysis presented here has theoretical implications that go well beyond cultural-products agglomerations as such and that provide important clues about all forms of agglomerated economic development in the modern economy, from high-technology manufacturing complexes such as Silicon Valley or Boston's Route 128, to business and financial clusters as found in central New York or the City of London.

THE CULTURAL ECONOMY

Culture and Economy

The cultural economy can be broadly described as a group of sectors (equivalently, cultural-products industries) that produce goods and services whose subjective meaning, or, more narrowly, sign-value to the consumer, is high in comparison with their utilitarian purpose. Bourdieu (1971) refers to the outputs of sectors like these as having socially symbolic connotations. It must be stressed at once that there can be no hard and fast line separating industries that specialize in purely cultural products from those whose outputs are purely utilitarian. On the contrary, there is a more or less unbroken continuum of sectors ranging from, say, motion pictures or recorded music at the one extreme, through a series of sectors whose outputs are varying hybrids of the cultural and the utilitarian (such as office buildings, cars, furniture, kitchen utensils), to, say, iron ore and wheat at the other.

There has long been intense debate about whether or not cultural products whose origins lie in business-oriented systems of supply can have any genuine merit as expressions of artistic or intellectual accomplishment. In the case of the cinema, echoes of this same debate resonate around the claims that are sometimes made about the superiority and authenticity of the *film d'auteur*, in contrast to the allegedly debased products that emanate from the bureaucratized factory-like studios of Hollywood. Contemporary theoretical commentary from scholars like Becker (1982), Crane (1992), or Latour and Woolgar (1979) inclines to the view that this sort of broad normative distinction is invidious. In brief, we need at the outset to understand all cultural activities in indicative terms as immanent social phenomena. This signifies in turn that the moment of genesis of even the most rarified forms of artistic or intellectual accomplishment, just as much as of the most commercialized forms of entertainment, is rooted in concrete conditions of life. If this argument is correct, it suggests that there can be no necessary *a priori* distinctions between the merits of different cultural products simply on the basis of the social contexts out of which they arise. This proposition does not insinuate that we cannot pass critical judgments in any given instance. Rather, it extends the field of judgment by leading on to the observation that every domain of social life, including capitalism itself, is a legitimate site of cultural production, and potentially a site of even the highest levels of cultural achievement. But if capitalism is just another site of the production of culture, it does not follow that it produces just any culture. To the contrary, the ever-expanding streams of cultural products that emerge from contemporary capitalist business enterprise are deeply inflected by this point of social origin, and this observation provides important clues about both the successes and the failures of these products on different levels of cultural interpretation, an idea that is explored further in the following section.

Fordism, Post-Fordism, and the Cultural Economy

Over much of the twentieth century, cultural-products industries were of comparatively minor economic significance compared to the great leading industries driving national growth and development. This was especially the case in the first half of the century as so-called fordist mass production shifted into high gear and as sectors like cars, machinery, and petrochemicals moved to the forefront of economic expansion.

The rise of fordism was accompanied by all-out product standardization and the pervasive deskilling of workers as central efficiency-promoting strategies (Braverman 1974). These technical aspects of mass production suggest, at first glance, that it was (and is) unlikely to be much adapted to the generation of the aesthetic and semiotic content that is the hallmark of cultural outputs. In the period of high fordism, indeed, a number of critics, most especially adherents of the Frankfurt School (e.g., Adorno 1991; Horkheimer and Adorno 1972), were giving voice to sharp condemnations of commercial culture on the grounds that its vacuity, meretriciousness, and "eternal sameness" induced a sort of ideological stupor in consumers. Even in the era of fordism, however, there were theoretical currents that sought to combine the basic productive dynamics of mass production with ambitious forms of cultural expression, as manifest, for example, in the work of the Bauhaus School and various less-is-more aesthetic programs. All that being said, and while business practices in the motion picture industry of the pre–World War II period were certainly greatly influenced by the ethos of fordism, they never embraced full-blown mass production as such. There was, to be sure, a prevailing attitude among the top echelons of Hollywood executives that fordist principles of manufacturing could eventually be applied to the production of motion pictures, and a number of the studios actually did try to reorganize elements of their internal operations along the lines of a large car factory. Studio managers enthusiastically endorsed this quest for efficiency, and they succeeded in streamlining many kinds of work processes. However, they were unable to push the process to its logical end and install mechanized assembly-line methods, for the very good reason that no commercially viable film can be exactly like any other.

In the years immediately following the Second World War, the flirtation of Hollywood executives with mass production was brought sharply to an end. The system now started to evolve in a different direction altogether, prefiguring as it did some of the essential features of today's so-called new economy. This turn of events followed on the heels of a number of crises that are described in detail in later chapters. The important point for now is that over the 1950s and 1960s, and even though fordism was still in full swing in the United States at large, the entire Hollywood motion picture industry restructured in ways that made it vastly less concentrated in functional terms than it had been before the war. The large studios (or majors) themselves never actually disappeared in this process, though they were subject to considerable downsizing as many of the activities that they had previously carried on in-house were steadily externalized. As a corollary, the production system was significantly reconstituted as a congeries of many small and medium-sized firms linked together in shifting coalitions by flexible production networks. The majors, for their part, took on a variety of new roles, one of the more important of which was to provide central coordinating services to the vertically disintegrated networks proliferating around them.

As these events were occurring, and as part of their inner logic, local labor markets in Hollywood were also being reorganized, above all, by the elimination of many types of workers from permanent studio payrolls. These workers were in some instances reemployed in smaller firms; in other instances (e.g., elite creative workers) they became freelance contractors of their own labor. In any case, long-term employment security in Hollywood was severely curtailed by these events, though it should be added that in contrast to certain other cultural-products industries, such as clothing or jewelry, Hollywood has never had much of a tendency to generate low-wage, low-skill jobs, in large measure because the long-standing guilds and unions have been notably successful in erecting institutional barriers to wage-cutting by employers. The basic labor of making a film was now, too, significantly reorganized on a project-oriented basis (Grabher 2001), with shifting, temporary teams of creative workers and associated technical workers engaging with one another in personalized, open-ended systems of interaction.

By the early 1980s, these sea changes in productive organization and local labor markets in the Hollywood motion picture industry were becoming increasingly evident in a large number of other sectors in the advanced capitalist countries. Various technology-intensive, service-oriented, and crafts sectors were most directly affected by these changes, and the overall trend itself was rapidly labeled by students of industrial organization as the expression of a mounting shift to flexible specialization or post-fordism, or some combination of the two (Hirst and Zeitlin 1992; Leborgne and Lipietz 1988; Piore and Sabel 1984). Today, these labels seem generally to have given way before the more neutral notion of the "new economy." Above all, a new creative economy comprising many different kinds of design-intensive, cultural-products sectors now began to move to the leading edges of economic expansion and innovation in the American economy at large.

Like the restructured Hollywood motion picture industry, these cultural-products sectors are typified by an abundance of small and medium-sized firms caught up in extended transactional networks, sometimes in association with larger firms that carry out basic functions of financing, coordination, marketing, and distribution. Despite this shift in favor of smaller firms, large-scale producers of selected cultural products have by no means disappeared; rather, in many cases, they have become yet more common as globalization has intensified. These complex features of productive organization in the cultural economy are mirrored in final markets in which a limited number of hit products (films, recordings, computer games, books, and so on) float within a mass of highly differentiated offerings addressed to a wide variety of specialized niche markets.

THE CULTURAL ECONOMY AND THE CITY

The great expansion of commercialized cultural production that has occurred over the last couple of decades has been very largely based in major urban centers. Places like Los Angeles, New York, London, Paris, Berlin, Rome, or Tokyo have always been important hubs of cultural production. Today, the same places, along with other burgeoning world cities like Beijing, Hong Kong, Seoul, Bombay, or Mexico City, are assuming even greater importance as foci of the global cultural economy, and they are the sites of diverse creative industries such as publishing, fashion, music, architecture, graphic arts, and, of course, film. Cultural-products industries, in short, are preeminently attracted to large metropolitan areas, and the most successful of all are almost always concentrated in cosmopolitan cities with extended global influence (Scott 2000a).

Within any given metropolitan area, firms in these industries typically gather together in tightly defined quarters or districts. More accurately, their locational pattern in the metropolis is usually characterized by a dense nucleated core of specialized producers surrounded by a more scattered pattern of firms, sometimes extending to the outer edges of the built-up area. Hollywood is just such an industrial district within the urban fabric of Los Angeles. The propensity of firms in cultural-products sectors to converge together in distinctive spatial clusters within the city is above all a reflection of an organizational structure in which each individual unit of production is organically caught up in a wider system of socioeconomic interactions, on which it depends for survival. Above all, firms have a strong incentive to come together in communities or ecologies within the city because mutual proximity often greatly enhances the availability of agglomeration economies and increasing-returns effects (or in a less technical language, benefits that accrue to producers precisely because they are close to other producers). By clustering together, firms are able to econo-mize on their spatial interlinkages, to reap the multiple advantages of spatially concentrated labor markets, to tap into the abundant information flows and innovative potentials that are present wherever many different specialized but complementary producers are congregated, and so on (Scott 1988a, 1988b; Storper 1997). Clustering is especially prone to occur in cases where the relations between firms cannot be planned over extended periods of time so that useful inter-firm contacts need to be constantly pro-grammed and reprogrammed. The formation of complex institutional arrangements and social conventions within and around industrial districts is also a factor that tends to reinforce the durability of localized production sys-tems on the landscape. Concomitantly, vibrant agglomerations of cultural-products industries become magnets for talented individuals from other areas. Capable and aspiring neophytes recognize that personal and profes-sional fulfillment in their chosen line of work can best be attained by migrat-ing to a center where that sort of work is well developed and highly valued (Menger 1993; Montgomery and Robinson 1993). Thus, visual artists are attracted in droves from all parts of the world to Paris and New York, and aspiring scriptwriters, film directors, actors, and so on, to Hollywood. In this manner, new aptitudes flow continually into particular clusters from outside, thus helping to enlarge their production capabilities and to refresh their pools of talent.

The spatial systems of production, work, and social life that emerge in this way are often permeated with symbolic and sentimental assets deriving from the distinctive historical associations and landmarks that invariably come into being in any area of dense human interaction, much as in the manner described by Firey (1945). Similarly, any urban area that is colo-nized by cultural-products industries will tend to accumulate place-specific cultural associations as the symbologies embedded in goods and services produced in the same area are absorbed into the local urban landscape. Producers in any given cultural-products agglomeration, then, no matter what its final outputs may be (films, television programs, recorded music, fashion clothing, etc.), will always tend to draw to some extent on local social traditions, mental associations, and icons. This very process is impor-tant in authenticating and differentiating cultural products in the percep-tion of the consumer (Molotch 1996). Equally, the meanings lodged in these products engender both real and fictional images of their places of origin, and these images are frequently re-assimilated in different ways back into the urban field. One example of this phenomenon is the romanticized image of Hollywood itself, not as the rather humdrum working environ-ment that it actually is, but as the "home of the stars." Another is provided by the frequent association, both metaphorical and literal, of Los Angeles with Ridley Scott's film *Blade Runner* (Davis 1990; Wollen 2002). In this manner the ever-growing fund of symbolic assets embedded in the local environment functions as a source of inputs to new rounds of cultural production and commercialization, leading in turn to further symbolic elaboration of the urban field, and so on.

Synopsis and Envoi

These introductory remarks set the scene for the detailed investigation of the Hollywood motion picture industry that ensues. The discussion as a whole comprises five main thematic arguments each of which addresses a specific aspect of the ways in which the history, geography, economic structure, and cultural energies of the Hollywood motion picture industry combine to sustain its long-term competitive advantages. The arguments are briefly summarized in the following points.

1. The historical origins of Hollywood present a number of puzzling questions. The first task, then, is to decipher how Hollywood made its historical and geographical appearance as a unique industrial district, and how it subsequently developed and grew. I show how Hollywood emerged as the main center of U.S. motion picture industry (in competition with New York) after about 1915, and how its pioneering model of film production helped to ensure its success by generating an expanding system of agglomeration economies. By the 1920s, the classical studio system of production was firmly in place and Hollywood had risen to unequaled ascendancy on national and international markets.

2. The studio system defines the "old" Hollywood. In the decades following the Second World War, a "new" Hollywood came into being as the studio system was transformed, and as a more diffuse organizational pattern of production came to the fore. As this occurred, the role of Hollywood as a concentrated industrial district was greatly enhanced, and its place-specific competitive advantages intensified. A critical moment in this process was the great extension of disintegrated, flexible production systems in Hollywood, and the radical shift in the role of the majors as they began to function more and more as fountainheads of financial and coordination services for independent producers in combination with overall marketing and distribution activities.

3. Industrial districts are made up not only of the units of production from which they draw their principal identity (in the case of Hollywood, film production companies) but also of the myriad firms in adjunct sectors that provide the critical physical inputs and services needed to keep the entire system operating. In several different parts of the book, we probe into the nature and dynamics of some of the more important of these

sectors in Hollywood, including soundstages, set design and construction, prop houses, digital visual effects, agents and talent managers, and so on. All of these sectors are bound directly and indirectly to the motion picture industry through complex webs of spatial and functional relationships.

4. Without labor, the production system is nothing but an empty shell. Moreover, the Hollywood production system depends on particularly large numbers of employees, and on the availability of an immense diversity of skills. A lengthy account of the formation and structure of the Holly-wood labor market is provided, with special stress being laid on its propensity over the last half century to become ever more unstable and risky. An analysis of the guilds and unions that play such an important role in defining the employment relation is also furnished.

5. An efficient productive base is one of the primary conditions for the economic success of any industrial district. Another is that effective marketing and distribution of final products must be assured. Firms in Hollywood have been notably aggressive on the marketing front, and have built up an extensive system of distribution channels through which their outputs flow smoothly to the rest of the world. The performance of the distribution system is therefore analyzed at length, and its tendencies to oligopoly are highlighted. This part of the argument takes us directly into questions of globalization, including a number of sensitive issues raised by the worldwide diffusion of American culture and its reception in other countries.

These five themes interweave with one another throughout the book, in a discussion that shows in great detail how Hollywood became, and continues to be, the largest and most influential cultural-products agglomeration in the world, but also how it has become increasingly susceptible to various forms of erosion around the edges. The argument hinges centrally on the critical role of agglomeration economies and localized increasing-returns effects. These benefits constitute much of the glue that holds Hollywood together as a spatial unit, and they endow all producers in the agglomeration with potent competitive advantages. I make various attempts to get at these phenomena by means of questionnaire data, statistical analysis, and case studies. However, the paucity of published statistics on the motion picture industry, and the barriers that stand in the way of obtaining detailed firm-based data, impose severe limits on how deeply the inquiry can go. My method, rather, is to proceed by piling up, point by point, a mass of rather disparate empirical evidence in an inductive argument that I hope is convincing overall but that admittedly falls short of finality. There is little in this book by way of direct advice to policy makers about how to protect and enhance the competitive advantages of Hollywood or other cultural-products agglomerations, though the discussion is replete with theoretical asides that suggest how critical aspects of these tasks might be accomplished. It thus

offers to policy makers everywhere a point of departure for thinking about
the cultural economy generally as a source of local economic growth and
development and as an increasingly important nexus of job creation opportunities in contemporary society.

Finally, a brief word about centers of cinematographic production other
than Hollywood is in order at this point. Hollywood may well be the largest
and most influential cultural-products agglomeration in the modern world,
but it is by no means the only one. For the foreseeable future, Hollywood
will almost certainly continue to control much of the global film industry.
Yet numerous other agglomerations producing both motion pictures and
television programs exist in other countries, and some of these are giving
evidence of new-found dynamism. From time to time over the decades, producers in these other agglomerations have sought to challenge the market
supremacy of Hollywood. It is entirely within the bounds of credibility that
some of them will one day begin to crack the wall of competitive invulnera-
bility that seems to surround American motion pictures, just as they have
done at various periods in the past. Also, above and beyond the main markets dominated by Hollywood production companies, there are numerous
alternative niches, both actual and latent. These niches, as we shall see, furnish opportunities for the production of many kinds of specialized films, and
they provide a strategic platform from which more aggressive market contestation by firms outside of Hollywood can be attempted. The problem
here is the relative underdevelopment of film marketing and distribution
systems other than those that serve Hollywood producers. In this regard,
the Hollywood majors retain a forceful but by no means unassailable stran-
glehold over world markets for cinematographic products.

It is conceivable, of course, that globalization, by making it possible for
existing major producers to extend their market reach even further, will
bring in its train a continued expansion of Hollywood's competitive achievements. However, if the basic theoretical ideas on which the present book is
based carry any force at the end of the day, it seems probable that global patterns of commercialized cultural production will become more variegated in
the future, not less so. I comment at length on this prognostication in the
final chapter of the book, where I also deal with some of its wider political
implications. One of the significant implications of this alternative structure
of global cultural production, should it begin to materialize in significant
ways, is that it is liable to take much of the wind out of current debates
about cultural imperialism. An outcome like this would potentially open a
wider space for what I believe is now a more fruitful line of debate, namely,
the meaning of the massive process of the commercialization of culture—
wherever its geographic points of origin—that is in progress all around us,
and its progressive and regressive implications for social and political life in
the twenty-first century.

CHAPTER TWO

Origins and Early Growth of the Hollywood Motion Picture Industry

THE FIRST STIRRINGS of Hollywood as a center of motion picture production occurred in the years from about 1907 to 1914. Then, from 1915 down to the early 1930s this burgeoning cluster evolved into the dense agglomerated complex of production activities that subsequently came to be known as "classical" Hollywood. The present chapter deals with this critical period in the historical geography of Hollywood via two broad investigative thrusts. One of these concerns a brief general identification of a conceptual lens through which issues of the genesis and growth of localized industrial systems can be viewed in some theoretically coherent manner. The other revolves around an attempt to marshal a large body of information on the emergence of the industry in this corner of Southern California so as to achieve an interpretative reconstruction above and beyond a simple descriptive ordering of empirical outcomes in time and space. Needless to say, these tasks are fraught with much difficulty. For one thing, the conceptual framework that I offer is in large degree provisional and speculative. For another, the historical record of the business activities of early film production companies is extremely uneven, and gaps are especially evident in regard to the kind of data that might shed light on the specifics of the industry as an evolving agglomeration. Inevitably, then, the explanations that follow sometimes stand on fragile ground.

With these provisos in mind, I attempt to show how Hollywood developed over the first three decades of the twentieth century from a loose and rather chaotic collection of motion picture shooting activities into a dense interlocking system of production companies, anchored in geographic space by its own virtuous circle of endogenous growth. After its initial emergence, Hollywood (which at this time was no more than a straggling suburb some seven miles from downtown Los Angeles) rapidly established itself as the preeminent center of motion picture production not only in the United States but also the world. By the late 1920s, the classical studio system of production was firmly established, and Hollywood was now poised at the threshold of a golden age that would continue through the Second World War until the late 1940s (Schatz 1988). This remarkable series of events has been subject to investigation time and time again from the perspective of the film historian. In spite of a wealth of literature in this regard, there remains an important set of unresolved questions about just why Hollywood came to the fore as a center of the American film industry in the first instance, and how it established its early supremacy over a number of other equally likely (or unlikely) production locales. At the heart of these questions there lies the further issue of how it was that Hollywood came to be constituted as a peculiar kind of industrial district generating streams of localized competitive advantages that have sustained it as the world's premier center of motion picture production for close to a century.

WHY HOLLYWOOD? THE BIRTH AND DEVELOPMENT OF INDUSTRIAL CLUSTERS

Observations on the Early Motion Picture Industry

The very earliest stirrings of the motion picture industry in Europe and North America at the end of the nineteenth century have been documented at length elsewhere (e.g., Bordwell et al. 1985; Jacobs 1939; Musser 1994) and most of the details need not detain us here. At the turn of the century production in the United States was concentrated in the New York–New Jersey metropolitan area, and this is where the two leading firms at this time, Edison Manufacturing Company and the American Mutoscope and Biograph Company, were located. Films made by these and other companies comprised diverse short subjects projected in storefront theaters or nickelodeons. In the first decade of the twentieth century, audiences grew rapidly, and the number of production companies expanded greatly in the New York–New Jersey area as well as in other parts of the Northeast. In these early days of the industry, open-air stages lit naturally by the sun were widely utilized for photography, though indoor shooting of films using artificial light was practiced. It was also common for production companies to shoot films on location in urban or natural settings, and filmmakers were constantly searching for suitable background scenery. The cold, harsh winters of the Northeast presented obvious problems for early filmmakers in this respect, and so every year, teams of camera operators and actors would fan out from the main studios across the southern and western states, and even further afield, in order to enlarge their sphere of filming opportunities.

One location that early on attracted filmmakers from the Northeast was Southern California; and without any question, the climatic and other physical attributes of the region made it a favored venue at this time. Certainly, in the period from about 1907 to 1915, knowledgeable people in and around the industry were increasingly ready to proclaim the virtues of

Southern California as a location for the motion picture industry, not only because of the region's warm sunny climate and mild winters but also because of the diversity of landscapes that it offered (cf. Spencer 1911). This argument, indeed, has become enshrined in a conventionalized story about the development of the motion picture industry in Hollywood that is now more or less repeated without much further elaboration from one study to another (see, for example, Jacobs 1939; Palmer 1937; Ramsaye 1926; Sklar 1975; Torrence 1982; Zierer 1947). Some analysts have thrown a further argument into the ring related to the formation of the New York–based Motion Picture Patents Company (see below) and the strong desire on the part of independent motion picture producers to put as much distance as possible between themselves and the company, given its aggressive enforcement of the patent rights that it held on critical cinematographic equipment (Hampton 1931; Jacobs 1939). A much repeated but surely improbable gloss on this story suggests that a decisive factor in the choice of Los Angeles as a shooting locale was that it was close to the Mexican border, and hence producers who were violating the Patents Company's rights could easily make their escape whenever the authorities appeared on the scene. In addition, Sklar (1975) has suggested—perhaps not unreasonably—that the open-shop labor market arrangements of Los Angeles in the period up to about 1935 were an attraction to motion picture producers from the Northeast. Hampton (1931), by contrast, has claimed that San Francisco should have had a clear locational advantage over Los Angeles as a center of motion picture production, for the puritanical atmosphere of Southern California in the early years of the twentieth century made it distinctly inhospitable to the early motion picture industry and the people associated with it.

To what extent, we may ask, do explanatory sketches of these sorts really account for the emergence of the motion picture industry in Hollywood? Do the factors typically advanced constitute a set of necessary and sufficient conditions, or are they merely contingencies in a much more complex set of historical processes that might just as easily have led to altogether different outcomes? Of course, we must always take seriously the reasons that people give for their own decisions. Many representatives of the motion picture industry at the beginning of the twentieth century were unquestionably persuaded as to the superiority of Southern California as a production locale, and clearly acted on their convictions. Does this truth about the matter provide us with an adequate basis for explanation, as certain idealist historians and geographers might suggest (Guelke 1974)? Alternatively, is the genesis of the motion picture industry in Hollywood merely a matter of historical and geographical accident? Before we address questions of these sorts directly, let us look briefly at the broad issue of the formation and logic of industrial districts or regional productive agglomerations in general. Armed with whatever insights this exercise might offer us, we can then come back to the specific problem of Hollywood and the American motion picture industry at the beginning of the twentieth century.

The Dynamics of Locational Agglomeration

The essential features of any industrial agglomeration are represented, first, by the dense gathering together of many individual units of production in one place, and second, by the existence of strong functional interdependencies and overspill effects (i.e., externalities) linking these units together. The basic externalities at issue here reside in the inter-firm networks, the local labor markets, and the learning effects that are commonly to be found in agglomerated industrial communities (as already indicated in chapter 1). These externalities are frequently amplified by the physical and institutional infrastructures that almost always take shape within and around any given industrial agglomeration. In these ways, the agglomeration as a whole tends to generate streams of benefits in the form of increasing-returns effects that bolster the competitive advantages of every individual unit of production out of which it is composed.

There is a fair amount of agreement across a broad literature about these main points, though there is much debate as to the specifics of how each one of them actually plays out in any given instance. That said, there is surprisingly little in the existing literature by way of systematic analysis of the genetics of industrial agglomerations, notwithstanding a wide scattering of empirical observations about individual cases. Silicon Valley in Santa Clara County is perhaps the classic reference here. Just as stories about the origins of Hollywood have crystallized around a bundle of conventionalized anecdotes mainly focused on Southern California's climatic advantages, so has the standard account of Silicon Valley's birth concentrated on a basic formula about the combined activities of William Shockley (the founder of Shockley Transistor Corporation in Palo Alto), and Frederick Terman (the entrepreneurial dean of Stanford University's School of Engineering) in the mid-1950s. Sturgeon (2000) has recently pushed the Silicon Valley story back to events in the early teens of the last century, but without for all that deepening our explanatory understanding of the problem at large.

Let me hasten to state at the outset that I am not questioning the veracity of these accounts *qua* statements of historical fact. The point at issue here is a theoretical one. Most statements that I am aware of about the origins of industrial agglomerations rely ultimately on one or other of two interrelated approaches that in effect circumvent a genuinely analytical result. The first is the principle of *post hoc ergo propter hoc*. In this approach, explanatory emphasis is placed on the observed sequence of events along with the explicit or implicit claim that the sequence itself must represent the essential system of causality. In this sort of narrative, any agglomeration can in principle be accounted for in terms of a handful of founding events out of which all else flows. The second can be characterized as the "locational factors" approach. Here, various empirical attributes of a locale (e.g., physical characteristics, natural resources, human capital) are measured and then used to assess the *ex post facto* likelihood that a given type of industrial agglomeration will have taken root there (cf. Scott and Storper 1987).

Of course, the history of every industrial agglomeration can be told in terms of a succession of locational events; and of course, prior natural and social conditions may well have big effects on a region's developmental destiny. My argument here is that there is necessarily another and more fundamental set of issues to be settled before we can really understand industrial agglomerations in genetic terms. This argument turns on the intertwined problems of (a) when and how a simple accumulation of production units at any place begins to manifest signs of an endogenous developmental dynamic, and (b) how this place then pulls ahead of actual or latent competitors, and how it subsequently acquires a dominant position in extended markets, sometimes over long periods of time. There may be strong locational factors underlying the initiating events of this process; or there may be none (i.e., the initiating events are random); it may even be that the initiating events are a result of a misperception on the part of relevant decision makers. The important analytical issue, however, is not so much how the seed of the agglomeration is planted, as how, once its locational coordinates have somehow or other been established, the emerging local economic system is subject to a structured and self-reinforcing process of growth and development. In conceptual terms, we must distinguish between the planting of the seed and the blooming of the organism as a working, organized system. In other words, the detection of incipient locational activity at any place (e.g., in Hollywood or Santa Clara County) can usually not be taken, in and of itself, as the foundation of an explanatory account about its subsequent emergence as a dynamic agglomeration.

The discussion can be usefully extended by reference to the theoretical models of Arthur et al. (1987) and David (1985). These analysts show that many social processes start off as purely random events, but then steadily lock into systematically structured, path-dependent outcomes. For example, there are in principle several different and equally efficient ways of laying out typewriter keyboards, and at the turn of the last century, various options were available to consumers. However, as David argues, once the QWERTY system achieved a certain level of social acceptance, its further diffusion was by the same token made more likely because of the self-reinforcing mechanism of market lock-in. This example can be transformed into locational terms as follows. Imagine that a new industry has come into being and let us assume—to raise the analytical stakes as high as they can go—that the first firms to make their appearance in the industry have located on the landscape at random. Additional units enter the system one by one, but if agglomeration economies are at work, their choice of location will become progressively less random. Hence as each production unit enters, the probability, p_i, that it will choose the ith location or region is a function of the constellation of agglomeration economies at that same location, which in turn is related to (but is qualitatively different from) the number of units already there. This leads to a logic in which small random events can have a critical impact on the eventual spatial configuration of the entire system, which further implies that if the experiment is run repeatedly, many different final outcomes are likely to be observed. Over the long run, in any given experimental trial, and as more and more units enter the system, the locational pattern will lock into a structure dominated by one agglomeration because of the influence of localized increasing-returns effects. But at the outset, all locations have the same probability of becoming this dominant agglomeration.

Even if this account reduces the concrete processes of agglomeration to a probabilistic black box, it has the merit of providing a sense of an evolutionary logic in time and space. On this basis, moreover, it is possible in theory to identify three major phases in the development of any industrial agglomeration. The first phase involves an initial geographical distribution of production units over the landscape, possibly at random, possibly as a result of some preexisting geographic condition. The second and more important phase begins when one particular location starts to pull ahead of the others and to form a nascent agglomeration. This turn of events again can be the result of purely random processes, or it may stem from some peculiar conjuncture in the agglomeration's developmental logic. The latter point can be illustrated by reference to the aircraft industry in Los Angeles in the mid-1930s when Donald Douglas began producing the DC-3, which could fly faster, further, more cheaply, and more safely than any other aircraft of comparable size on the market at that time. Partly as a consequence of this breakthrough (and, once more, not because of climatic advantages), Los Angeles started to surge decisively ahead of production centers in Michigan, New York, and Pennsylvania, which had until then been the main foci of aircraft manufacture in the United States (Scott 1993b). A third phase can be identified, following this sort of breakthrough moment, in which the agglomeration, building on its intensifying competitive advantages, extends and consolidates its market reach, while other locations enter a period of comparative stagnation or decay. Note that we cannot necessarily predict which of the locations identified in the first phase of this process will become the dominant agglomeration of the third phase, except to say that it will have achieved this status by reason of its superior command of localized increasing-returns effects. In this manner, a historical process that begins as an open window of locational opportunity ends by lock-in to one dominant agglomeration (Scott 1986). Even so, new windows of locational opportunity can open up in yet later phases of development when, as sometimes happens, large-scale shifts in technologies, product designs, markets, and so on, begin to undercut the supremacy of the heretofore leading agglomeration.

Despite its rather abstract logic, this account of the formation of industrial agglomerations offers us a number of important clues about the early historical geography of the motion picture industry in the United States. The problem we now face is how to exploit this account in order to identify critical turning points in the industry's evolution while at the same time respecting the full complexity of events as they actually occurred on the ground. In order to achieve this difficult synthesis, we first of all need to review the simple empirical record of Hollywood's early development.

THE EARLY MOTION PICTURE INDUSTRY IN THE UNITED STATES

From New York to Los Angeles

As we have seen, the most important motion picture production companies in the United States in the first decade of the twentieth century were located in the New York–New Jersey metropolitan area, with subsidiary centers in Chicago (primarily, Essanay Studios and the Selig Polyscope Company) and Philadelphia (the Lubin Film Company).

In 1908, a core group of firms, under the leadership of the Edison Manufacturing Company and the American Mutoscope and Biograph Company, established a cartel officially designated the Motion Picture Patents Company, but more popularly known as the Trust (Allen 1976; Balio 1976b; Bowser 1990; Brownlow 1979; Cassady 1982; Izod 1988). The other production companies involved in this enterprise were Essanay Studios, Kalem Company, Lubin Film Company, Selig Polyscope Company, and Vitagraph Company, together with three distributors, Kleine Optical Company, Méliès, and Pathé Frères. The Trust functioned as a holding company for the patents owned by its members, and this effectively gave it monopoly control over the then most advanced equipment for both shooting and projecting films. The Trust was accordingly able, through its licensing operations, to exert massive control over the production, distribution, and exhibition of motion pictures in the United States. Its level of control was augmented in 1910 when it established the General Film Company to distribute its members' products throughout the United States. General Film was notorious for the influence it exerted over its licensed exhibitors, threatening to cut off their supply of films should they attempt to deal with independent companies. For a time, the Trust even managed to establish itself as a monopsony for Eastman Kodak film. These arrangements enabled the Motion Picture Patents Company to earn unusually high revenues while at the same time shackling the business activities of competitors outside the Trust. One outcome of this state of affairs was that members of the Trust were induced to make an ultimately self-defeating calculation to the effect that their competitive advantage lay more in cultivating their monopoly powers than in improving the quality and appeal of their films. This calculation not only opened the Trust to the scrutiny of regulators in the Department of Justice, but also encouraged its rivals to pursue what turned out in the end to be a superior competitive model. The ultimate consequence was that by 1915 the Trust had ceased to be a major force, and by 1918 it was disbanded entirely.

Meanwhile, members of the Trust and independent companies alike were dispatching teams every winter to carry out location shooting in the southern and western parts of the United States, where the weather was more propitious. For a time, Jacksonville, Florida, was a favored location, and in the early teens Kalem, Lubin, Selig, Thanhouser, and Vim Comedy, among others, were active in the area (Ponti 1992). Southern California was initially selected as a shooting locale when the Selig Polyscope Company came to Los Angeles in the winter of 1907–08 to film *The Count of Monte Cristo*. This was the first of many visits over the next few years by production companies based in the Northeast in search of temporary winter havens for outdoor filming. The first permanent studio in Southern California was constructed by Selig in 1909 in the community of Edendale (now Glendale) just to the east of Hollywood. A number of other companies also built studios in the region; these included the New York Motion Picture Company in 1909, Biograph in 1910, Nestor, Vitagraph, and the Independent Motion Picture Company in 1911, and Mack Sennett's Keystone Studio and Lubin in 1912 (Bowser 1990; Clarke 1976; Florey 1923, 1948; Jessen 1915; Slide 1994). In view of the fact that some of these firms were members of the Motion Picture Patents Company, it makes little sense to claim that they came to California in search of refuge from the company's agents. By 1912, according to Clarke (1976), there were 17 production companies at work in Los Angeles. However, most of these companies were headquartered in the Northeast, and the biggest studios by far were all still located in the New York area, which remained at this time the main center of motion picture production in the United States. It is one of the ironies of modern Hollywood, given the recurrent complaints over the last couple of decades about "runaway production," that its own earliest stirrings came about as a result of a process of locational decentralization.

Hollywood Emergent

An alert observer scanning the motion picture production industry in the United States in the year 1912 or 1913 would have noted the continued dominance of New York, the relatively minor recent clustering of decentralized production units in Jacksonville and Los Angeles, and a scattering of studios in many other parts of the country. In California, outside of Los Angeles, the American Film Company was flourishing in Santa Barbara, an offshoot of Essanay was making Broncho Billy films in Niles in the Bay Area, and the Balboa Studios were just getting off the ground in Long Beach. On the basis of this information, and supposing, for the sake of argument, that premonitions about the modern theory of locational agglomeration were already in the air, our fictitious observer would have no doubt hazarded a best guess to the effect that the main creative and commercial center of the motion picture industry would probably continue to be New York (which, furthermore, contained the country's largest concentration of writers, actors, producers, scene decorators, stagehands, and so on), and that other parts of the country would at best function as subsidiary satellite locations. Alternatively, even if our observer invested a high degree of faith in the virtues of mild sunny climates as a decisive factor in the success of the motion picture industry, he or she would surely be likely to suggest Jacksonville, Palm Beach, Phoenix, Niles, Santa Barbara, San Diego, and a dozen other similar places as being just as attractive as Hollywood, if not more so.

The initial accumulation of motion picture production companies in Los Angeles up to about 1912, then, can perhaps best be thought of as a rather arbitrary outcome, one that could as easily have occurred at a great many other locations. I would add the speculation that this outcome was probably also encouraged by casual but self-reinforcing gossip about the merits of the region for camera work as itinerant film crews reported back to their peers in the Northeast. In this sense, we can in part see the development of the industry in California as an illustration of the notion of self-fulfilling prophecies as propounded by Krugman (1991). At the same time, there was certainly no lack of promotional propaganda about the merits of Southern California as a location for the motion picture industry, much of it from self-interested boosters in the region. Whatever the case may be, the important point to be stressed here is that there is little or no evidence to suggest that the motion picture industry in the region up to this stage was anything but a distant satellite of New York. Not until the turbulent years from about 1912 to 1915 does the industry in Southern California really begin to show signs that a process of internal transformation and developmental change was occurring. This is a period marked by considerable business effervescence as many new production facilities were established and as others disappeared through bankruptcy or merger. More than anything, Hollywood was now starting to function as an incipient agglomeration with its own distinctive production system and local labor market, and with innovative capacities (in terms of both commercial practices and film content) that seemed to set it well apart from the more established studios of the Northeast. By 1915, as figure 2.1 shows, Hollywood and its surrounding area were beginning to assume the geographic shape of a prototypical industrial district. This trend was reinforced by the

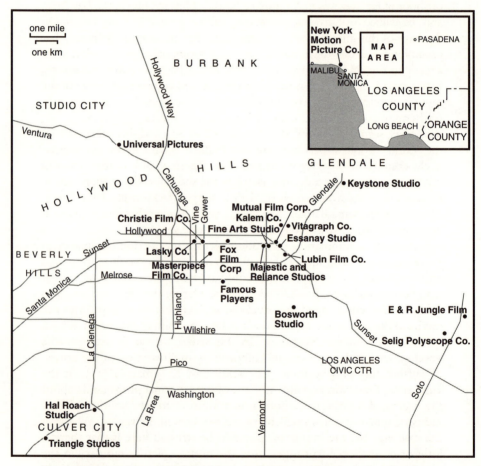

Figure 2.1. Locations of motion picture production companies in Los Angeles, 1915. Addresses were obtained from a great diversity of publications, directories, and web pages. The information shown is probably not complete.

arrival of a number of critical figures from New York, each of whom helped to establish a dynamic Hollywood cinema as such. One of these figures was Cecil B. DeMille, who came to Los Angeles in 1913 on behalf of the Lasky Feature Play Company, and proceeded to film *The Squaw Man* in a barn at the intersection of Selma and Vine Streets. *The Squaw Man* became the first Hollywood film to enjoy major international success. A year later, Zukor's Famous Players Company also established production facilities in Hollywood; in 1916 it merged with the Lasky Company, forming the Famous Players–Lasky Corporation, the forerunner of Paramount, Hollywood's first true major. In addition, in 1915, the Fox Film Corporation set up operations in Hollywood, and Carl Laemmle launched Universal Pictures, which he established on a large lot at Universal City in the San Fernando Valley. Lasky, Zukor, Fox, and Laemmle were among the first Hollywood moguls. All four were Jewish immigrant entrepreneurs with modest backgrounds in sales and showmanship, in contradistinction to the more patrician figures (with the exception of Lubin) who were associated with the Motion Picture Patents Company.

While the business practices of the members of the Trust were centrally focused on equipment licensing revenues, the new production companies of Hollywood were much more concerned with film content and audience appeal (Jones 2001). One index of the difference between the two groups is that members of the Trust tended to resist the production of feature films in favor of less demanding short films, whereas the leading independents were much more aggressive in developing feature films—though we should probably not try to press this particular point of contrast too far.[1] Another significant difference is that the Trust was much more opposed than the independents to the emerging star system in the motion picture industry, and many of its members refused to divulge personal information about or even the names of their main performers. Yet as early as the mid-teens, independent producers were discovering that stars could be an important device for branding films and thereby helping to expand and stabilize markets. At the same time, firms belonging to the Trust rented out their films by the foot irrespective of content, a practice that underlines their relative insensitivity to the market value of content and product quality. The Hollywood independents, by contrast, started at an early stage to concentrate on feature films and to promote individual stars, while simultaneously building strong narrative dynamics into the films that they made (Allen 1976; Hampton 1931).

One of the decisive moments of this trend was the production of *Tess of the Storm Country* by the Famous Players Film Company in Southern

[1] In 1915, four of the leading independent companies, Famous Players, Fox, Lasky, and Universal, produced on average 37 feature films each. The members of the Trust produced on average 13 feature films each. These data were calculated from Hanson (1988).

California in 1914, a film that propelled Mary Pickford into superstar status. The vitality of the nascent Hollywood cluster was further fortified when Charles Chaplin went to work for Mack Sennett's Keystone Studio in 1913. To be sure, Chaplin moved on in 1914 to the Essanay studio at Niles in the Bay Area, only to return to Hollywood in 1916 with the Mutual Film Corporation, and then to set up his own studio (at the intersection of La Brea and Hollywood Boulevards) in 1918. Other Hollywood stars who came to prominence at this time were Douglas Fairbanks, William S. Hart, and Roscoe Arbuckle, representing, respectively, the swashbuckling adventure films, westerns, and comedies that were now (among other genre films) pouring out of Hollywood. Above all, the figures of Thomas Ince and D. W. Griffith tower over this historical moment. They exerted an influence on both the business and aesthetic practices of Hollywood production companies that alone was sufficient to push them to the leading edge of the industry.

Ince can be seen as one of the principal harbingers of the full-blown studio system. He arrived in Southern California in 1911 to produce cowboy films for the New York Motion Picture Company, establishing a studio known familiarly as Inceville in Santa Monica at the point where Sunset Boulevard meets the Pacific Ocean. Ince was the first producer to attempt to industrialize the whole filmmaking process and to push it beyond the rather simple set of craft practices that had largely constituted it up to that point. Instead of the makeshift methods and improvisation that were widely characteristic of film production at this time, Ince developed more systematic procedures based on his perfection of the continuity script. Above all, he separated the conception of motion pictures from their production, and broke the shooting process down into disconnected segments that he then reassembled into the final film at the postproduction stage. The continuity script thus functioned much like an industrial blueprint. On these foundations, an advanced division of labor started to make its appearance in the motion picture industry, and the elements of a modern managerial model of production were installed (Bordwell et al. 1985; Staiger 1982). The net result was to endow film production companies with a greatly enhanced ability to control the entire fabrication process, and, above all, to exert discipline over the conduct of talent workers like writers, directors, and actors.

If Ince is notable for his managerial creativity, D. W. Griffith is celebrated above all for his influence on the whole conception of cinematic entertainment. He is credited by Florey (1923) and O'Dell (1970) with developing the close-up, the flashback, and fade-out techniques in cinematography, among other innovations. Griffith's career is a long and complicated one. After an already active professional life in motion pictures on both the East and West coasts, Griffith achieved his most important directorial success in

1915 with the production of *Birth of a Nation* for the Epoch Producing Corporation. Shot at the Fine Arts Studio located at the intersection of Hollywood and Sunset boulevards, the film is reputed to have cost $85,000, making it five times more expensive than any other film made up to that time (Clarke 1976; Stern 1945). Moreover, it earned gross revenues of over $18 million, far more than the earnings of any other motion picture of the silent era, so that it stands on record by a very large margin as the first blockbuster. *Birth of a Nation* also helped to make cinema acceptable to the respectable middle class in America, which had hitherto largely considered the medium to be an offensively inferior form of entertainment (Izod 1988; Slide 1994). This surge in Hollywood's business fortunes and reputation helped to push the entire complex to the undisputed forefront of motion picture production. In 1916 Griffith developed an even more grandiose project into which he poured all of his profits from *Birth of a Nation*. This was the film *Intolerance*, produced on the enormous budget for the time of $2 million. Although the film failed commercially, the economic energies that it set in motion via its huge cast and lavish sets (built on a lot just across the street from where *Birth of a Nation* had been produced) sent sizable ripples through the local community. These two films together stand not only as monuments to early cinematic art, but also as major business experiments that contributed significantly to Hollywood's forward momentum. If there is any breakthrough moment to be discovered in the development of Hollywood as a productive agglomeration, it can surely be best identified with these two films of D. W. Griffith.

More generally, Hollywood's critical take off as an industrial complex hinges around the year 1915 when an extraordinarily potent combination of commercial and cultural forces—in addition to Ince and Griffith—came together, and when Hollywood was finally transformed from its status as a simple branch-plant extension of New York's motion picture industry to a composite system with a strong endogenous dynamic of development. After 1915, the number of workers and establishments in the Hollywood motion picture industry shot up both absolutely and relative to the rest of the country. The *Motion Picture Studio Directory* of 1918[2] records a total of 37 studios in Los Angeles, 45 in New York, and a scattering in other places, including 7 in Jacksonville and 6 in Chicago. By 1919, 80 percent of the world's motion pictures were being made in California (Davis 1993). Two years later, in 1921, according to the first *Biennial Census of Manufactures* published by the U.S. Bureau of the Census, the motion picture industry in California as a whole had 68 establishments employing

---

[2] Published in Los Angeles by the *Motion Picture News*.

5,329 workers, as compared with New York state's 20 establishments and 3,922 workers.

It would certainly be a stretch of economic logic to try to account for this growth purely by reference to the physical characteristics of Southern California; at most, they played a contingent and less than necessary role. Rather, the rise of Hollywood can best be seen as a consequence of the vigorous system of productive organization that evolved out of the disparate collection of branch plants that had drifted into the area in the six or seven years before 1915. The physical geography of Southern California is in fact irrelevant to the question of how the dominating economic and cultural power of the Hollywood motion picture industry came to be socially constructed, and it cannot be sufficiently reiterated that a mature motion picture industrial complex might have sprung up virtually anywhere in the United States in the early years of the twentieth century. However, once the forces of agglomeration are set in motion at any location, systemically rooted competitive advantages help to sustain an upward spiral of growth and development, while making it increasingly difficult for other locations to capture markets. In many respects, New York, with its decisive first-mover advantages, might well have been expected to forge ahead as the main production center in the United States, just as primary metropolitan areas in Western Europe e.g., London, Paris, and Berlin maintained their lead as centers of motion picture production in their respective countries despite their cold and humid winters. (If climatic conditions were so critical to success at this time, we would also need to explain not only why the French film industry did not migrate in any important degree to the Côte d'Azur, but also how the industry, despite its location in Paris, managed to dominate world trade in motion pictures up to World War I [Jarvie 1992; Thompson 1985].) New York producers enjoyed the benefits of a head start, but squandered their initial advantages by pursuing a business strategy that undermined the possibilities of long-term competitive success. By contrast, the Hollywood independents, many of whom were aggressively opposed to the Trust, pioneered an alternative and vastly more successful strategy based on the cultivation of mass audiences by means of decisive business, stylistic, and content innovations. The superior dynamic of individual and collective development that came to function in Hollywood, in combination with the self-imposed shackles that hindered the maturation of the motion picture industry in New York, allowed the former to catch up with and then greatly to surpass the latter.

These remarks are in a sense a translation into place-specific terms of the developmental model of the motion picture industry proposed by Jones (2001). In Jones's model, the origins of the industry as a going concern are analyzed in terms of three main variables, namely, the coevolution of entrepreneurial careers, institutional rules, and competitive dynamics, representing the underlying developmental axes of any viable community of producers. Jones's analysis is not concerned with issues of economic geography as such, but much the same set of variables that she proposes has been deployed here to account for Hollywood's rise as a spatial agglomeration. As Mezias and Kuperman (2000) have argued, in addition, the multiple overspill effects that flow systematically through thriving agglomerations help to maintain high levels of local business vitality, and certainly were a significant factor in Hollywood's emergence. An essential point that lies at the core of the present investigation is that such overspill effects will always greatly intensify any existing propensity for firms to cluster in geographic space.

CONSOLIDATION: TOWARD THE GOLDEN AGE OF HOLLYWOOD

The final years of World War I saw a slowing of the pace of motion picture production in United States, and even after the war was over, the industry remained depressed for some time. With the dawning of the 1920s, however, the industry entered a new period of growth, most of which was now concentrated in Hollywood.

Among the important events of this period were the formation of the early majors in addition to Fox, Paramount, and Universal. In 1918, the Warner Brothers Company opened its first West Coast studio on Sunset Boulevard. The following year, the United Artists Corporation was founded by Charles Chaplin, Douglas Fairbanks, D. W. Griffith, and Mary Pickford as a distribution company to handle their independently made films (Balio 1976b). CBC Sales Film Corporation was established in 1920, and renamed Columbia Pictures in 1924. In the same year, Metro-Goldwyn-Mayer was born out of a complex merger operation, and RKO, which similarly had its origins in a series of mergers, was formed in 1928. By this time, the main outlines of classical Hollywood were in place, and its rise to international preeminence assured. Already, in the mid-1920s, 30% of the industry's total revenues were being generated by exports (North 1926). It was in the mid-1920s, too, according to Koszarski (1990), that "Hollywood" started to be used to designate the American motion picture industry at large.

The data laid out in table 2.1 help to summarize the main economic trends in the motion picture industry in the 1920s and on into the 1930s in the United States. The data are consistent with the notion that California had by this time shifted into a sort of second phase of development, characterized by rapid absolute growth and increasing national shares of both employment and productive capacity. Note in particular that in 1921

TABLE 2.1
Employment in Motion Picture Production, United States and the States of California and New York, 1921–37

	United States		California		New York	
	Employment	Establishments	Employment	Establishments	Employment	Establishments
1921	10,659	127	5,329	68	3,922	20
1923	9,904	97	7,137	48	1,734	16
1925	11,518	132	n.a.	72	n.a.	18
1927	16,013	142	12,852	78	1,907	21
1929	19,602	142	n.a.	n.a.	n.a.	n.a.
1931	14,839	140	11,182	71	2,594	26
1933	19,037	92	16,417	39	1,748	24
1935	27,592	129	23,278	75	3,240	24
1937	34,624	83	30,408	35	2,883	21

Source: United States Department of Commerce, Bureau of the Census, *Biennial Census of Manufactures.*
n.a. = not available

California had just under 50% of all employment in the U.S. motion picture industry, but that by 1937 its share had grown to 87.8%. The industry correspondingly stagnated in New York, with its share of employment falling from 36.8% to 8.3% over the same period. Not only was Hollywood consolidating its technical, commercial, and cultural domination of the entire motion picture industry at this time, it was also widening and deepening its roots in the local area. It was in the 1920s that the basic distinction—still in use—between majors and independents came into being,[3] and by 1930 the Hollywood production system could be succinctly described as comprising eight majors together with a surrounding constellation of smaller independents. The majors themselves were further subdivided into the so-called "big five" (Twentieth Century Fox, MGM, Paramount, RKO, and Warner Brothers), and the "little three" (Columbia, United Artists, and Universal Pictures), the distinction between them deriving from the fact that the former group owned extensive first-run exhibition facilities while the latter did not.

The spatial distribution of majors and independents in and around Hollywood in 1930 is displayed in figure 2.2. In comparison with figure 2.1, the pattern here shows that a modest westward shift into central Hollywood had taken place in the intervening fifteen years and that a considerable locational intensification of the industry had occurred. Observe, in particular, the conspicuous clustering of production companies in the vicinity of Gower Street between Sunset and Santa Monica Boulevards. Many production companies making cheap B movies converged together in this area, most of them small independents, though Columbia was also one of their number. As a consequence, the area was widely referred to as Poverty Row, or alternatively, Gower Gulch in reference to the large number of cowboy films made locally and the throngs of costumed actors on the street seeking work as extras (Fernett 1973; Mezias and Mezias 2000; Pitts 1997). Figure 2.2 also indicates that some of the majors had by 1930 located in the geographic periphery of the main Hollywood complex, where they could find cheap land for their space-intensive soundstages and back lots.

As the majors grew by acquisition, merger, and internal expansion over the 1920s, they evolved into increasingly vertically integrated corporate entities. In the first place, the big five studios were aggressively engaged in vertical integration of all three main phases of the motion picture business, namely, production, distribution, and exhibition. By the late 1920s the big five controlled significant segments of the entire industry and exercised something close to monopoly power over first-run theaters. In cases where they did not own the theaters, they were nevertheless able to circumvent

[3] The term "independent" in this context is to be distinguished from its earlier usage to designate a production company that was not a member of the Motion Picture Patents Company.

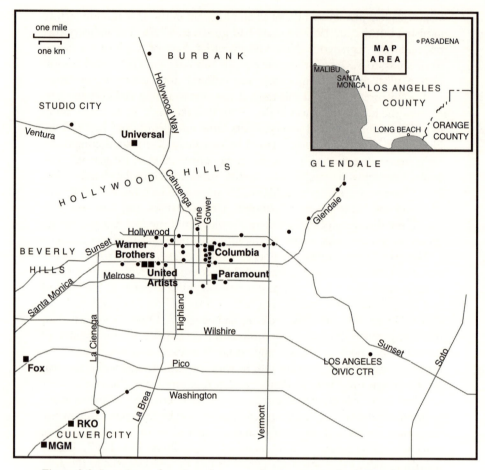

Figure 2.2. Locations of motion picture production companies in Los Angeles, 1930. Majors are represented by squares. Addresses were obtained from a great diversity of publications, directories, and web pages. The information shown is probably not complete.

open market competition by means of blind-booking and block-booking strategies (Huettig 1944). In the second place, the production phase itself was also subject to a high level of vertical integration. Thus, in the major studios all the main tasks of filmmaking—writing, directing, acting, sound-stage operation, musical composition and performance, film editing, and so on—were largely brought together under one structure of ownership and employment, and the most talented workers were signed up to long-term contracts, usually of seven years' duration. Some of the effect of this second form of vertical integration on plant size is revealed in figure 2.3,

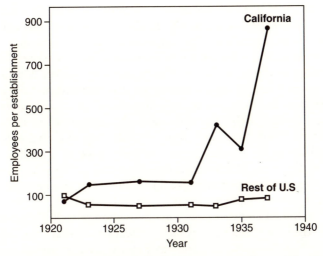

Figure 2.3. Average size of establishments in the motion picture industry in California and the rest of the United States, 1921–37. Source of data: U.S. Department of Commerce, Bureau of the Census, *Biennial Census of Manufactures.*

which shows that after the 1920s, the average number of employees per establishment in California's motion picture industry began to increase dramatically, rising from 165 employees in 1927 to just over 850 in 1937.

These two types of vertical integration in the motion picture industry in the 1920s and 1930s complemented and reinforced one another. On the one hand, the majors were in control of the entire motion picture commodity chain and could find outlets for their films irrespective of quality, hence allowing for stability in the organization of production. On the other hand, their contractual control of the most popular performers ensured that quality was sufficiently high on a sufficient number of occasions that mass defections of audiences did not occur. As the next chapter shows, the Paramount Decree of 1948 undercut this model of productive organization and ushered in a new Hollywood in which vertical *dis*integration was now the main trend in the evolution of productive organization (Storper and Christopherson 1987).

Still, it would be a mistake to think of the major studios in the 1920s and 1930s as being totally integrated over the vertical chain of production. They certainly embodied most of the basic functions of filmmaking, and they maintained a mass of permanent employees on their payrolls, but they also displayed a degree of flexibility in regard to certain production tasks that they could not efficiently internalize on a permanent full-time basis. Some types of employees at this time, even talent workers and skilled craftspeople, were hired as temporary or freelance labor by the studios, and Koszarski (1990) points specifically to the frequency of this practice in regard to cinematographers. Other types of workers that the studios often had recourse to on a subcontract or freelance basis were writers, dancers, character actors, extras, and so on. The studios were subject, as well, to the normal ebb and flow of labor turnover among their rank-and-file employees; their locations at the heart of a dense and suitably socialized pool of workers certainly helped to keep down the costs they had to bear as a result of these fluctuations. In addition, a wide array of specialized services and suppliers to the motion picture industry were to be found in Los Angeles at this time. One local business directory published in 1928 has multiple listings under headings like film editing, film laboratories, orchestras, agents, cowboy equipment, costumes and props, and animals, though we have no way of knowing from the information provided what was purchased by the majors and what by independent production companies. The majors lent out directors, stars, and other elite workers to one another from time to time, and jointly established the Central Casting Corporation in 1925 to bring order into the deployment of temporary labor in the industry. They also rented out studio space to independents so as to improve the return on their fixed capital investments (Fernett 1988). These observations suggest that classical Hollywood represented a rather more complicated and diffuse organizational pattern than is set forth in those accounts that insist on its character as a monolithic structure of vertically integrated majors and mass production. That said, much further historical research is clearly needed on this matter, and especially on the interplay between organizational forms on the one side and external and internal economies on the other side in the Hollywood of the 1920s and 1930s, regarding both the majors and the much-neglected independents.

Over the 1920s and 1930s, then, Hollywood can be described as a distinctive industrial district imbued with multiple spillover effects flowing from its internal transactional order and the dense, many-sided local labor market that had developed in the urban community around it. This local labor market grew greatly in size as migrants from all over the United States and the rest of the world moved into Los Angeles in search of work in the motion picture industry. Among them, we must count the great number of gifted foreigners drawn to Hollywood by its rewards and gratifications, and whose ranks included, if we consider only directors of the 1920s, such first-rank talent as Ernst Lubitsch, Friedrich Wilhelm Murnau, Michael Curtiz, Alexander Korda, and Victor Sjöström (Robinson 1968, 1977).

Like industrial districts everywhere, Hollywood also acquired an idiosyncratic superstructure of institutions in response to diverse needs for coordination and collective order as it developed and grew. In 1922 the main production companies collaborated with one another to establish the Motion Picture Producers and Distributors of America, or MPPDA (the antecedent of today's Motion Picture Association of America), as an instrument of joint representation. One of the principal early functions of the MPPDA was to regulate what threatened to become an explosive public relations crisis as general perceptions of Hollywood's moral tone in the mid-1920s (hot on the heels of a series of scandals) became ever more negative (cf. Anger 1975; Shindler 1996). In 1930 the MPPDA formally adopted the so-called Hays code, a set of self-imposed ideological and moral injunctions, as a preemptive strike against extra-industry regulation. The MPPDA was also greatly exercised by labor relations issues, and in 1926, it helped to engineer the Studio Basic Agreement, representing one of the first efforts on the part of the industry to ensure orderly management-labor interactions. The agreement was a simple two-page document, signed by nine production companies and five unions in Hollywood, that laid out a framework for adjudicating grievances and other disputes (Ross 1941, 1947).[4] Shortly after signing the Studio Basic Agreement, and in an attempt to head off full-blown labor organizing activities in Hollywood, the studios created the Academy of Motion Picture Arts and Sciences in 1927 to function essentially as an overarching company union (Nielson and Mailes 1995). The Academy, as initially constituted, had five branches representing producers, writers, directors, actors, and technicians. It failed to establish any credibility as a labor organization, and in the wake of the Great Depression, when the studios demanded that workers across the board take deep pay cuts, it steadily gave ground to independent unionization movements (Ross 1947).[5]

In spite of this concentrated development of productive activity and institutional order in Hollywood, the head offices of all the major production companies remained in New York. This arrangement provided top executives with a strategic base to deal with vital issues of finance, while they tried, not always successfully, to keep a watchful eye on the decisions of studio managers in Hollywood. This locational split in the industry's

---

[4] Signatories (on the management side) were Universal Pictures, MGM, First National Pictures, Famous Players–Lasky, FBO Studios, Producers' Distributing Corp., Warner Brothers, Educational Film Exchanges, and Fox Film Corporation, and (on the union side) the International Alliance of Theatrical and Stage Employees, the United Brotherhood of Carpenters and Joiners, the International Brotherhood of Electrical Workers, the International Brotherhood of Painters and Paperhangers, and the American Federation of Musicians. This information was obtained from a copy of the agreement in the archives of the Alliance of Motion Picture and Television Producers.

[5] The Academy, which still exists, has long since abandoned its original goals, and is now mainly known for its patronage of the annual Oscar awards.

functions was to last until well into the 1970s. On these foundations, Hollywood entered its golden age, a period of "mature oligopoly" (Balio 1976a) that lasted from the late 1920s to the late 1940s, when both the Paramount Decree and the development of television heralded an extended period of crisis and a reversal of earlier trends to vertical integration. The beginning of the golden age is marked symbolically by Warner's release of the first sound feature film, *The Jazz Singer*, in 1927 (Gomery 1976), though this in and of itself was only one expression of a continuing series of technical, organizational, and aesthetic innovations (from technicolor to Busby Berkeley's extravagant choreography) that reached into every corner of the motion picture industry. Hollywood was now manifestly dominated by the major studios, each of which came to acquire distinctive stylistic features, ranging from the lavish *mise en scène* typical of MGM films to Paramount's urbane comedies and Columbia's cut-price Westerns. The motion pictures that streamed from Hollywood's production system at this time evinced an unequaled command of narrative economy and visual storytelling that captivated popular audiences all over the world, though they were also roundly condemned by European intellectuals such as Adorno, Horkheimer, Duhamel, and Gide (Benjamin by contrast took more tolerant attitude) for the cultural and political quietism that they were alleged to induce. Hollywood's revenge, so to speak, can be regularly observed every Friday and Saturday evening outside the art house cinemas of Berlin, Paris, and London, as the avatars of the same European intellectuals line up to see the very same films today.

Conclusion

In this chapter, I have tried in both theoretical and empirical terms to convey something of the origins and growth of the Hollywood motion picture industry. In particular, the argument presented here can be taken as an attempt to add historical and geographical substance to the kind of location theory that comes out of the work of Arthur (Arthur et al. 1987) and David (1985), with its synthetic description of agglomeration economies, path dependency, and lock-in.

On the theoretical side, I have suggested that an analytic genetics of industrial districts must go beyond the simple description of sequences of locational events and delve forthrightly into the question of when and how virtuous circles of increasing-returns effects come into existence. A related important point is that static "location factors" approaches are deeply flawed, especially when they take an explanatory form of the type $a \rightarrow b$, where a is a suggested list of the spatial attributes of any given place and b is the claimed locational consequence. For the kinds of developmental problems at issue here, a more potent line of attack is to focus on the dynamics of cumulative causation and the ways in which the competitive advantages of particular places emerge endogenously, out of their own forward momentum. This way of proceeding recognizes that there may well be preexisting social or natural conditions that help us to account for the first seedlings of growth in any given place; but it also recognizes that this same moment of inception may be nothing more than a random outcome, with any one of a number of alternative locations being equally likely at the outset to evolve into a dominant agglomeration. By the same token— and Hollywood is the perfect example of this point—the actual shift of a given agglomeration into a leading competitive position often bears no relationship whatever to any conditions that may have exerted an influence on its initial location. This is another way of saying that the increasing-returns effects and competitive advantages that push development forward are at least in part derived from the agglomeration's own functional evolution as internal webs of synergy-generating relationships build up within it.

On the empirical side, I have tried to outline a brief historical geography of Hollywood showing how it shifted in the mid-teens of the twentieth century from being a branch-plant extension of New York's motion picture industry to an economically sustainable agglomeration in its own right. Much of this shift can be explained by the formation of a highly successful business framework and culture of cinematographic production in Hollywood combined with a powerful endogenous dynamic of development. It is no doubt the case that the early movie pioneers in Los Angeles really did believe that the region's sunshine and mild winters offered uniquely ideal conditions for film shooting activities, and certainly once they arrived there they made ample opportunistic use of the local landscapes. But Southern California does not have a monopoly on sunshine, mild winters, and varied landscapes, and numerous other locations in the U.S. South and West might just as easily have acquired (and some did acquire for a time) a reputation among early production companies as the place to be in the winter season. In brief, there might well have been an altogether different geography of the motion picture industry in the United States in the twentieth century from the one that actually came to pass. Among other possibilities, had the early business history of the motion picture industry played itself out in a different key, there is every reason to suppose that New York might have capitalized on its first mover advantages and retained its preeminence throughout the succeeding century.

After about 1915, however, the die was cast. The Hollywood production complex now surged ahead rapidly, and over the next decade it decisively consolidated its ascendancy. Much of Hollywood's success in these and succceeding years can be ascribed to its steadily accumulating assets (as represented by the wealth of sunk costs in its firms, in its talent, and in its collective order) and to the streams of economies of scale and scope that accordingly flowed forth. These developments laid the foundations for a golden age that lasted until the late 1940s. But even as the old Hollywood fell into crisis after 1948, a new Hollywood started to rise again on its ashes. The new Hollywood gradually and painfully reorganized itself around a highly disintegrated network model of production that actually intensified the play of agglomeration and has been one of the important foundations of its continued competitive success down to the present day.

CHAPTER THREE

A New Map of Hollywood

SOMETIME IN THE 1980S, entertainment industry analysts began to refer more and more insistently to a "new Hollywood," in contradistinction to the old Hollywood that had thrived over the prewar decades on the basis of the classical studio system of production (Gomery 1998; Litwak 1986; Schatz 1983; Smith 1998). This new Hollywood emerged slowly and painfully out of the profound restructuring of the old studios that occurred from the 1950s to the 1970s, and that finally resulted not only in a new business model but also in a new aesthetics of popular cinema. Over the last two decades of the twentieth century and on into the twenty-first, there has been a complex deepening and widening of the trends first recognized in terms of the new Hollywood, and this chapter is an attempt to shed some light on the way these processes are currently working themselves out.

Hollywood has always been identified, in one of its principal representations, as a disembodied bundle of images. But it is, too, a distinctive geographic phenomenon, which, right from its historical beginnings, has assumed the form of a dense agglomeration of motion picture production companies and ancillary services, together with a distinctive local labor market, within the wider context of Southern California. This persisting geographic base has been the arena of many and perplexing transformations over the last few decades. In addition to the breakup of the old studio system, five principal changes have had particularly strong impacts. These are:

1. The intensifying bifurcation (as I shall argue) of the Hollywood production system into makers of high-concept blockbuster films on the one side, and more modest independent filmmakers on the other.
2. The merging of the majors into giant media conglomerates whose scale of operation is nothing less than global.
3. The intensifying geographic decentralization of film-shooting activities away from the core complex of Hollywood.
4. The proliferation of new markets based on the packaging and repackaging of intellectual properties.
5. The penetration of new computerized technologies into all stages of the motion picture production and distribution process.

These changes, dealt with throughout the rest of the book, represent particularly important background in the present chapter, where the recent growth and development of the Hollywood motion picture industry are discussed in terms of the organizational structure of the Hollywood production system as a whole, the changing logic and dynamics of Hollywood's competitive advantages as a dense agglomeration of firms and workers and associated institutions, and the ways in which Hollywood distributes its outputs to wider markets.

ECONOMIC GEOGRAPHY AND THE NEW HOLLYWOOD DEBATE

The key research on the economic geography of the new Hollywood was carried out by Susan Christopherson and Michael Storper in the mid-to-late-1980s (Christopherson and Storper 1986; Storper 1989; Storper and Christopherson 1987). The basic argument set forth by these two authors revolves around the transformation of the classical vertically integrated studio system of Hollywood into the much more vertically disintegrated production complex that it has become today.

Christopherson and Storper describe the old studio system in terms of a dominant group of seven majors, each of them vertically integrated across production, distribution, and exhibition. They also characterize the actual work of making films under the studio system as a mass production process (see also Bordwell et al. 1985). They then go on to argue that the restructuring of this system was induced by two main factors: the *Paramount* antitrust decision of 1948, and the advent of television in the 1950s. The *Paramount* decision forced the majors to divest themselves of their extensive theater chains (cf. Cassady 1958),[1] and television drained off the audiences that had previously flocked to motion picture theaters. The net effect, according to Christopherson and Storper, was a dramatic rise in competitiveness, uncertainty, and instability in the motion picture industry, followed by the breakup of studio-based mass production, whose peculiar process and product configurations could no longer sustain profitable operations. Instead, the system was succeeded by a new order in which the majors divested themselves of much of their former productive capacity and contractual engagements, and became the nerve centers of

[1] *Paramount* did not, however, sever the link between production and distribution (Robins 1993). Had it done so, the entire subsequent history of Hollywood would almost certainly have turned out quite differently. Among other possible outcomes, the degree of concentration in the distribution segment of the industry might well have been reduced, thus opening up a wider market space for independent films of all kinds, and possibly inhibiting the majors' shift into blockbuster productions.

vertically disintegrated production networks. In this process, large numbers of small, flexibly specialized firms sprang up in a wide range of subsectors of the motion picture industry, providing both direct and indirect inputs of all kinds to the majors. This turn of events allowed the majors to cut their overheads, to pursue ever more diversified forms of production, and eventually to flourish in the new high-risk Hollywood (cf. Kranton and Minehart 2000). Recently, Caves (2000) has described this same kind of development in the creative industries generally as a contractual model of business activity. In Christopherson and Storper's account, the breakup of the studio system and the emergence of a new flexibly specialized Hollywood was allegedly associated with a "loss of control by the majors over production" (Storper 1993, p. 482), though they also note that the majors continued to play important roles in Hollywood as centers of financing, deal-making, and distribution. The authors go on to aver that with the reconstitution of the production system as a transactions-intensive congeries of small and specialized but complementary firms, the agglomerative forces holding the entire complex together in geographic space were reinforced and its regional competitive advantages secured. Sedgwick (2002) has added the gloss that in the wake of the *Paramount* decision, the majors also began to concentrate much more heavily than they had done in the past on making large-budget hit films with high production values.

The Christopherson-Storper story represents the first really serious attempt to understand the organizational and locational foundations of Hollywood as a productive agglomeration, and it must be given high marks for its pioneering analysis, especially in view of the fact that the shifts the authors were trying to understand were far from having fully emerged and were still very much subject to confusing cross-currents. Their basic characterization of the new Hollywood in terms of shifting networks of small, flexibly specialized firms provides us with eminently useful insights, notwithstanding the criticism to which this idea has been subject of late. Analysts such as Aksoy and Robins (1992), Blair and Rainnie (2000), Smith (1998), Véron (1999), and Wasko (1994), have all questioned the emphasis on flexible specialization, and have instead asserted that contemporary patterns of production in Hollywood can only be understood as an expression of the economic power and leverage of the majors. Other recent work that has laid stress on the continuing muscle of the majors has been presented by Balio (1998), Gomery (1998), Litman (1998), Maltby (1998), and Schatz (1997), among others.

In actuality, it is fair to argue that Christopherson and Storper paid insufficient attention to the durability and importance of the role of the majors in the Hollywood production system, though they certainly did not overlook this aspect altogether. For their part, a number of the critics—notably, Aksoy and Robins—can be faulted for their radical depreciation of the role played by small producers, amounting virtually to an exercise in ejecting them from any meaningful analysis of contemporary Hollywood. Aksoy and Robins are right to maintain that oligopoly never ceased to exist in Hollywood (though its foundations were greatly shaken over the 1960s and 1970s). However, they fail to identify the sources of the majors' market power, which at least since the Second World War has resided to a large extent in the internal economies of scale that characterize their distribution systems (Huettig 1944). The market power created in this manner is by no means incompatible with an efficient and dynamic production system based on flexible specialization *à la* Christopherson and Storper. In fact, in Aksoy and Robins's account, we lose sight altogether of the production system itself as a dense regional complex made up of thousands of intricately interdependent firms, and, by the same token, of the independent segment of the industry as an important locus in its own right of innovation, skilled work, and many and varied final products.

I shall attempt to demonstrate in this chapter that a more accurate portrayal of Hollywood today involves acknowledgment of the important roles played by large and small firms alike—by the majors, by independent production companies, and by the firms that supply both majors and independents with specialized service inputs. Also discussed briefly is the rapid globalization of Hollywood, a phenomenon that is reinforcing the importance of Southern California as a center for the more creative segments of motion picture production (because of expanding markets), while also starting to undermine less creative segments of the agglomeration (as a consequence of runaway production).

An Analytical Taxonomy of Firms

At the outset, we need to clarify some of the conceptual language that has already made its entry in the previous section, and to use this exercise as a platform for a more disciplined description of the motion picture industry. This will help us, in addition, to overcome some of the more enervating elements of the one–sided debates in the literature about the extent of flexible specialization versus large-scale oligopolistic production and distribution in Hollywood today.

In a very schematic way, any modern production system may be represented in terms of the size of its basic units of production (establishments) and the standardization (or variability) of their outputs. This idea is represented in figure 3.1, where scale and standardization represent orthogonal axes defining a space within which any given unit of production can then be

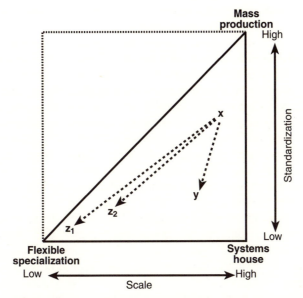

Figure 3.1. Schema of basic organizational possibilities in industrial systems: x and y represent old- and new-style studios, respectively; z_1 and z_2 represent common kinds of independent production companies or service suppliers. Dashed lines with arrows point to the situation after vertical disintegration.

situated. Three paradigmatic outcomes relative to these axes are identified in the figure. One of these is designated by *mass production*, which is exemplified by plants or establishments that produce standardized outputs in large quantities. Another is represented by, *systems houses* which can be defined as large-scale production units turning out limited numbers of extremely variable and complex products (like space satellites or block-buster films).[2] The third case is labeled *flexible specialization*, which refers to small production units that focus on a relatively narrow line of business (for example, independent motion picture production, costume design, or film editing), but where the specifications of each particular job, or batch of jobs, are different from all preceding jobs. (A fourth paradigmatic case, cor-responding to the upper left corner of figure 3.1, can conceivably be iden-tified with small-scale process industries—Adam Smith's pin factory comes to mind—though this case would seem to be of limited empirical interest today.) In reality, we rarely observe pure examples of these paradigmatic cases. Rather, actual production systems are usually composed of more or

---

[2] The term is taken from the jargon of the aerospace industry; see Scott (1993b)

less hybrid production units, representable by points at intermediate positions relative to the vertices in figure 3.1.

In spite of the notion developed by several analysts that the Hollywood studios had moved into something like paradigmatic mass production by the late 1930s, a brief scrutiny of their actual working operations reveals that this was not quite the case. Even less is it plausible to claim, as some have done (cf. Creton 1994, 1997), that the system approximated to *fordist* mass production. Notwithstanding the efficiency gains that flowed from finely grained technical divisions of labor, the use of continuity scripts, the constant reutilization of formulaic plot structures, and the move toward regular production schedules, filmmaking in the classical studio era was never standardized in any ultimate sense. We might argue, rather, that the classical studio can be represented by a location somewhere in the vicinity of point x in figure 3.1, which is to say that its technical and organizational configuration was marked by quite high levels of scale and a degree of routinization, but nothing equivalent, say, to the typical Detroit car assembly plant churning out identical models by the tens of thousands.

The old studios were nonetheless very much characterized by vertical integration over virtually all segments of the industry. Storper and Christopherson (1987) are probably correct to invoke the *Paramount* decision and the advent of television as being major factors in the destabilization of the industry's markets and its consequent restructuring, though the fact that very similar processes of breakup were proceeding at the same time in the music recording industry and in television broadcasting (cf. Hirsch 2000; Scott 1999) suggests that there may well have been more general trends at work. In addition to the rupture between distribution and exhibition, two other main organizational effects flowed from vertical disintegration in the motion picture industry. The first was the transformation of the studios themselves into something closer to systems houses, that is, large-scale (though relatively downsized) establishments now focusing on the production of many fewer and increasingly grandiose films. The point labeled y in figure 3.1 represents a typical case. The second was the emergence of masses of small independent production companies and service providers, as represented by points z_1 and z_2 in figure 3.1. This second category of firms comprises flexibly specialized producers and near relations in the sense that they concentrate on making a narrow range of outputs in comparatively limited quantities, and in ever-changing shapes and forms. With the disintegration of the old studios after the 1940s, firms of this type colonized an enormous number of different production niches, and they have continued to push out the organizational boundaries of Hollywood, a notable recent instance being the formation of a vigorous digital visual effects sector in the 1980s and 1990s (see chapter 6). As we have noted,

TABLE 3.1
Feature Films Released in the United States by Majors and Independents

	Releases		
	Majors	*Independents*	*Total*
1980	134	57	191
1985	138	251	389
1990	158	227	385
1995	212	158	370
2000	191	270	461

Source: Motion Picture Association of America, *2000 US Economic Review* (http://www.mpaa.org/useconomicreview/2000economic/index.htm).

Note: In this table, the term *majors* refers to both the majors proper and their subsidiary releasing companies.

even in the age of the classical Hollywood studios, small specialized firms were not uncommon, but in no way did they achieve the significance, either as independent film producers or as specialized suppliers, that they have now.[3]

The Hollywood production system today can hence be described in terms of a prevailing pattern of major and independent film production companies (see table 3.1), intertwined with ever-widening circles of direct and indirect input suppliers. These firms interact with one another in complicated ways as any given motion picture production project moves through its three main stages of development, namely, (a) preproduction, involving elaboration of the initial idea, scenario preparation, the raising of finances, set design, casting, and so on; (b) production proper (shooting), an intense period in which large numbers of workers are mobilized in directing, acting, camera-operating, and numerous allied functions from set construction to lighting and makeup (DeFillippi and Arthur 1998); and (c) postproduction, namely, photographic processing, film editing, sound editing, and so on. In practice, as the discussion will now show, the Hollywood production companies engaged in this sort of work can be segregated into two distinctive functional groups, represented on the one side by the majors and associated smaller firms (both subsidiaries and independents), and on the other side by a mass of independent production companies whose sphere of operations rarely or never intersects with that of the majors.

[3] Mezias and Mezias (2000) suggest that in 1929, vertically integrated firms controlled about 80% of the market.

A Bifurcated Production System

The World of the Majors

At the present time, there are seven major studios in Hollywood: Metro-Goldwyn-Mayer, Paramount Pictures, Sony Pictures Entertainment (Columbia-Tristar), Twentieth Century Fox, Universal Studios, Walt Disney, and Warner Brothers. These seven majors are joined together in the Motion Picture Association of America (MPAA), which functions as an exclusive cartel promoting their interests.

The majors have traditionally concentrated on the financing, production, and theatrical distribution of motion pictures, but over the last few decades they have actively diversified their operations, and they now earn as much if not more of their revenues through their specialized divisions in such fields as television programming, home video, multimedia, theme parks, and merchandising. Most of the Hollywood majors today constitute operating units within even larger multinational media and entertainment conglomerates (Litman 2001; see figure 3.2). Three of these—the News Corporation (which owns Fox), Sony (Columbia Tristar), and Vivendi (Universal)[4]—are foreign-owned. As Acheson and Maule (1994), Balio (1998), D. Gomery (1998), Prince (2000), Puttnam and Watson (1998), and Wasko (1994) have suggested, the growing complexity of these conglomerates can be ascribed to attempts to internalize the synergies that are frequently found at intersections between different segments of the media and entertainment (and hardware) industries. The modern media entertainment conglomerate accordingly functions as a sort of parallel in economic space to industrial clusters in geographic space, that is, as an organized economic collective, with the difference that if in the one case the relevant synergies are activated under the umbrella of common ownership, in the other they owe their genesis to geographic proximity. Figure 3.2 sketches out the ownership relations between the Hollywood majors and their parent companies, as well as between the majors and their most important subsidiary film production and distribution companies. However, the figure refers only to the feature-film operations of the majors and makes no reference to other divisions, such as television programming or home video production (but see next chapter for additional details).

The majors, as currently constituted, engage in feature-film production with varying degrees of vertical integration and disintegration of the relevant tasks. One way in which they proceed entails integrated in-house development, shooting, and editing using their own creative staffs and

---

[4] At the time of writing, the future of Vivendi is extremely uncertain, and there appears to be a high probability that it will renounce its ownership of Universal.

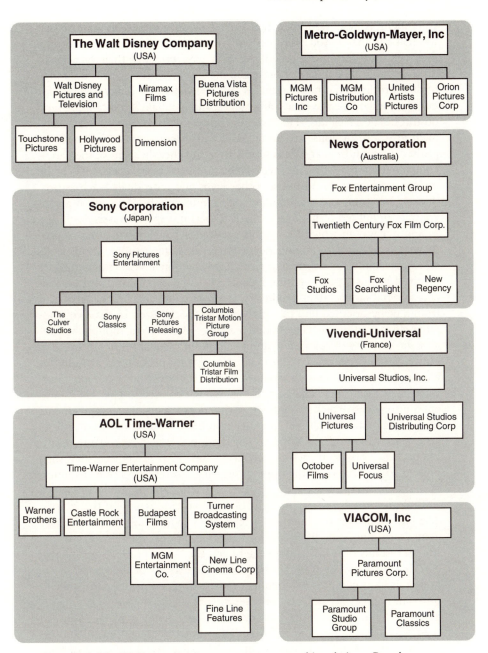

Figure 3.2. The Hollywood majors: corporate ownership relations. Based on information from various directories, reports, and web sites.

equipment as basic resources. It is important to note in this context that whereas the majors today are certainly more vertically disintegrated than their prewar forerunners, they never fully gave up all of their capacity to produce motion pictures in-house, and in most instances, the vertical range of their production capacity remains quite considerable. Many of them, for example, still own large-scale soundstages, and maintain significant pre- and postproduction facilities.[5] However, in contrast with the prewar years, each main group of in-house studio facilities today represents an independent profit center whose mandate is simply to treat other divisions of the parent company on a par with all other potential lessors. Equally, even when the majors produce a film in-house, other firms and individuals (such as producers, directors, and set designers) are commonly brought in on a subcontract or limited-term contract basis to perform specific tasks.

Another way in which the majors proceed is to work with smaller production companies, in arrangements where the latter assume various levels of responsibility for organizing overall production tasks. The companies involved in this type of venture include both the majors' own subsidiaries and selected independent producers, in projects that may range anywhere from a niche-oriented film to a high-budget blockbuster. In these collaborative alliances, the majors work under a range of protocols, though in probably the majority of cases these grant significant control to the majors over critical production and editing decisions. Typical procedures include financing, production, and distribution deals, coproduction pacts, joint ventures, split rights agreements, and "first look" contracts. The majors also enter into negative pickup contracts with independents, that is, agreements to acquire films (negatives) that have already been completed and to assume the tasks of distribution and marketing. Many independents assemble packages of scripts, actors, directors, and other assets that they then present to the studios in the hope of securing a production or distribution agreement, though few are ever successful (Acheson and Maule 1994).

Table 3.2 sheds important light on the evolving world of the majors. The table indicates the number of releases by majors and their subsidiary companies at five-year intervals since 1980. Note that the release or distribution of films is to be distinguished from the actual production of films, and that the majors release films made by themselves or their subsidiaries as well as films in which independent production companies participate in different degrees. By contrast, releases by subsidiaries owned by the majors are overwhelmingly produced by smaller independent companies. Many of these subsidiaries (e.g., Castle Rock, Miramax, New Line, Orion Pictures) began their existence as independents; others (like Fox Searchlight or Universal Focus) were set up as auxiliary units from the start. Table 3.2 reveals

---

[5] MGM, by contrast, owns no studio facilities whatever, preferring to rent these as and when they may be needed.

TABLE 3.2
Films Released by Majors and Their Subsidiaries, 1980–2000

	Releases by majors less releases by subsidiaries	Releases by majors' subsidiaries	Subsidiary releases as percentage of major releases
1980	94	0	0
1985	103	12	11.7
1990	109	27	24.8
1995	127	85	66.9
2000	104	75	72.1

Source: Calculated from information in Academy of Motion Picture Arts and Sciences, *Annual Index to Motion Picture Credits.*

Note: Subsidiaries involved in these counts are Castle Rock Entertainment, Dimension Films, Fine Line Features, Fox Searchlight, Miramax, New Line Distribution, October Films, Orion Pictures, Orion Film Classics, Paramount Classics, Sony Classics, Tristar Pictures, Triumph Releasing, Twentieth Century Fox International Classics, United Artists Films, Universal Focus, and Warner Classics. Some of these entities have operated as independents at various times, and some are no longer in existence. They are included in the present counts only for years when they actually functioned as subsidiaries of majors. Buena Vista Pictures is the principal distributing arm of Disney and is treated as a major. The discrepancies observable between the data given in table 3.1 and table 3.2 stem from the different sources used.

that since 1980, the number of films released by the majors proper has remained more or less constant at close to a hundred a year, whereas the subsidiaries have greatly increased production, in parallel with increasing activity in the independent sector.

Thus, although the majors continue to dominate the entire industry, and to maintain a significant degree of in-house production capacity, they also rely more and more on smaller subsidiaries and independent production companies to spread their risks, to diversify their market offerings, and to sound out emerging market opportunities. The business strategies of the motion picture industry majors in this respect strongly resemble those of majors in the music business (Dale 1997; Hirsch 2000; Negus 1998; Scott 1999).

The World of the Independents

The independent segment of the industry represents an important and flourishing element of the Hollywood complex. As the information set forth in table 3.1 suggests, independent film production has increased greatly over the last two decades, with the period of most intense growth being the early to mid-1980s when a boom occurred, fueled by the growth of ancillary markets, especially in television (Prince 2000). Independent production companies make films for both domestic and foreign markets, for presentation in any and all formats (theatrical exhibition, television, or home video). They cater to a great variety of market niches, and their out-puts include art films for specialized audiences, genre movies of all kinds, documentaries, television commercials, and direct-to-video films (includ-ing the numerous pornographic films made by firms clustered in the San Fernando Valley). The distribution of films made by independent produc-ers is handled for the most part by independent distribution companies, many of them highly specialized with respect to market niche (Donahue 1987; Rosen and Hamilton 1987).

According to *County Business Patterns*, some 3,500 establishments were engaged in motion picture and video production (NAICS 51211) in Los Angeles County in 2000, and their average size was just 14.4 employees. Almost all of these establishments, of course, consist of independent pro-duction companies, some of which are allied with majors but most of which operate in an entirely separate sphere of commercial and creative activity. Thus, in face-to-face interviews with representatives of many different firms it was found that significant numbers—almost certainly the majority—of Hollywood independents rarely or never come into contact with a major. This observation is confirmed by results from a postal survey of indepen-dent production companies in Hollywood carried out in the summer of 2001. Out of a total of 115 respondents, 83 (72.2%) indicated that they had *not* engaged in any production deals with majors over the previous twelve months, and it was evident that some of those who responded posi-tively were actually making a very liberal interpretation of the term "major." Additionally, the average response to a question asking firms to rate the direct and indirect dependence of their business upon either the production or distribution divisions of majors on a scale ranging from 1 (no dependence) to 5 (high dependence) was a rather low 2.8.

A Bipartite or Tripartite System?

At first glance, then, the motion picture production system of Hollywood appears to consist of two tiers of productive activity: the majors and the inde-pendent companies that work with them, and the many independents that have little or no contact with the majors. These two tiers, however, are far from being hermetically sealed off from one another. First, some indepen-dent production companies work in both, while others move erratically in and out of the sphere of operation of the majors. Second, there are obvious symbioses between the two in the sense that each generates externalities that are of value to the other, including important flows of new talent from the lower end of the system to the top. In fact, we might well want to revise any description of the Hollywood production complex as a bipartite system by redefining it in terms of *three* different tiers (see chapter 8), consisting of

(a) the majors proper, (b) an intermediate circle of companies as represented by the majors' own subsidiaries combined with independents allied to the majors, and (c) companies that work entirely independently of the majors. The middle tier provides a shifting but evidently widening bridge between the two more clearly definable segments as represented by the majors proper and the pure independents.

THE GEOGRAPHY AND DYNAMICS OF THE HOLLYWOOD PRODUCTION COMPLEX

A Schematic Overview

Hollywood is neither just a metaphor nor just a business model; it is also a unique geographic entity, with a very distinctive structure as a production locale. As such, one important approach to understanding its character and evolution is offered by the contemporary theory of industrial districts and regional development. Since there already exists a large general body of literature on this issue (see, for example, Cooke and Morgan 1998; Porter 2001; Scott 1993b; Storper and Scott 1995), I shall be brief in what follows.

The key elements of the Hollywood production complex today can be described by reference to four main functional and organizational features (see figure 3.3):

1. A series of overlapping production networks in various states of vertical disintegration. The nodes of these networks are composed of majors (and their subsidiaries), independents, and providers of specialized services from script writing to film editing.
2. A local labor market comprising a large number of individuals differentiated according to skills, sensibilities, and forms of habituation. This labor market is constantly being replenished by new talent from all over the rest of North America and the world.
3. An institutional environment made up of many organizations and associations representing firms and workers.[6] A number of governmental and quasi-governmental agencies are also involved with the industry in different ways. Some of these organizations exert considerable influence over the developmental trajectory of the industry.

---

[6] Some of the more important of these institutions are the International Alliance of Theatrical and Stage Employees, the Director's Guild, the Producers' Guild, the Screen Actors' Guild, the Writers' Guild, the Academy of Motion Picture Arts and Sciences (which organizes the annual Academy Awards), the Alliance of Motion Picture and Television Producers, the American Federation of Television and Radio Artists, the American Film Marketing Association, the Motion Picture Association of America, and the Entertainment Industry Development Corporation.

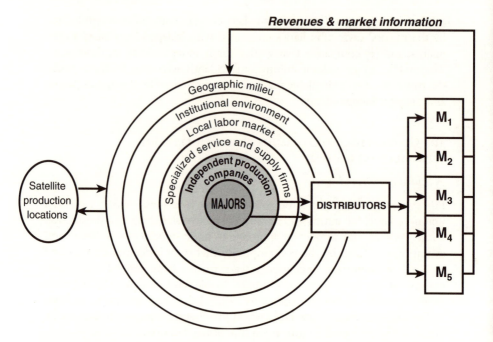

Figure 3.3. Schema of the Hollywood motion picture production complex and its external spatial relations. M_1, M_2, . . . , M_5 represent markets differentiated by niche and by geography.

4. A regional milieu whose peculiar geographic and historical features emerge in part in relation to the phenomena identified in points 1, 2, and 3, and that is a repository of crucial resources for the industry. These range from the cinematic traditions that are embedded, as it were, in the very fabric of Hollywood as a production locale, through the background landscapes of Southern California, to the synergy-laden potentials offered by proximity to the region's many other cultural-products industries, such as multimedia, music, fashion clothing, furniture design, and so on (Molotch 1996).

These four points all allude to important positive externalities underlying the Hollywood production complex, endowing it with strong competitive advantages in the form of increasing returns to scale and scope (i.e., size and diversity) and positive agglomeration economies. Such advantages are fundamental in maintaining the status of the region as the leading center of motion picture production in the world today. They are also major elements of an organizational-geographic framework that functions as a hotbed of creativity and innovation for the industry (cf. Scott 1999). Like many other regional industrial complexes with similar structural frameworks, Hollywood evinces a periodic tendency to lock into relatively fixed configurations over time; yet so far in its long history, the industry has always in the end managed to overcome the many crises of adjustment that have been sparked off by periodic shifts in basic technological and market conditions, like the invention of talking movies or the development of new digital technologies, not to mention the *Paramount* decree.

Two other brief remarks complement the discussion of figure 3.3, and will be picked up again in detail later on. First, in spite of the centripetal locational pull of Hollywood, expanding streams of production activities have been moving to distant satellite locations at least since the 1980s in a process of decentralization or "runaway production." Second, distribution represents an especially critical adjunct to production. Without effective distribution, the production system could attain neither the scale nor the scope that make it such a formidable source of competitive advantages today.

Development and Growth, 1980–2000

All of this productive activity calls for an enormous variety of worker skills, service inputs, and entrepreneurial effort, and Southern California offers an extraordinarily dense concentration of these assets. Most of the industry is clustered in a relatively small geographic area centered on Hollywood itself, but it also spills over into other parts of the region. Figure 3.4 shows the locations of individual production companies in the region. Observe the dense swath of firms sweeping from Burbank in the north and east through the central pivot of Hollywood to Beverly Hills and Santa Monica in the west. Remarkably few production companies are located outside this dense primary cluster.

The motion picture industry has grown greatly in Los Angeles County over the last few decades, as indicated by figures 3.5 and 3.6, which trace changes in employment and number of establishments in motion picture production and allied services since 1980. The information presented in these two figures is defined in terms of the old standard industrial classification (SIC), as opposed to the new North American industrial classification system (NAICS) that succeeded it in 1997 (see appendix to this chapter).[7] Employment in SIC 7812 in Los Angeles County remained more or less stable over the period 1980–2000, with 39,318 employees at

[7] As it happens, SIC 7812 (Motion Picture and Video Production) is perfectly matched by NAICS 51211, and thus we can extend any data series under the former rubric beyond 1997. SIC 7819 (Services Allied to Motion Pictures) has no corresponding NAICS codes, so the data series defined under this rubric cannot be continued after 1997.

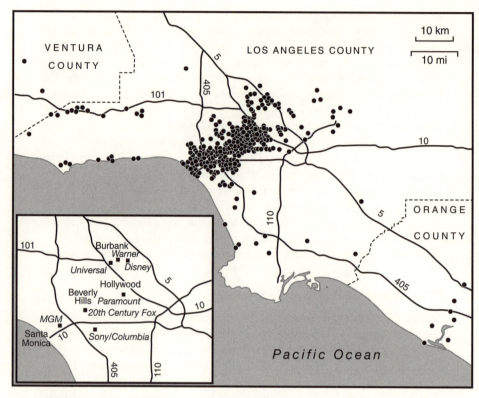

Figure 3.4. Motion picture production companies in Southern California. The inset shows locations of the majors. Sources of address data: *Blu-Book, 2001* (Los Angeles: Hollywood Reporter), and *Producers* (Los Angeles: Ifilm).

the start of the period and 38,951 at the end; by contrast, the number of establishments in the same sector increased massively, from 983 to 3,309. Employment in SIC 7819 grew from 10,946 to 120,000 between 1980 and 1997, and the number of establishments in the same sector expanded from 509 to 2,326, which clearly reflects the great rise in demand for intermediate inputs to the industry, including special effects and other digital services (Hozic 2001; Scott 1998a). Thus, taken as a whole, motion picture production and service activities (SIC 7812 plus SIC 7819) in Los Angeles County grew at a rate of 194% for employment and 248% for number of establishments from 1980 to 1997. This trend runs parallel to the considerable increase in the total number of films produced in the United States over the same period (from 214 in 1980 to 684 in 2000, according to MPAA records). The global deregulation of television in the

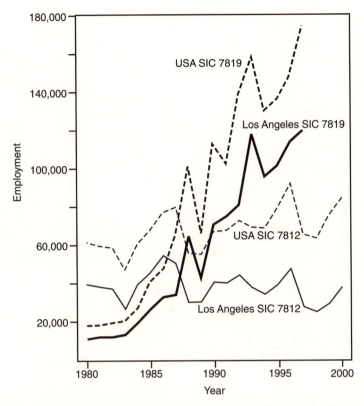

Figure 3.5. Employment in the motion picture industry, Los Angeles County and the United States. SIC 7812 = Motion Picture and Video Production; SIC 7819 = Services Allied to Motion Pictures. Source of data: U.S. Department of Commerce, Bureau of the Census, *County Business Patterns*.

1980s and 1990s unquestionably also helped to stimulate this expansion. In the same period, a significant downsizing of establishments occurred in SIC 7812, in association with a corresponding increase in average establishment size in SIC 7819. In the former case, establishment size in Los Angeles County fell from 39.9 to 9.0 employees on average; in the latter, it rose from 21.5 to 51.6. It is tempting to interpret these data in terms of continued vertical disintegration in production and enlarged opportunities for reaping internal economies of scale in associated service providers, but in the absence of suitable statistics at the individual firm level, analysis of the precise mechanisms at work here must await further research.

Figures 3.5 and 3.6 indicate that the growth of the motion picture industry in Southern California has been accompanied by a parallel expansion

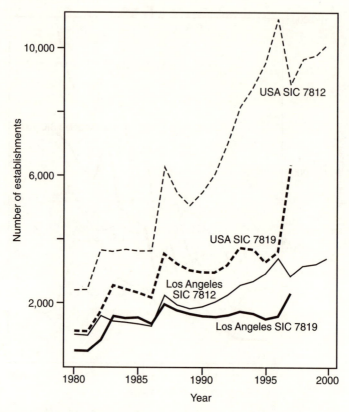

Figure 3.6. Number of establishments in the motion picture industry, Los Angeles County and the United States. SIC 7812 = Motion Picture and Video Production; SIC 7819 = Services Allied to Motion Pictures. Source of data: U.S. Department of Commerce, Bureau of the Census, *County Business Patterns*.

of the industry (and most notably by an increase in the number of small establishments) in the rest of the United States. Even so, Southern California remains the primary agglomeration in the country, followed in distant second place by New York. In 1980, combined employment in SICs 7812 and 7819 in Los Angeles County represented 63.3% of the U.S. total. In 1997, the figure was 61.4%. Hence, not only did the industry continue to grow in absolute terms in Los Angeles over the 1980s and 1990s, but it maintained its high level of relative geographic concentration as well. More recently, as the economic downturn of the early 2000s has taken hold, it appears that employment in motion picture production in the United States has declined rather sharply. Certainly, data for Los Angeles County released by the state's Employment Development Department show that employment in the industry declined sharply from 2000 to 2002.[8] Some significant share of this decline must also be ascribed to the decentralization of production activities from Hollywood to satellite locations in recent years. However, available statistical information does not permit any precise apportionment of the overall decline in employment to the one or the other factor.

Satellite Production Locations

Decentralization occurs for two main reasons: the search for realistic outdoor film locations (which has always been a feature of the industry's operations), and the search for reduced production costs (a more recent phenomenon). In the vernacular of contemporary Hollywood, firms engaging in these two types of decentralization are referred to as "creative runaways" and "economic runaways" respectively (Monitor 1999).

A number of studies have shown that decentralization of film-shooting activities to reduce costs has been observable at least since the early 1980s (Coe 2001; EIDC 2001; ITA 2001; Monitor 1999). At the present time, much of it is directed to Canada, Australia, Britain, and Mexico, with Canada receiving 81% of the total. The Monitor Company (1999) estimates that the total dollar loss to the United States as a result of economic runaways was $2.28 billion in 1998. The presumed Canadian share of this total is $1.85 billion. By contrast, the Canadian Film and Television Production Association estimates that total revenues from foreign film shooting in Canada in the 1999–2000 season was just $1 billion (CFTPA 2001).[9] Even given the discrepancy between these two estimates, the total loss to Hollywood is evidently of major proportions, and the point is underlined by the fact that of 1,075 U.S. film and television projects surveyed in 1998, 285 or 26.5% involved runaway production to foreign countries (Monitor 1999). According to EIDC (2001), most of this activity is currently accounted for by television program production, with movie-of-the-week presentations being the staple item.

Figure 3.7 provides a simple analytical language for thinking about this issue. The central elements of the figure are average cost curves for a particular package of production tasks (in the present instance, film shooting) at two different locations: the home base (i.e., Hollywood), and a satellite location. The cost curves depict typical increasing- and decreasing-returns effects as a function of the size of any given package, with c_1 representing production in Hollywood, and c_2 production in the satellite location.

---

[8] More details can be found at http://www.calmis.cahwnet.gov/htmlfile/county/califhtm.htm.

[9] "Runaways" resurface in Canada as "export value."

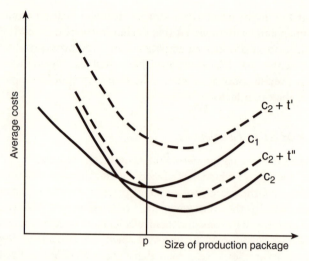

Figure 3.7. Analysis of runaway production: c_1 is the average cost curve for a given package of production tasks in Hollywood; c_2 is the average cost curve for the same tasks at a satellite location; t' and t'' are unit costs of transacting between the two locations.

We may assume that there are fixed setup costs at the satellite location so that c_2 is greater than c_1 at relatively low levels of production; but because of various cost advantages at the satellite location, c_2 falls below c_1 at higher levels. Among these advantages we may count relatively low wages, low rental rates for soundstages and equipment, advantageous foreign exchange rates, governmental tax credits and subsidies, and so on (ITA 2001). Additionally, any shift of production from the home base to a satellite location entails transactions costs, including expenses for transport of personnel and equipment, communications charges between the home base and the satellite as production is proceeding, and perhaps most importantly, implicit costs due to diminished managerial and creative control by the Hollywood-based production company over day-to-day work activities and hence over the quality of the final product. These transactions costs (which may, like production costs, be subject to increasing and decreasing returns) are apt to be particularly onerous where a high-budget feature film is concerned, but relatively low in the case of, say, a more routine television program with limited production values, especially where a series is involved so that the basic package specifications can be repeated over and over again. The interplay between average production costs and transactions costs at different levels of scale determines whether runaway production is economically feasible in any given case. As shown in figure 3.7, a strong production cost advantage at the satellite location can be completely eliminated where transactions costs are high (t'); then, as transactions costs are lowered there will be a greater and greater incentive to shift production to the satellite location. Eventually, if average transactions costs fall from t' to t'', as in figure 3.7, production at the satellite is likely to occur for task packages larger than p. A noteworthy corollary of this argument is that small task packages are more likely to resist decentralization than large.

This exercise helps to clarify the interactions between the various cost factors brought into play in runaway production relative to the size and complexity of the tasks to be completed. In view of this analysis, we can gain a clearer grasp of just why (relatively standardized and often serialized) television program production has been hitherto more susceptible to runaway production than feature films. And we can extend the analysis by allowing the number of possible satellite locations to increase. For example, a significant appreciation of the Canadian dollar, from its current exchange rate of around C$1.54 per US$1.00 to C$1.15 per US$1.00 will just offset the reputed 25% cost advantage of Canada for film production, therefore making substitute satellite locations more attractive. In view of this logic, there is every likelihood that Hollywood will continue indefinitely to lose certain kinds of production to one country or another, subject to the availability of adequate soundstage facilities and crews at alternative locations. A dramatic parallel case can be found in the Los Angeles clothing industry, where a steady increase in offshore "full-package" contracting has been occurring since the late 1980s (Kessler 1999; Scott 2002).

So far, runaway production has not seriously undermined the vitality of the Hollywood film industry, and it may well never become life-threatening, at least in the more creative segments of the industry. This inference is based on two presumptions: first, that the towering competitive advantages of Hollywood in pre- and postproduction work will continue to prevail; and second, that films requiring close supervisory control and complex customized inputs at all stages of production will continue to constitute a significant core of the industry's product range. Accordingly, and even though the great flow of shooting activities to Canada has unquestionably given a developmental boost to the motion picture industries of Toronto and Vancouver, where most of the work takes place (cf. Coe 2000), there seems little reason to suppose that the locational attractions of Hollywood are on the point of dissipation. In the same way, it is surely implausible to claim, along with Clough (2000, 2002), that as a consequence of the increasing use of special effects and digital technologies in the industry, its center of gravity in California may be shifting toward the Bay Area. The claim is yet more implausible in view of the extensive development of a robust cluster of digital media and special effects firms in Southern California over the last decade or so (see chapter 5).

In brief, Hollywood's competitive advantages—deriving from its overlapping transactional networks, the skills and creativity of its workers, its dense institutional underpinnings, its roots in a supportive regional milieu (one of whose attributes is the diverse and striking visual imagery of Southern California), and its proximity to related cultural-products industries—would appear to afford it some durability as a going concern. Its current vibrancy is yet more assured when we add to these advantages, the benefits that it derives from its unparalleled distribution system (Wildman and Siwek 1988). Accordingly, the pronouncements of Aksoy and Robins (1992, p. 19), to the effect that "Hollywood is now everywhere . . . production now moves almost at will to find its most ideal conditions, and with it go skills, technicians, and support services," and of Hozic (2001, p. 153), who talks about "Hollywood's exodus into worldwide locations," are both exaggerated and premature.

Motion Picture Distribution and Marketing

Distribution is a vital element of the Hollywood motion picture industry, and one of the sources of its massive success on global markets. These issues are of sufficient importance to merit a chapter in their own right (see chapter 8); I will make only a few brief remarks here to complete this first descriptive mapping of Hollywood today.

The majors own many individual distribution offices scattered over the United States and the rest of the world. As we might expect, Los Angeles is the main hub of this segment of the industry, and it is from this location that the distribution system as a whole is controlled. In 1999, Los Angeles County could claim 22,399 employees and 299 establishments in NAICS 51212 (Motion Picture and Video Distribution), compared with 5,270 employees and 407 establishments in the rest of the United States. Los Angeles thus has about 80% of total employment and 40% of all the establishments in this sector in the United States today. These figures include independent distributors as well as the distribution facilities of the majors.

Not surprisingly, the bifurcation that is characteristic of production activities in the Hollywood motion picture industry is also—and even more—characteristic of distribution. As table 3.3 indicates, nine of the top ten film distributors in the United States are either majors or subsidiaries of majors, and the one independent shown in the table (USA Films) has only recently displaced MGM from the top ten. The point is brought home by an examination of detailed box-office statistics for films distributed in the United States. For independent distributors, the average domestic box office per film was $3.8 million in the year 2000, and for majors it was $55.6 million.

TABLE 3.3
Top Ten Film Distributors in the United States, 2000

	Number of films released	Domestic box-office revenue ($ millions)	Average per film ($ millions)
Buena Vista (Disney)	19	1,089	57.3
Universal	15	1,053	70.2
Warner Brothers	22	863	39.2
Twentieth Century Fox	14	849	60.6
Paramount	12	792	66.0
Dreamworks	10	668	66.8
Sony	22	664	30.2
Miramax (Disney)	25	507	20.3
New Line (Warner)	14	388	27.7
USA Films	17	202	11.9
Totals:	170	7,075	41.7

Source: Hollywood Reporter, Film 500, August 2001.

The gap between these two figures is so great that there might well be a *prima facie* case for inferring that the majors are in some sense crowding the independents out of more lucrative markets (Daly 1980). The business concentration of the majors is magnified by what Cones (1997) refers to as their "creative accounting" practices, where revenues are skimmed off at the distribution phase, thus reducing the flow-back to production and by the same token diminishing claims for payment by outside contractors (writers, directors, actors, and so on) based on a percentage of production companies' revenues.

Distribution, then, is the segment of the industry where oligopoly is most in evidence. This feature has its roots in the internal economies of scale that are inherent to distribution activities, especially where, at least in the case of the majors, they assume the form of extensive networks with strong central management and widely diffused regional offices. As a result, these networks can be organized on the basis of repetitive operating rules and routinization of the transmission of the variable product. The economics of blockbuster production, with its associated logic of high-intensity, saturation marketing and distribution, greatly intensifies this tendency to concentration. In a study of motion picture distribution in Canada, Globerman and Vining (1987) have claimed that because there is rotating leadership among the larger distributors, and low barriers to entry at the bottom end of the system, the market is "workably competitive." Whatever the situation in Canada may be, the very marked concentration in the distribution sector in the United States and the apparent difficulties of outsider penetration into the top tier of the sector mean that significant impediments to competition exist. This situation, as I argue more fully later, can scarcely be qualified as being anything but oligopolistic.

Hollywood today is a large-scale, many-sided, cultural-production and franchising complex, disgorging an endless variety of products designed for many different market niches. The linchpin of the entire system is the high-concept, mass-appeal blockbuster, that is, a big-budget film with a simple but climactic central narrative, an uplifting finale, a major star presence, and many marketable assets (Branston 2000; Garvin 1981; Wasko 1994; Wyatt 1994). The market for all films is risky, and the high-concept blockbuster has especially insecure prospects. Only a few such films actually recoup their costs directly from theatrical exhibition, but the ones that do generally compensate for the ones that do not (de Vany and Walls 1997). In addition, the studios now also reap huge revenues from the repackaging of films for home video, broadcast, and cable television licensing, and from product placements and spin-off products such as recorded music, games, toys, fashions, books, novelties, and theme park rides.

. . .

Hollywood in its current incarnation is one of the most remarkable examples of a successful industrial agglomeration anywhere in the world—for its size and complexity, its longevity, its global impact, and the mystique that surrounds its products. It is especially noteworthy and puzzling because unlike many other case-study industrial districts (Silicon Valley, Orange County, or Boston's Route 128, for example), its outputs trade on a purely cognitive register. Hollywood, in short, is one of the most arresting examples of the burgeoning cultural-products agglomerations that are on the rise all over the world today, no matter whether their stock-in-trade is film, multimedia, music, fashion, or any other vehicle of aesthetic and semiotic expression.

APPENDIX TO CHAPTER 3
COMPARISON OF SIC AND NAICS CODES FOR MOTION PICTURE
    PRODUCTION AND DISTRIBUTION SECTORS SINCE 1972

The SIC (Standard Industrial Classification) system as laid out in various versions of the *Standard Industrial Classification Manual* (published by the U.S. Office of Management and Budget) was the prevailing official industrial classification in the United States for most of the postwar period. Major internal revisions of the SIC system were carried out in 1972 and 1987.

In 1997, the SIC system was replaced by NAICS, the North American Industry Classification System (see http://www.census.gov/epcd/www/naics.html).

Table A3.1 provides a guide to the changing industry classifications pertinent to motion-picture production and distribution in the United States for the periods 1972–87, 1987–97, and 1997 onward. Each official revision of the classification system typically results in a number of discontinuities as new and non-commensurable codes compared to the earlier system are introduced and old ones are discarded; in other cases, the codes remain unchanged. Comparability of codes across different classifications is indicated in table A3.1 by means of horizontal alignment.

TABLE A3.1
SIC and NAICS Codes for Production and Distribution of Motion Pictures and Television Programs, 1972, 1987, and 1997

1972 SIC code and description	1987 SIC code and description	1997 NAICS code and description
—	—	5121 MOTION PICTURE AND VIDEO INDUSTRIES
781 MOTION PICTURE PRODUCTION AND ALLIED SERVICES	781 MOTION PICTURE PRODUCTION AND ALLIED SERVICES	—
—	7812 Motion Picture and Video Tape Production	51211 Motion Picture and Video Production
7813 Motion Picture Production, Except for Television	—	5121101 Motion Picture Production (Except for Television)
7814 Motion Picture and Tape Production for Television	—	5121102 Motion Picture and Video Production for Television

(*continued*)

TABLE A3.1 (*Cont.*)

1972 *SIC code and description*	1987 *SIC code and description*	1997 *NAICS code and description*
7819 Services Allied to Motion Picture Production	7819 Services Allied to Motion Picture Production	—
782 MOTION PICTURE DISTRIBUTION AND ALLIED SERVICES	782 MOTION PICTURE DISTRIBUTION AND ALLIED SERVICES	—
—	7822 Motion Picture and Videotape Distribution	—
7823 Motion Picture Film Exchanges	—	—
7823 Motion Picture Film Exchanges	—	—
7824 Film or Tape Distribution for Television	—	—
7829 Services Allied to Motion Picture Distribution	7829 Services Allied to Motion Picture Distribution	—
—	—	512120 Motion Picture and Video Distribution
—	—	51219 Postproduction Services and Other Motion Picture and Video Industries

CHAPTER FOUR

The Other Hollywood: Television Program Production

TELEVISION EMERGED as a going concern in the United States over the 1940s and early 1950s, and right from the start proved itself to be a fierce competitor of the motion picture industry. In these early years of its commercial life, television program production remained largely separate in both geographic and functional terms from the older motion picture industry. To begin with, the television industry sprang up for the most part in New York, which was already the home of the three major broadcasting networks (ABC, CBS, and NBC), and which was also the main production locale of the live shows that then predominated in television programming. In addition, television was initially perceived with considerable hostility by the Hollywood motion picture studios. In the immediate postwar decades the two industries became locked in an intense competitive battle as more and more consumers turned to television as their preferred form of distraction, with consequent severe drops in attendance at motion picture theaters. This phenomenon set off one of the most intense crises in the history of the motion picture industry, and, along with the Paramount Decree of 1948, helped to undermine the old business model that had propelled the studios forward in their prewar glory days (Gomery 1994; Sklar 1975).

By the end of the 1950s, however, these lines of separation and antagonism were becoming increasingly blurred as the major Hollywood studios started to realize the potential of the new medium as an outlet for their own products. In particular, the studios now set about establishing specialized television programming divisions in order to capitalize on their own creative capabilities. Hence, as the New Hollywood emerged from the trials and tribulations of the 1950s and 1960s, television program production and motion picture production became irrevocably intertwined, and a major shift of the former from New York to Hollywood occurred. As early as 1960, some 40% of network programming was being produced by firms located in Hollywood, and today, the figure is over 90%. Even if the principal U.S. networks continue down to the present time to be headquartered in New York, Southern California is now unquestionably the heartland of American television program production.

The Business Context: Production and Distribution of Television Programs

Corporate Structures and Production Relations

Television program production in Hollywood is dominated by much the same set of multinational firms that control the motion picture industry. Figure 4.1 displays some relevant ownership and organizational relationships for eight of the most important multinational corporations with stakes in the U.S. television business. Except for General Electric, these corporations are all directly involved in motion pictures as well as television program production (cf. figure 3.2). No attempt is made in figure 4.1 to identify all of the television-related activities of these firms; only principal program production facilities are shown, together with their relationship to the corporate owner. Each of the eight designated firms owns at least one and sometimes several facilities of this sort, and these are typically organized as specialized stand-alone divisions, like CBS Productions, Columbia-Tristar International Television, MGM Television, NBC Studios, Spelling Entertainment, and TBS Productions. These divisions are to be distinguished from the actual television networks (including ABC, CBS, and NBC) that are also owned by firms designated in figure 4.1.

Beyond this dominant group of corporations and their subsidiaries, television program production in the United States is represented by a large number of independent firms. The latter operate mostly outside the orbit of the large media corporations, though there is a privileged inner core that works frequently in partnership with major producers, either in some sort of financing deal or in direct creative collaboration. Unlike the Hollywood majors, whose motion picture and television program production activities are usually conducted in separate divisions, many independent firms combine these activities under one roof. Thus, of the 1,175 production companies listed in the *Hollywood Creative Directory: Producers* for 2001, 762 or 64.8% are on record as being engaged in both activities. Interviews with representatives of numerous companies suggest that it is small and medium-sized independents that are most likely to function on this dual register, and that they do so as a way of mitigating the market uncertainties that they face. By maintaining a capacity to switch from the one activity to the other and back again, these firms are able to widen their sphere of possible markets without unduly overstretching their core competencies. Larger units of production, by contrast, usually face more stable and durable demands, and so they have more incentive to specialize.

Television programs come in a wide variety of formats, from documentaries and news programs to game shows and movies-of-the-week, though prime-time serials are the staple item. Both majors and independents turn out programs for transmission. The majors enter frequently into financing

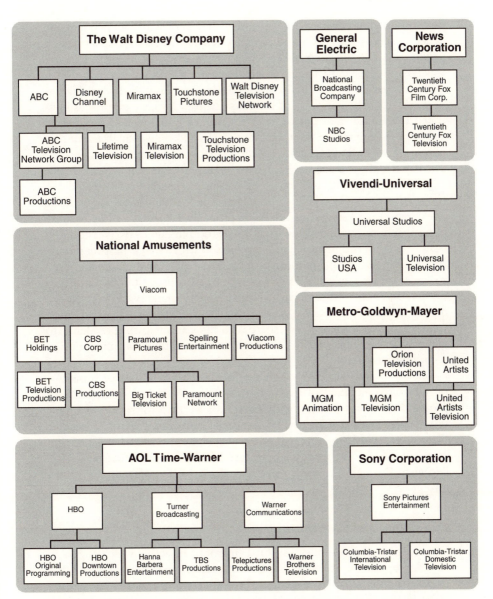

Figure 4.1. Major media corporations and their holdings of television program production facilities. U.S. holdings only are shown. Sources: Various directories, company reports, and web sites.

or coproduction deals, either with other majors or with independents, in order to spread their risks and tap into new talent. As in motion picture production, the loose collaborative networks that come together in this way typically break apart again and regroup in some other configuration as individual projects come and go, leading to constantly revolving alliances of producers. The enormity of the risks involved in this enterprise is illustrated by the fact that only a small fraction of initial plans for serialized shows ever go into the pilot program stage, and only a small fraction of pilot programs ever become actual shows. Most shows themselves are canceled after only one season. Successful serials, however, offer some degree of productive stability, and key personnel such as producers, writers, directors, and actors can be kept on the payroll over extended periods of time when a show has a long run. Television programs are usually cheap to make in relative terms, with a prime-time show absorbing up to two million dollars per hour of programming, in comparison with a major motion picture (lasting, say, two hours) that can cost upwards of fifty million dollars. Even so, most shows rarely make a profit when first broadcast and hence they depend on successful performance in secondary markets to make up the deficit. Although television shows tend to embody lower production values than feature films, they share with films an increasing tendency to generate spin-off products in the form of games, toys, fashions, musical recordings, and so on.

Television programs are invariably distributed by specialized broadcast or network companies (or by program syndicators) that deliver individual programs to local television stations or cable systems for relay to viewers' sets. Transmission is executed via terrestrial broadcast infrastructures and by satellite, which in some cases are owned by specialized independent companies and in other cases by the television networks themselves. Of late years, the major networks have also been actively integrating upstream into program production.

Deregulation and Reorganization

The technological and organizational environment within which television program production operates has been profoundly reshaped by the course of deregulation over the last couple of decades. The year 1977 was especially pivotal, marked as it was by the deregulation of cable systems, which then began to grow by leaps and bounds. According to the *Statistical Abstract of the United States*, only 29.9% of all households owning a television set had access to cable in 1980, but by 1998 the figure was 67.2%. Audience access to satellite broadcasts has similarly increased greatly. The net result of this expansion in the types and extent of distribution channels has been a considerable intensification of competitiveness in television program distribution and a proliferation of companies like Comedy Central, E!

Entertainment, HBO, the History Channel, Lifetime, MTV, and Show-time, offering specialized programming as an alternative to the material carried by the traditional networks.

These trends in turn have induced much variegation over what was widely referred to in the past as the vast wasteland of network television, dominated as it was by just three major companies with minimal product differentiation between them (see also Bourdieu 1996; Litman 1979). Nowadays, by contrast, a great diversity of programming alternatives is available to viewers, with content providers seeking out ever more finely divided market niches for specialized programming. The shift is all the more evident in view of the major networks' established policy of airing programs that concentrate on the middle of the market (thereby maximizing advertising revenues). More specialized networks, especially when they transmit under pay-TV arrangements, can focus on the viewing preferences of much smaller and more narrowly defined groups of individuals (cf. Deakin and Pratten 2000; Vianello 1994). Concomitantly, even while the three major networks continue to dominate the industry, their audience share has declined greatly over the last couple of decades as viewers have defected to other channels that serve their specific needs more adequately. Hence, in the 1985–86 season the three networks had an aggregate audience share of 73%, but their share had dwindled to 41% by 1999–2000 (Gitlin 1994; Staiger 2000; Walker and Ferguson 1998).

A second important wave of deregulation in 1991 made it possible for television networks of every type to enter aggressively into program production in addition to distribution. Until that year, the financial interest and syndication rules (fin-syn rules in everyday parlance) had forbidden the networks from maintaining a financial stake in the materials that they broadcast, with the exception of first-run programs (Cantor and Cantor 1992; FCC 1980). The same rules made it illegal for networks to set up in-house syndication arms. The relaxation of the fin-syn rules accordingly cleared the way for the integration of program production and network activities, just as in the early 1980s, the Justice Department's increasing tolerance of infractions of the 1948 *Paramount* decree encouraged major Hollywood studios to reenter the theatrical exhibition side of the business (Chipty 2001). With the relaxation of the fin-syn rules, therefore, all the existing major networks established specialized program production facilities within their corporate structures. Concurrently, a number of the large motion picture studios set up their own television broadcast networks. Twentieth Century Fox led the way in this matter, having already launched a network in 1986 in anticipation of more relaxed fin-syn regulations, and this move was followed in the 1990s by Paramount (UPN) and Warner (the WB network). In the same spirit of internal synergistic diversification, the Walt Disney Company purchased the ABC network in 1995.

These tendencies are manifest not only in the changing organization charts of the main media businesses in the United States today, but also in the changing corporate origins of the programs transmitted by the networks. As table 4.1 indicates, prime-time programs broadcast by ABC, CBS, and NBC in recent years have increasingly been made by the same companies' internal programming divisions. In the 1987–88 season, the three networks broadcast 66 prime-time shows per week, none of which was produced in-house. By 2000–01, they were broadcasting 65 prime-time shows per week, of which 30.8% were produced internally.

Note that the latter figure is closely comparable to the 36.2% of feature films released by the Hollywood majors that are produced in-house. This observation offers a hint that there may be limits to further vertical integration over production and distribution in the television industry. To be sure, the networks, like the motion picture majors, have strong incentives to engage in some degree of vertical integration, especially because they can then vigorously promote internally produced shows without having to

TABLE 4.1

Prime-Time Television Shows Produced and Broadcast by ABC, CBS, and NBC (by season)

Season	Total prime-time shows broadcast by the three networks	Shows where network is producer or coproducer	
		Number	Percent
1987–88	66	0	0.0
1988–89	63	1	1.6
1989–90	71	2	2.8
1990–91	75	2	2.7
1991–92	70	4	5.7
1992–93	67	6	9.0
1993–94	73	11	15.1
1994–95	72	12	16.7
1995–96	73	11	15.1
1996–97	81	11	13.6
1997–98	77	13	16.9
1998–99	70	20	28.6
1999–00	69	23	33.3
2000–01	65	18	27.7
2001–02	65	20	30.8

Source: Calculated from program information contained in Hollywood Reporter, TV Preview (published annually).

Note: Shows exclude news and current affairs programs.

share the corresponding benefits with third parties. However, the extent to which the networks can continue to integrate program production into their internal operations without damaging their long-term viability is almost certainly bounded by the need to keep harvesting new material and talent in the effort to stay one step ahead of the competition in the vast markets that they serve. Independently made programs provide one of the important instruments by which this kind of diversity can be secured. Further evidence in regard to the benefits of organizational diversity is provided by recent changes in British television, which has traditionally been vertically integrated. As a consequence of deregulatory legislation passed in 1990, the old BBC and ITV television monopolies have been induced to move in the direction of vertical disintegration; however, they have resisted full vertical disintegration, and the resulting mix of programs produced both in-house and by independents has apparently had very beneficial effects on the size of the audience (Barnatt and Starkey 1994; Ursell 2000). In other words, some combination of vertical integration and disintegration seems to be the most successful formula for large operators in the television industry under current market conditions, except where very unusual circumstances prevail. Thus, a highly specialized network, like E! Entertainment (which is based in Los Angeles), produces the entirety of its programming in-house, but this is because an extremely good match exists between the devoted audience of 18-to-34-year-olds that the network has cultivated over the years and its narrow core competency focused on celebrity interviews and show business news.

Two main tendencies have been revealed in these remarks. One is the great expansion in the number of channels available to television viewers since the end of the 1970s. The other is the vertical merging that is taking place between program production facilities and the television networks in response to the relaxation of the fin-syn rules. The first of these tendencies has been associated with a great expansion in the number of independent production companies serving the many new programming opportunities that have recently made their appearance. The second has been somewhat less beneficial to independent program producers, for it means that they have found it increasingly difficult to gain access to those parts of the distribution system controlled by the major networks. As suggested, however, there is some prospect that the networks' shift into higher levels of vertical integration may start to moderate in the not-too-distant future as they attempt to balance the competing demands of the search for rent-generating internal synergies with the need to remain open to a diversity of creative influences.

Taken as a whole, then, the television program production industry has strong resemblances to the motion picture industry in that it is dominated by a limited number of majors embedded in even larger conglomerates together with complementary swarms of small independent producers. However, this judgment must be nuanced in various ways. One particular point of contrast between television program and motion picture production is that firm concentration indexes are significantly smaller in the former than they are in the latter. According to the *Economic Census* of 1997, the four-firm concentration ratio in NAICS 5121102 (Motion Picture and Video Production for Television) was 22.1% for the United States as whole. This figure is far below the ratio of 53.6% for NAICS 5121101 (Motion Picture Production except for Television). The eight-firm concentration ratios were 30.6% and 60.6%, respectively. These contrasts presumably reflect the differential play of internal economies of scale and scope in the two sectors, with television program producers being generally involved in much less grandiose projects than their counterparts in the motion picture industry.

The Growth and Geographic Incidence of Television Program Production in the United States

The National Context

The U.S. television program production sector, as represented by NAICS 5121102, earned total revenues of just over $10 billion in 1997. In the same year, the sector employed 33,668 workers in 4,044 establishments. Total revenues in the motion picture sector (NAICS 5121101) were also just over $10 billion in the same year, though the latter employed almost 50% more workers than the former. Average establishment size in NAICS 5121102 was 8.3 workers and in NAICS 5121101 it was 10.5, again suggesting that distinctive differences of scale exist between the two sectors.

Unfortunately, the detailed employment history of the television program industry in the United States over the last few decades is difficult to track because of the periodic changes that have been made to official industry definitions over the course of the years (see appendix to chapter 3). The old Standard Industrial Classification System recognized television program production as a sector in its own right only after 1968, when both SIC 7814 (Motion Picture Production for TV) and SIC 7813 (Motion Picture Production except TV) were first defined. Then, from 1987 to 1997, the two sectors were collapsed into the composite SIC 7812 (Motion Picture and Video Production). In 1997, the shift to the NAICS scheme once more identified television program production as a separate sector in its own right.

In spite of the incompatibilities that crop up because of these changes, official data sources can still be made to yield some useful insights about overall employment trends in television program production in the United States. These are summarized in figure 4.2, where, for comparative purposes, data for the motion picture sector are also included. Figure 4.2 shows that from 1968 to 1987, employment in SIC 7814 for the United States as a whole expanded greatly, if erratically, as did employment in SIC 7813. The two sectors evolved more or less in tandem over this period through a series of mutually divergent and convergent paths. A particular surge in employment in SIC 7814 is apparent in the late 1970s as deregulation sets in. Official data for SIC 7814 are unavailable after 1987, but we can get some sense of overall trends in the industry by examining the

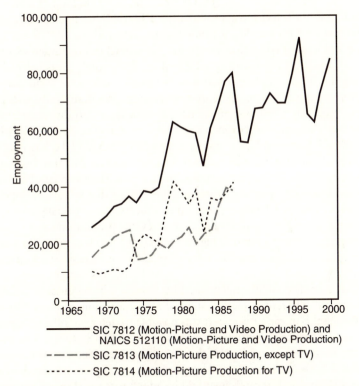

Figure 4.2. Employment in motion picture and television program production, United States, 1968–99. Note that prior to 1988, SIC 7812 had no official status in the Standard Industrial Classification; data imputed to SIC 7812 for the period from 1968 to 1987 are obtained by combining SICs 7813 and 7814. Source: United States Department of Commerce, Bureau of the Census, *County Business Patterns* (published annually).

composite sector SIC 7812, formed in 1988 by the amalgamation of SICs 7813 and 7814. As shown already in chapter 3, SIC 7812 experienced a notably large increase in employment after the late 1980s (from 55,795 in 1988 to 84,549 in 2000), and the television program production sector presumably accounts for a share of this growth. That said, employment in SIC 7812 has recently been subject to decline after attaining its peak figure of 92,374 in 1996.

The Los Angeles Complex

Los Angeles is by far the most important center for the production of television programs in the United States. In 1997, Los Angeles County employed 14,960 individuals in NAICS 5121102 (Motion Picture and Video Production for Television), 44.4% of the 1997 U.S. total. This figure may be compared with the 31,242 individuals employed in NAICS 5121101 (Motion Picture Production except for Television) in Los Angeles County in the same year, representing 62.2% of the U.S. total. Thus, while both sectors are highly agglomerated in Los Angeles, television program production is much less so than motion picture production. By the same token, modestly sized clusters of television program producers are much more likely to occur in places other than Los Angeles. New York, which has only 3.7% of total U.S. employment in NAICS 5121101, has 14.1% of employment in NAICS 5121102, still far behind Los Angeles, but significant for all that. This superior performance of television-related activities as compared with motion pictures in New York is due in part to the city's residual cluster of television program producers, but especially to its preeminence as a center of news and current events programming.

Los Angeles' domination of television program production in the United States stands out with special clarity if we examine its main stock in trade, namely, serialized television shows. The data for this exercise were taken from an extensive archive maintained by *Variety*, which contains information on 598 different television shows broadcast mainly in the 1980s and 1990s but also in earlier years.[1] It was possible to determine the geographic locations of the lead production companies for all but 36 of the shows contained in the *Variety* archive. Of the 562 shows identified in this manner, a massive 87.7% were developed by production companies located in and around Hollywood, though it should be added that the shows were not always shot in Southern California. New York ranks well below Los Angeles, with only 5.5% of shows being made there. A critical observation here is that 6.6% of all the production companies involved in these 562 shows are located in Toronto (though they are usually involved in coproduction

---

[1] *Variety*'s TV production chart can be accessed for a fee at http://www.variety.com.

arrangements with firms based in Los Angeles). This remark will be further elaborated below, but it provides a further insight into the rising tide of decentralization of film- and TV-shooting activities away from Los Angeles and their execution in other countries, above all, Canada.

THE OTHER HOLLYWOOD: LOCATION AND LINKAGE STRUCTURES

The detailed locational pattern of companies producing television programs in Southern California is virtually identical to that of motion picture production companies as shown in figure 3.4. Again, companies are primarily located in a belt running east and west, with its center corresponding to Hollywood. In the rest of Southern California outside this main axis, only a few scattered firms are to be found.

As in the case of the motion picture industry, this distinctive clustering of television program production companies can be seen as resulting from the collective benefits that come from the mutual proximity of many different but interrelated producers together with dependent pools of appropriately skilled and socialized workers. And as in the motion picture industry, these benefits are intensified by the existence of a number of local organizations that offer critical coordination and steering services. Certain of these organizations have already been identified in chapter 3, but special mention needs to made in the present chapter of the Academy of Television Arts and Sciences (ATAS). This particular institution is of central significance to the television industry in Southern California for its role as an instructional center, information broker, and lobbying organization. It is also the sponsor of the annual prime-time Emmy Awards. ATAS thus makes important contributions to the competitive advantages of the region as a center of the entertainment industry.

Centripetal Forces

Among the forces leading to the sort of geographic clustering observable among television program producers in Southern California, the existence of a dense structure of inter-firm linkages is often thought of as being of considerable importance. This is notably the case in situations where finely grained social divisions of labor are present, leading to the formation of especially dense webs of transactional relations between firms. The tendency to agglomeration that flows from this circumstance is augmented where the temporal rhythm of transacting is high and where final output specifications are extremely variable, leading to the need for producers to search continually for new suppliers of inputs. In situations like this, the spatially dependent costs of interlinkage are often quite elevated per unit of flow, so that firms have a strong interest in being as close to one another as possible in geographic space. Linkage structures of this type appear to be common right across the entertainment industry of Hollywood, and are presumably one of the main factors helping to hold the entire productive complex together in geographic space, though unfortunately, any attempt to subject this notion to rigorous empirical inspection comes up at once against the fact that appropriate data are extremely hard to come by.

By dint of persistent inquiry, however, I was able to obtain a unique source of data relevant to this issue from the producer of a television show that has achieved a high level of popularity over the last few years. The data represent detailed accounts of every purchase of materials, equipment, and services used as inputs to the show over a series of eighteen individual episodes. The show itself is marked by notably high production values, including the lavish use of special effects, and every episode under examination here was made entirely in Los Angeles. It therefore represents an ideal case study for an investigation of the relations between location and linkages in the television program production industry, and as we shall see, the data reveal the remarkable imbrication of the show as an economic activity within a system of local suppliers. As such, the present case study runs parallel to a somewhat similar investigation of the Potsdam-Babelsberg film industry carried out by Krätke (2002).

Each of the eighteen one-hour episodes cost on average about $2 million to produce, though this sum refers only to variable expenditures (including wages and salaries) and excludes fixed costs such as land, buildings, and managerial overheads. All equipment used in the show (cameras, lighting, sound recording systems, etc.) was leased, and the costs of leasing are included in the accounts to be examined here. Wages and salaries amount to about three-quarters of the show's total costs, with purchases of requisite inputs making up the other quarter. (Detailed breakdowns of wage and salary information were not made available.) The data for the 18 episodes under analysis here refer to 9,444 individual purchases from 534 different suppliers or vendors (so that on average each vendor was responsible for 17.7 individual transactions). The aggregate value of these transactions is $8.8 million, with the average and median transactions being rated at $931.80 and $325.00, respectively.

A frequency distribution of the dollar value of the transactions (table 4.2) reveals that the vast majority of them are extremely small, with 80.0% of them being below $1,000. They are, too, markedly heterogeneous in substantive content, and as many as 83.1% represent non-repeat orders. Out of all 9,444 transactions recorded, 40.0% are diverse inputs for use in the shooting phase of production (photographic supplies, camera and lighting equipment rental, props and scenery, wardrobe, etc.); another 23.2% involve postproduction expenditures (photographic processing, editing, voice-over, digital visual

TABLE 4.2
Frequency Distribution of Transactional Expenditures for the Case-Study
Television Show

Value of transaction	Frequency (as percentage)
$0–$1,000	80.0
$1,000–$2,000	11.5
$2,000–$3,000	3.6
$3,000–$4,000	1.7
$4,000–$5,000	0.6
$5,000–$6,000	0.5
$6,000–$7,000	0.3
> $7,000	1.8
Total number of transactions	9,444

effects, etc.); and the remaining 36.8% are nonspecific in that they represent items like security, vehicle rental, office supplies, and catering, whose precise relation to the shooting or postproduction phases of the work could not be determined.

Most of the individual transactions under investigation here evidently entailed rather complex decision-making processes. First of all, the data in hand clearly indicate that the overall structure of transacting is highly irregular over time. Second of all, and even when the production company has had previous business relations with the vendor, almost all transactions involve special detailed decisions in regard to the precise specifications of the selected input, its cost, the quantity bought, the timing of each purchase, and in many cases (e.g., for special effects or certain kinds of stage props) these operations absorb large amounts of labor time. These are characteristics that greatly reinforce the advantages of proximity within any system of transactional relations.

In fact, of the individual input transactions under analysis here, by far the greatest number involved vendors in Southern California. Only 6.2% of all transactions (10.8% by total value) came from outside the region. Moreover, as predicted by the spatial theory of inter-industrial linkages, with its emphasis on economies of scale in procurement patterns over space (Scott 1993a), the average value of inputs from inside the region is considerably smaller than the average value of inputs from outside ($883.55 versus $1,623.71). The locations of the individual vendors with addresses in the greater Los Angeles region are mapped out in figure 4.3. Many of these vendors, it should be recalled, provided multiple inputs to the case-study show, so that the number of vendors is much lower than the total number of transactions. The pattern revealed in figure 4.3 bears a strong resemblance to the spatial distribution of production companies

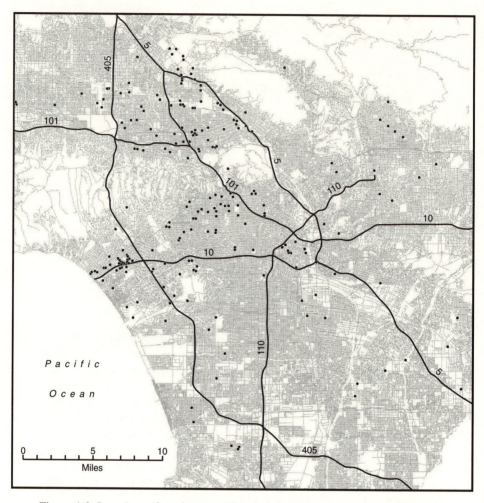

Figure 4.3. Locations of vendors providing inputs to the case-study television show.

generally in Southern California. As such, it covers the same band of territory stretching from Santa Monica through Hollywood proper (where the company that produces the case-study show is located) to Burbank. The pattern also extends somewhat beyond this area and into the San Fernando Valley, where many other auxiliary activities in the entertainment industry are located. Only minor occurrences of purchasing activity in the rest of the metropolitan area can be observed.

These remarks indicate that a tight locational symbiosis exists between the production company responsible for the case-study show and its main suppliers of materials, equipment, and services. In particular, the company's operations are deeply rooted in the economic environment of Hollywood via a great many small and irregular transactions (which accordingly are apt to have high unit costs). This enracination is especially forceful because so many of the individual transactions themselves involve peculiar kinds of inputs that are only likely to be found in the right quantities at the right times and with the right attributes in a large and specialized center of production. Very similar kinds of functional and spatial relationships presumably exist for other television program production companies in Southern California, thereby helping to keep them anchored to the wider regional economy. At the same time, however, various countervailing forces are increasingly making themselves felt so that despite the benefits of proximity to many different kinds of suppliers in Los Angeles, more and more companies are now carrying out basic production work at other locations.

Centrifugal Forces

The preceding exercise reveals the extraordinarily detailed grounding of the case-study television show in the wider economic system of Hollywood. While data on the workers employed in the show could not be obtained, it is evident that access to a large and appropriately multifaceted pool of labor has also been critical to the show's commercial viability. These two sets of relationships alone suggest that the production of television programs, certainly in its more accomplished forms, is subject to powerful agglomerative forces. The same tendency is no doubt reinforced by various creativity and innovation effects embedded in the transactions-intensive structure of production, and, as already suggested, by the many positive spillovers that flow from Hollywood's well-oiled institutional environment.

That said, any industrial cluster is also endemically subject to a variety of diseconomies, especially when it begins to mature and certain costs start to escalate. Eventually, as this process continues, more and more firms will tend to seek out alternative production sites. As already indicated in chapter 3, this phenomenon has long been evident in Hollywood in both the motion picture and television sectors, though it is especially strongly developed in the latter. It is also a phenomenon that can be observed in many other segments of the entertainment industry, including animation, special effects, musical composition and performance, and so on. Accordingly, and despite the long-standing centripetal attraction of Hollywood, much decentralization of entertainment-industry functions to satellite locations has gone on over the years, and has been accelerating rapidly since the mid-1990s.

As noted earlier, the phenomenon of creative runaways, reflecting the constant search for realistic outdoor locations and lower production costs, has always been a feature of the Hollywood entertainment industry. Economic runaways for purely cost-cutting purposes are now also beginning to erode employment, especially in the shooting phase of television program production. As Monitor (1999) has shown, the total number of U.S. television shows shot outside the United States in 1990 for cost reasons was 56, and by 1998 the number had grown to 185, representing a 230.4% increase over this nine-year period (see also EIDC 2001; U.S. Department of Commerce 2001).

While there have been expressions of concern about runaway production from Hollywood ever since the 1950s (cf. Bernstein 1957; Christopherson and Storper 1986), the industry has always in the past displayed a remarkable ability to recover from its periodic losses of employment as a result of decentralization and to expand to newer and higher ground. It is possible, however, that the current situation may present a more intractable set of challenges. In view of the logic already laid out in chapter 3, there is every likelihood that Hollywood will continue to lose film-shooting projects (especially relatively standardized television projects with limited input requirements) to lower-cost locations. The same process, however, does not imply any necessary reversal of growth at the managerial-*cum*-creative end of the production spectrum, which is still strongly tied in to the nexus of Hollywood itself. As in past periods when runaway production has intensified, there is currently much political concern about the problems it is creating in Hollywood, and various legislative actions to stem the tide are under consideration. On the basis of the discussion here, it might be reasonably argued that while relevant public intervention (e.g., subsidies, tax breaks, municipal support for new soundstage construction) may delay further decentralization, it is unlikely to stem the tide in the long run. Arguably, one of the best bets for Hollywood in terms of policies to promote continued growth and development would be to ensure that its central deal-making and innovative capacities remain healthy, thus helping to safeguard its position as the world's leading center of conception, design, and content development of popular culture.

Runaway production has unquestionably made substantial inroads into employment in television program production of Hollywood, and it has created painful dislocations in the lower half of the labor market. Still, the problem has not yet grown to full-blown crisis proportions, nor has it in any sense diminished the commercial or creative proficiencies of Hollywood. So long as Hollywood continues to forge ahead by cultivating its leading rather than its lagging edges, it will almost certainly survive as an agglomeration, though increasingly, perhaps, in symbiotic relation with a set of far-flung satellite locations. Over a more distant time horizon, it may well be that some of these locations will emerge more strongly as head-to-head competitors in final television program markets, but such competition will probably increase in any case as the entertainment industries of Europe, Asia, and Latin America press forward in their current quest to expand commercially and to contest global markets.

THE OTHER HOLLYWOOD AND THE WORLD

Television program production represents the "Other Hollywood" in the sense that it runs parallel to but lies in the shadow of the more familiar Hollywood that produces large-scale feature films. In spite of this circumstance, television program production has grown greatly in Hollywood over the last couple of decades, especially in response to the changes sparked by several major rounds of media deregulation. One of the more important of these changes has been the dramatic expansion in the number of television channels available to viewers, with, as a consequence, significant increases in the quantity and diversity of television shows produced. By the same token, competition has stiffened markedly across the industry in the last two decades. In Hollywood itself, these developments are bound up with a series of complex local outcomes represented above all by the dense clustering of television program producers along with their input suppliers at the core of a large and many-sided local labor market. This system is undergirded by webs of associations, institutions, and social networks that help to consolidate the powerful streams of agglomeration economies that emanate from it. Even so, some weakening of the local employment base has occurred in recent years as more and more shooting activities have shifted to other locations, and it is difficult to see how this trend can be reversed, given the cost dynamics involved. Thus, in an incipient way, Hollywood seems to be moving toward participation in the same types of global commodity-chain structures that characterize many other industries today, from clothing to aircraft. It may not be entirely far-fetched to speculate on a possible future scenario in which Hollywood starts to function within an extended spatial division of labor embodied in a worldwide mosaic of specialized production centers, though for the present its integrity as a self-sufficient cluster remains intact.

In view of these remarks, what might we conclude as to how the competitive dynamics of the entertainment industry are likely to work themselves out in a more insistently globalized future? One possible outcome, of course, is that the competitive supremacy of Hollywood will remain unchallenged, and may even intensify, though in the case of television program production, there is a credible counterargument to this line of thinking. Even though Hollywood-made television programs are familiar around the world, they have not penetrated foreign markets to anything like the same degree that American feature films have, and only about a quarter of U.S. television program revenues today are generated by exports (compared with half for motion-picture revenues). This contrast is due partly to the relative ease with which governments in other countries can regulate the content of local television programs, and partly to the well-known preferences of television viewers for homegrown fare. This means, as a corollary, that relatively vigorous television program production industries continue to exist in a number of different countries, even in the absence of a parallel motion picture industry. Producers in some of these countries are demonstrating an increasing capacity to make high-quality television programs, many of which—from British dramas, through Japanese cartoons, to Latin American telenovelas—are also widely exported (Collins 1993; Segrave 1998; Varis 1993). As this occurs, television program production agglomerations in a number of these countries appear to be gearing up for yet more energetic attacks on global markets.

CHAPTER FIVE

Dream Factories: Studios, Soundstages, and Sets

THE PHYSICAL NUCLEUS of film and television production activities is the studio and its associated soundstages. This is the arena where working conditions in the motion picture industry generally come most closely to resemble those of a factory environment. It is also the point where the greater part of the hectic labor of actual shooting is concentrated, and where large teams of assorted workers, from carpenters and painters through actors and camera crew to postproduction staff, come together on given projects. In the present chapter we look in detail at the functional and spatial charac- teristics of this important segment of the industry, and the ways in which it contributes to the overall dynamism of Hollywood. We also briefly examine the geography of a number of allied sectors.

THE STUDIO AS A NEXUS OF PRODUCTION ACTIVITIES

Studios and Production Companies

Strictly speaking, the term *studio* denotes nothing more than a specialized establishment or firm equipped with soundstage facilities for the shooting of films and allied products. In pre–World War II Hollywood, the majors owned huge lots containing multiple stages together with extensive backlots for open-air filming, and they accordingly came frequently to be referred to as *the* studios. However, many smaller studios (in the strict sense) have always been part of the basic infrastructure of Hollywood. The conflation of majors and studios is still common today, but in the present chapter, for the sake of clarity, I shall keep these terms entirely separate from one another.

As the majors downsized and externalized many of their former func- tions after World War II they also cut back severely on their land holdings and associated physical assets. In most cases, they sold off or redeveloped large swaths of their backlot areas. Some of these areas were divided up into smaller parcels; others became the basis of comprehensive land rede- velopment projects such as Century City (now a dense office complex) and Universal City (now a theme park). Up to the end of the 1950s the majors also owned spacious ranches on the periphery of Los Angeles, which were used mainly for making cowboy films. These, too, have largely disappeared, along with most of the independently owned movie ranches. The Warner Ranch and Disney's Golden Oak Ranch are among the few reminders still standing today of this formerly thriving aspect of the Hollywood production complex.

In spite of these cutbacks, the majors continue to retain by far the largest share of soundstage space in Hollywood today. The majors have thus continued right down to the present time to maintain a loose vertical integration of their film production activities and soundstage operations, with the exception of MGM, which gave up the last of its internal studio operations in the mid-1980s. I say "loose" vertical integration because the majors do not always automatically use their own stages for shooting their own films. Depending on strict cost accounting principles, the majors frequently resort to other studios for soundstage space, and they also aggressively rent their stages out to other production companies. At the same time, independently owned studios have come to occupy a position of increasing prominence within the motion picture industry as a whole, especially since the great surge in the construction of new soundstages in Hollywood during the 1990s. In contrast to the majors, independent studios are rarely or never vertically integrated with film production as such, and they subsist by renting out their facilities to production companies proper.

Soundstages and Their Operation

Since the earliest days of motion pictures, then, the studio has occupied a central position in the day-to-day work of the industry. To be sure, studio filming has always been complemented by location shooting in quest of realistic backgrounds, often in parts of the world quite distant from Hollywood. No matter what ups and downs may occur in the incidence of studio shooting relative to location shooting, however, the former has always taken pride of place as the industry's preferred modus operandi.

Studios vary greatly in their size and internal organization, but all are focused on the soundstage as the central element of their operations. The smallest studios in Hollywood have no more than one or two stages; the largest comprise upwards of 20 or 30 stages each. Stages are rarely smaller than 1,500 square feet in area, and at the extreme, they can attain to 30,000 square feet and more. Individual stages are housed in large hangar-like buildings, sometimes custom-built, sometimes converted from former factory or warehouse premises. Stages are usually multiuse facilities, and are variously used for shooting motion pictures, television shows, videos, commercials, and still photographs, as well as for occasional social events, though the largest stages of all are almost always strictly dedicated to feature film production.

Production activities on and around any given soundstage are of great complexity and call for meticulous planning and organization over all phases of activity, from the physical construction of background scenery, through actual shooting, to the final striking of the set. For especially complex feature films, these phases may stretch out over many months, though for less ambitious projects, such as commercials or still photography, a day or two may suffice. Dressing the set in advance of filming is often the most laborious and time-consuming part of the entire process (Grey 1966). The construction of even quite modest sets requires large inputs of labor from skilled carpenters, scene painters, plasterers, equipment operators, and other craftsworkers. The set must also be equipped with suitable props and whatever special effects may be needed to achieve the desired visual result. Certain types of conventionalized backgrounds, such as courtrooms, restaurants, executive office suites, and scientific laboratories, are in sufficiently large and recurrent demand that some studios keep them as standing sets for routine rental to production companies. Most of the larger studios also have stages equipped with tanks for the filming of on- or underwater scenes.

The actual work of shooting a film in the studio revolves principally around the actors and the camera crew under the guiding hand of the director. This moment in the production process also mobilizes large and diverse phalanxes of supporting workers who ensure that all the technical and organizational details of filming run as smoothly as possible. Two groups of workers of particular importance at this phase of the production process are the electricians and grips, who are responsible, respectively, for keeping all the electrical apparatus operating properly, and for shifting and adjusting the intricate lighting systems that are essential to modern cinematography. At the end of each working day, the "dailies" or rushes need to be developed for examination by the director and producer, and so ready accessibility to photographic processing facilities, either in the studio or nearby, is essential as shooting proceeds.

Complementary Studio Functions

Few studios, if any, limit their scope of operations simply to the renting out of soundstages. Most also provide complementary backup services for use by production companies working on the lot.

A widely though not universally established practice is for studios to integrate lighting equipment supply and grip services into their field of operations. Another involves the setting up of a studio mill offering facilities for carpentry, molding, and other crafts work. Production companies can either rent space and equipment in the mill or conveniently have the mill work done for them on a subcontract basis. Most studios are also able to provide office space for production personnel, and rooms for makeup and rehearsal. Major studios, in addition, often lease out office space over lengthy periods to independent production companies with whom they have special relationships.

The number and variety of studio-owned services on offer tend to increase greatly with increasing studio size. Larger studios typically propose a menu of rental opportunities that extends over costumes and props, screening rooms, and a vast array of technical equipment, including cameras, sound recording devices, cycloramas, wind and rain machinery, and postproduction facilities. In many cases, a studio commissary is also available where workers on the lot can take their meals. The largest studios of all—meaning the majors for the most part—are essentially full-service operations where virtually all of the equipment and materials for the preparation of studio sets and the shooting of films can be leased. They typically offer, in particular, full suites of postproduction facilities including cutting and editing machinery, ADR (automatic dialog replacement) stages for re-recording dialog, scoring stages, Foley stages for producing sound effects, dubbing and mixing equipment for the creation of the final film soundtrack, and so on (Clark and Spohr 1998). The majors and a few other large studios also retain backlot areas (much reduced from their prewar size, to be sure, but still quite extensive) that can be rented for open-air camera work. The backlots usually hold diverse standing sets representing commonly used backgrounds, such as a façade of brownstone houses, a Western street scene, or an open-air swimming pool and terrace.

A Close-up View

We can illustrate these remarks by looking at Warner Brothers studio, one of the largest in Hollywood.

The Warner Brothers opened their first West Coast studio in 1918 on Sunset Boulevard. In 1928, following the success of *The Jazz Singer*, the company moved to its current Burbank site (see figure 5.1). Today, the site covers some 110 acres incorporating an enormous array of activities including central administration, motion picture production, and cognate corporate functions such as Warner Brothers Records and Warner Brothers Television. On any given weekday thousands of workers can be found on the lot, some of them employees of the studio, others associated with firms engaged in business ventures with Warner Brothers or currently renting space or equipment.

The core of the lot is a complex of 28 soundstages, ranging in area from 10,000 to 30,000 square feet. Two of the stages are outfitted with large water tanks. At one end of this complex is a commissary, and at the other

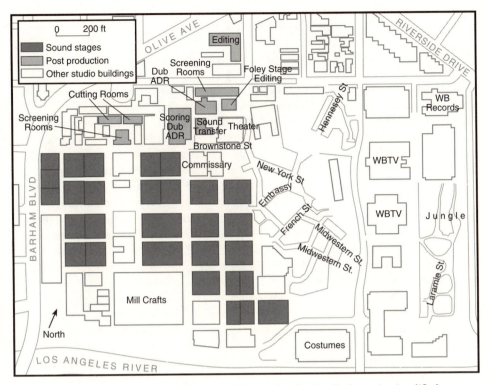

Figure 5.1. The Warner Brothers Studio in Burbank, CA. Redrawn in simplified form from Warner Brothers Studio Facilities *Directory of Services*, 2002–03.

end a large mill crafts building used for set construction and the production of physical special effects. A costume department is located on the south side of the lot. A cluster of buildings to the north harbors a full range of postproduction services, including screening and cutting rooms, editing suites, scoring, dubbing, ADR, and Foley stages, and sound-transfer facilities. Close by these buildings is a theater for film projection, combined with a museum. Much of the east side of the lot is given over to open-air standing sets, including a "jungle" and an associated lagoon, and archetypal streetscapes such as New York Street, French Street, Midwestern Street, and so on. Other activities and facilities that occur on the lot, but not labeled in figure 5.1, include equipment rental, a film archive, makeup and hairdressing facilities, dressing rooms, a photographic laboratory, and an art department, as well as numerous offices for administrative and production personnel.

The Spatial Distribution of Film Studios in Southern California

Southern California in Context

Without question, Hollywood contains the greatest concentration of studios and soundstages in North America and the world. Some indicative statistics are set forth in table 5.1, which shows the total area of soundstages installed at selected locations in the United States and Canada. Los Angeles as a whole is endowed with five million square feet of soundstage area at the present time, a figure far in excess of its main rivals in the United States, that is, New York, North Carolina, Miami/Orlando, and Chicago. Los Angeles actually has almost three times as much capacity as these locations combined. There is also considerably more soundstage space available in Los Angeles than in the whole of Canada. Nevertheless, Toronto and Vancouver have enough installed capacity to offer significant competition to the Hollywood studios, and Canada has been one of Hollywood's main challengers for studio work of late.

That said, the competitive advantages of Toronto and Vancouver reside not so much in their physical infrastructures as in the lower wages of Canadian workers and the fiscal incentives offered by the Canadian federal and provincial governments. Indeed, on the basis of interviews with a number of motion picture industry executives, it might be conservatively estimated that soundstage costs generally account for not much more than three percent of the total budget of most feature films. Important studio facilities can also be found in other parts of the world, many of which compete strongly for

TABLE 5.1
Total Area of Soundstages at Selected Locations in the United States and Canada

	Total soundstage area in square feet
United States:	
Los Angeles	5,049,000
New York	650,000
North Carolina	550,000
Miami/Orlando	282,000
Chicago	140,000
Canada:	
Vancouver	502,000
Toronto	500,000

Source: http://www.eidc.com/
Figure for Los Angeles corrected from 4,400,000.

Hollywood film-shooting projects. These include the Elstree, Pinewood, and Shepperton studios in the greater London area, the Boulogne Billancourt and Éclair studios in Paris, Cinecittà in Rome, and Babelsberg in Berlin, to mention only a few of the more prominent instances. Beyond these obvious competitors, there is much soundstage capacity at numerous other offshore locations (including Twentieth Century Fox's new studios in Baja California, Mexico, and Sydney, Australia). Not a few of these other locations are in countries with considerably lower wage levels than Canada or Europe. There is therefore some likelihood that the film-shooting activities of Hollywood production companies will eventually diffuse more rapidly to these other locations, especially as and when local suppliers can begin to provide more reliable adjunct services.

A Locational Analysis

Los Angeles is currently home to 72 different studios, with 369 soundstages in aggregate. Six majors (Disney, Sony, Twentieth Century Fox, Universal, and Warner Brothers) account for 132 of these soundstages, representing approximately 40% of the total square footage. Three television networks (ABC, CBS, and NBC) account for 35 stages between them and about 10% of the total square footage. The remaining stages are operated by independents of various sizes.

The locations of studios in the region are presented in figure 5.2. For the most part, the pattern shown, like that of the rest of the motion picture industry in Southern California, is strongly skewed toward the west and northwest of central Los Angeles. The pattern can be further roughly described in terms of three main zones drawn around the center of Hollywood. Within a three-mile radius of the central point, there is a core cluster of studio facilities, both small and large (including Paramount). This area, of course, was the original heartland of old Hollywood, and many of the studios there have been in continuous operation since the 1910s. This core area is succeeded by a second zone whose outer boundary extends some 7½ miles from the central point, and that coincides in part with the northern and western suburbs of Los Angeles in the pre–World War II years. This second zone is where most of the large studios were established in the 1920s and 1930s, and where much of the existing soundstage capacity of the region is still to be found. A third zone, containing mostly newer studios, extends to the edge of the metropolitan region. The relatively recent colonization of this outer area can doubtless be accounted for by the land-intensive nature of studio operations and the ever-escalating land prices at more central locations. Even so, and in spite of the increases in overall capacity that have occurred over the last decade or so, 77.8% of all soundstage area in the Los Angeles region, and well over 70% of all studios, still lie within the two inner zones depicted in figure 5.2 (see also table 5.2).

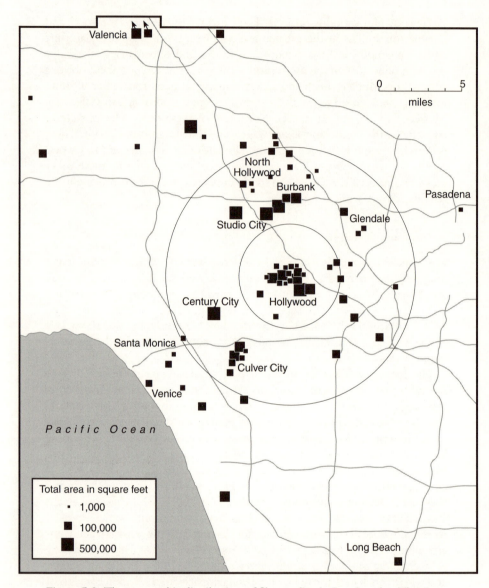

Figure 5.2. The geographic distribution of film studios in Los Angeles. The size of the squares is proportional to the logarithm of the total soundstage area of any studio. Circles are drawn with radii of 3 miles and 7½ miles from the center of Hollywood. Source: Various directories, trade journals, and web sites.

TABLE 5.2
Frequency Distribution of Studios and Soundstage Areas in Los Angeles by Geographic Zones, Based on the Center of Hollywood

Distance from origin in miles	Number of Studios	Percent	Cumulative percent	Total area (square feet)	Percent	Cumulative percent
0.0–1.5	11	15.3	15.3	745,701	14.8	14.8
1.5–3.0	10	13.9	29.2	595,860	11.8	26.6
3.0–4.5	11	15.3	44.5	2,042,564	40.5	67.0
4.5–6.0	8	11.1	55.6	236,470	4.7	71.7
6.0–7.5	12	16.7	72.3	305,651	6.1	77.8
7.5–9.0	5	6.9	79.2	47,789	0.9	78.7
9.0–10.5	5	6.9	86.1	70,310	1.4	80.1
10.5–12.0	2	2.8	88.9	325,000	6.4	86.5
12.0+	8	11.1	100.0	679,170	13.5	100.0
Totals	72	100.0	—	5,048,515	100.0	—

Let us now attempt to understand this complex pattern in somewhat more analytical terms by means of regression analysis. The technicalities of the analysis are laid out in the appendix to the present chapter, and only the main substantive results are presented here. The most statistically forceful of these results indicates that the total soundstage area in any given studio increases steadily, and as a general tendency, with distance from the center of Hollywood. This is an anticipated finding based on the widely observed interplay between land intensity and land prices in urban land use studies, and runs parallel to a very similar result for film studios in the Paris region (see appendix). The regression equations presented in the appendix also reflect the rather obvious point that studios owned by a movie major or television network tend to be much bigger than independent studios. Studios used for making feature films are typically even larger than those used for making television programs. In addition, the regressions add statistical weight to the casual observation that the southeast quadrant of figure 5.2 has an anomalously low density of soundstage activities. It is not hard to find the reason for this outcome. The southeast quadrant of figure 5.2 cuts across both the central business district of Los Angeles, with its peak land prices, and the low-income residential neighborhoods of the south-central area of the city. The few studios that do occur in this area are mostly located in and around the downtown area.

The LA Center Studios, which is located on the east side of Los Angeles' central business district, can be taken as a representative case of these downtown facilities. This is one of the newest studios in the region. Its lot accommodates a large expanse of soundstage space (over 100,000 square feet), which is somewhat unexpected given the high land values in the immediate vicinity. However, overall studio operations are compressed at high density onto a relatively small area of land. In particular, the core building on the lot consists of a converted high-rise office building, itself a unique asset in terms of the opportunities that it offers for filming special scenes and backgrounds. LA Center Studios is also notable for its efforts in pioneering a middle road between internalized and externalized auxiliary supply services. This intermediate course is somewhat reminiscent of the inside contracting system that prevailed in certain large factories in Europe and the United States in the nineteenth century (cf. Englander 1987). The system as currently set up at LA Center Studios is based on a series of joint ventures with individual service suppliers. The latter occupy premises on the lot and sell their services on an independent basis to production companies using the lot; they are also free, however, to sell services to companies at other locations. Suppliers engaged in this experiment provide a wide range of services and equipment, from travel and transportation coordination, through props and heavy equipment rental, to postproduction facilities of all kinds.

INDEPENDENT SERVICE SUPPLIERS OF ADJUNCT SERVICES

Many studios, as already noted, provide a range of auxiliary services in addition to soundstage rental space, though the same services are also almost always available as well from the specialized independent suppliers that abound in and around Los Angeles. On occasions, independent suppliers may have a location on a studio lot; more commonly they are to be found at sites outside the studios themselves, but nevertheless in close proximity.

Photographic processing laboratories provide one notable example of this clustering of auxiliary service suppliers around studio lots in Los Angeles. A particularly dense concentration of such laboratories can be found in and around the innermost clump of studios shown in figure 5.2. Set design and construction offer a further and particularly important example of the same tendency. As we have seen, set construction is often carried out in studio-owned crafts facilities. At the same time, there are currently some 50 independent set design and construction firms operating in the Los Angeles area, most of them combining the two functions under one roof. Sets produced by these firms are usually constructed in modular form so that they can be easily transported to the studio where they are to be finally assembled. The same firms also often produce analog special effects. Many of them are also engaged in the production of themed entertainment backgrounds, for other purposes including restaurant decors, shop window displays, trade show layouts, and so on.

The overall spatial pattern of set design and construction firms in Los Angeles is displayed in figure 5.3. The locations of these firms are rather obviously aligned with those of the studios, though they are somewhat more inclined to occupy peripheral areas of the city. Hence, as shown in table 5.3, as many as 52.0% of all set design and construction firms in Los Angeles are located outside the 7½ mile radius of the designated central point, as compared with 27.7% of studios. Observe that there is a rather strongly developed agglomeration of set design and construction firms in the vicinity of Burbank and North Hollywood, coinciding with a distinctive cluster of studios. This area also lies close to residential neighborhoods with high densities of immigrant Latino workers, who appear, on the basis of fieldwork observations, to be the preferred labor force in at least some segments of the set construction sector. In fact, set-construction activities, as such, represent a sort of transitional sector where the Hollywood motion picture industry starts to shade into the sweatshop economy generally of Southern California.

Finally, a small but vital activity associated with both soundstage operations and set design and construction is represented by the stage props sector. The majors, of course, have large internal props departments, but a number of

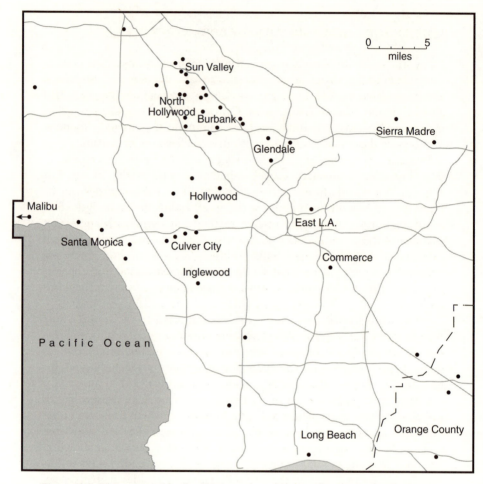

Figure 5.3. The geographic distribution of set design and construction firms in Los Angeles. Source: Various directories, trade journals, and web sites.

independent suppliers (or prop houses, as they are known in the trade) also operate in and around Hollywood (see figure 5.4), providing an enormous range of items such as cast-off surgical instruments, military equipment, old industrial machinery, furniture, posters, and so on (Bloch 2003). There are actually three individual clusters of prop houses in Los Angeles. The first of these, dating from the earliest stirrings of Hollywood as a motion picture complex, is located close to the intersection of Gower and Santa Monica Boulevards, where the original studios are to be found. A second, rather indistinct cluster occurs in association with studio activities in Culver City. A third cluster, of relatively recent origin, but now the largest of the three, is located close to the complex of studio activities in Burbank and North Hollywood (figure 5.4). The distinctive clustering of prop houses is in part explicable by the advantages of proximity to studios, and in part by the circumstance that the set decorators and set dressers, who typically search for the props needed in any particular production, have a habit of moving from prop house to prop house in quest of just the right object. This peculiar form of comparison shopping is an inducement (as it is in certain retail sectors) for suppliers to cluster together in space and thus to take advantage of the economies of scale that their joint proximity offers to users of their services.

STUDIOS AND SATELLITE PRODUCTION LOCATIONS

The studios are the hidden engine room, so to speak, of the entire Hollywood production system. They are hidden, in fact, in two different senses. On the one side, the detailed mechanics involved in actually shooting a film on a soundstage are largely invisible to the viewers of motion pictures; on the other side, the studios themselves are almost always tightly fenced in behind high security barriers and armies of guards so as to protect the property and to ward off the curious.

Precisely because they are such an organizationally and spatially distinctive element of the production process, soundstage operations, together with many of their associated functions, are increasingly susceptible to disarticulation from the rest of the system, and currently display a growing proclivity to decentralization away from Los Angeles into other parts of the world. This trend, by the way, does not signify that studio operations are insensitive to the play of external economies, but rather that the rele-

TABLE 5.3

Frequency Distribution of Set Design and Construction Firms in Los Angeles by Geographic Zones, Based on the Center of Hollywood

Distance from origin in miles	Number of firms	Percent	Cumulative percent
0.0–1.5	0	0.0	0.0
1.5–3.0	2	4.0	4.0
3.0–4.5	5	10.0	14.0
4.5–6.0	7	14.0	28.0
6.0–7.5	10	20.0	48.0
7.5–9.0	5	10.0	58.0
9.0–10.5	6	12.0	80.0
10.5–12.0	3	6.0	86.0
12.0+	12	24.0	100.0
Totals	50	100.0	—

vant externalities can be relatively easily reconstructed elsewhere, certainly in comparison to those that sustain the main creative, financial, and decision-making functions of Hollywood. To repeat, however, the trend is being driven more by labor cost differentials and financial incentives than it is by the rental costs of soundstages themselves. In this respect, motion picture studios bear a close resemblance to other labor-intensive and cost-sensitive industries in Los Angeles, like clothing or furniture, which have seen so much of their central productive capacity dispersed to low-wage off-shore locations of late (Scott 1996, 2002).

In the long run we can probably expect much further expansion in

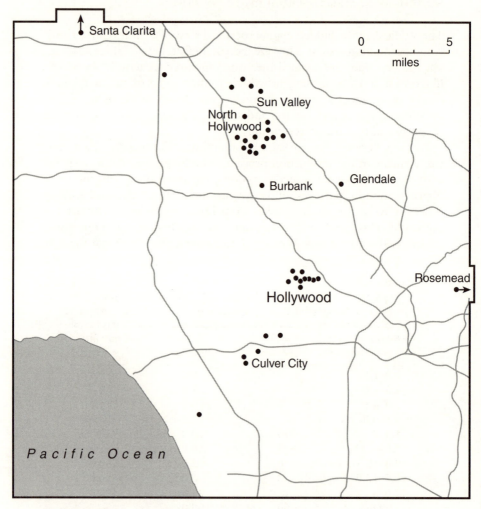

Figure 5.4. The geographic distribution of prop houses in Los Angeles. Redrawn from Bloch (2003).

the number and capacity of satellite studio locations and their use by Hollywood production companies. This trend may conceivably also stimulate the emergence of a regional or international division of labor in the motion picture industry generally. The incipient stages of this process seem already to be well under way.

APPENDIX TO CHAPTER 5
REGRESSION ANALYSIS OF SOUNDSTAGE CHARACTERISTICS IN
   LOS ANGELES

Three basic characteristics of sound studios in Los Angeles were subject to analysis by means of regression. These characteristics (the dependent variables of the regression) are represented by (a) total stage area in square feet, (b) total number of stages, and (c) average soundstage area (total stage area divided by the number of stages). The units of observation are individual studios.

Four independent variables are deployed in an attempt to account for these characteristics. They are: (a) the distance in miles of any given studio from the center of Hollywood, as indicated in figure 5.2, (b) ownership by a major (1 if yes, 0 otherwise), (c) ownership by a television network (1 if yes, 0 otherwise), and (d) an index identifying whether or not any given studio is located in the southeast quadrant of the axis system whose origin coincides with the center of Hollywood (1 if yes, 0 otherwise).

Each regression ranges over 72 observations. Data for the independent variables are analyzed in their natural units. Data for the dependent variables are in all cases transformed to natural logarithms. The results of the regression analyses laid out in table A5.1 are highly meaningful in

TABLE A5.1
Regression Results for Soundstage Characteristics

Variable	Regression 1 (Total stage area)	Regression 2 (Number of stages)	Regression 3 (Average stage area)
Distance to central point	0.082**	0.018	0.070**
Major studio	3.201**	2.149**	1.051*
TV network	2.259**	1.274**	0.985*
Southeast quadrant	−0.800*	−0.245	−0.555*
Constant value	9.231	0.807	8.424
Adjusted R^2	0.331	0.376	0.174

*significant at the 0.05 level.
**significant at the 0.01 level.

empirical terms and for the most part statistically significant, even if the adjusted R^2 values are on the low side. Four brief interpretative remarks are in order:

1. When the effects of all other independent variables are held constant, distance from the central cluster exerts a very significant and positive influence on any studio's total soundstage area. Distance also has positive impacts on the number of stages per studio (but not significantly so), and on average soundstage area (significantly).
2. All three dependent variables are positively and significantly related to ownership of any studio by a major.
3. Similar relations exist when a television network holds ownership, except that the impact is, in the case of all three regressions, less marked than for majors.
4. If a studio lies in the southeast quadrant of Los Angeles, it tends to score less highly on each dependent variable than would otherwise be expected. However, the relationship is not statistically significant in the case of the regression for number of soundstages.

We may compare these results with a regression equation presented in Scott (2000b) where the relationship between soundstage area and distance from the city center is presented for the Paris region. The precise form of the equation is $\ln(A_i) = 5.33 + 1.23D_i$, where A_i is total soundstage area of the ith studio in square feet, and D_i is the distance of the same studio in miles from central Paris. The parameter governing soundstage area with respect to distance is markedly greater for the Paris case than for Los Angeles (cf. table A5.1), which is to be expected in view of the much steeper land price gradient in Paris as a function of distance from the center.

CHAPTER SIX

The Digital Visual Effects Industry

SPECIAL EFFECTS have always played an important part in the theater and the cinema as devices for intensifying production values and heightening dramatic impact. Until quite recently, such effects were invariably produced in physical or analog form. Traditional special effects include simulated sounds, artificial bodily appendages, *trompe l'oeil* models and background paintings, lighting arranged to blur or pinpoint particular scenes, and so on. Over the 1980s and 1990s, great strides were made in simulating these and other kinds of special effects by means of computer-based technologies, thereby greatly extending and deepening their overall range of applications. The current chapter focuses on a particularly important subset of special effects, namely, graphic images (or *digital visual effects*) generated by computers and used as inputs to the entertainment/media industries generally. The discussion will trace the recent historical emergence and geographical characteristics of the digital visual effects sector in the United States as a whole, with special emphasis on empirical aspects of the dominant agglomeration of producers that has sprung up in Southern California and its interrelationships with the motion picture industry.

This is no easy task, given the absence of official sources of statistical data on the special effects industry as a whole, or even any reasonably complete compendium of firms and their geographic locations. In this account, then, I synthesize information from many scattered secondary sources as well as primary data gathered in an extensive questionnaire survey and in a large number of face-to-face interviews. Two main analytical goals motivate this effort. The first, and most important, is to provide an account of the broad logic of organization, location, and performance in the digital visual effects sector and to show how this logic leads to the overwhelming agglomeration of the industry in Southern California, and more specifically in Hollywood. The second is to use digital visual effects as a case study of the multiple and many-tiered input sectors that support the entertainment industry in Hollywood and that are essential building blocks of the local system of competitive advantages.

The Rise of a Digital Visual Effects Industry

A critical event in the development of a visual effects capability in the American cinema was the appearance of the film *Jaws* (Universal Pictures, 1975). Although the visual effects in *Jaws* were created by means of physical and mechanical operations, the intensely spectacular yet convincing images that they produced established a new standard of narrative power and commercial success for Hollywood feature films. There followed a rapid succession of high-concept blockbuster films over the 1980s and 1990s, each with successively more elaborate effects. To be sure, the animated film industry had long before this been producing feature-length films offering dense and striking visual experiences. But these films were built up entirely from hand-crafted images entailing labor-intensive ink-and-paint operations, and their high costs of production imposed severe limits on their commercial viability (Scott 1984). The Walt Disney Company was one of the few firms able over the long term to make a going concern of traditional animated films and to produce commercially successful animated feature films.

In the early 1980s, the development of new computer graphics technologies started to make it physically and economically feasible to create and manipulate digital visual images on a large scale. This turn of events stimulated the first stirrings of a digital visual effects industry, which subsequently, over the 1980s and 1990s, grew at a very rapid pace. The new industry came into being at a point of intersection between the older special effects sector and animated-film production. As it made its historical appearance, the industry came to consist principally of independent firms offering customized services on a contractual basis to major clients. Some of the more successful early digital visual effects firms were Industrial Light and Magic, Dream Quest Images, Stetson Visual Services, and Visual Concept Engineering. The first of these firms was originally founded in Southern California but then shifted to Marin County in the San Francisco Bay Area in the late 1970s. The other three firms were from the start located in Southern California. The major motion picture studios also invested in captive (vertically integrated) facilities, though they continue to rely on external suppliers of visual effects as much as they do on their own in-house production capacity. Captive facilities themselves typically work both for the companies that own them and for outside clients on a subcontract basis. Independent production, however, is dominant in the digital visual effects sector, and the overall high level of organizational fluidity that this affords is a reflection of the uncertainties that are endemic to the entertainment industry generally, subject as it is to extremely competitive business conditions and the hazards of production before the full magnitude of audience reaction is known. In these circumstances, vertical disintegration helps to reduce levels of risk for both suppliers and buyers of visual effects services by allowing them to engage in flexible contracting and re-contracting with one another in the never-ending search for new combinations of creative inputs and innovative energy.

A further critical moment in the development of the digital visual effects industry was the production of *Who Framed Roger Rabbit?* (Touchstone Pictures, 1988, special effects by Industrial Light and Magic), which combined live action and animation with hitherto unequaled realism and dramatic impact. *Who Framed Roger Rabbit?* established a new standard of accomplishment for digital visual effects and marked a continuing evolution in their status from background to foreground on the screen. In fact, the digital visual effects industry at the present time covers an extremely wide range of activities, from unobtrusive touch-up services to massive visual engineering. The latter trend can be observed in films like *Titanic* (Paramount Pictures and Twentieth Century Fox, 1997) or in full-blown animated features like *Monsters, Inc.* (Disney-Pixar, 2001) or *Shrek* (Dreamworks, 2001). *Titanic* alone provided work for more than sixteen different visual effects firms. In Japan, a thriving digital visual effects industry has coalesced around *anime*, or animated films in comic-book idiom. At the same time, applications of digital visual effects techniques are by no means confined to the motion picture industry, but are also important in many allied fields such as television, advertising, web design, computer games, and multimedia generally. Indeed, a significant functional symbiosis between the computer games industry and the motion picture industry is now occurring as more and more films are made on the basis of successful games, and as blockbuster films generate spin-off games.

A Brief Profile of the Industry

Something on the order of 750 to 850 digital visual effects firms exist in the United States at the time of writing. The precise number is difficult to ascertain because of the incompleteness and ambiguity of available information. For present purposes, I have compiled a list of 780 individual digital visual effects firms for the United States as a whole, using a great diversity of sources, including business directories, trade journals, and internet sites.[1] Individual entries were subject to laborious cross-checking and direct verification by means of telephone, mail, and e-mail, and many of the more obviously outlying cases were weeded out. The final list of 780 firms is still

[1] One of the more important sources of information on digital visual effects firms is *Blu-Book Film, TV and Commercial Production Directory* (Los Angeles: Hollywood Reporter, annual). Much useful information can also be gleaned from the Hollywood Creative Directory web site at http://www.hcdonline.com and the Cinefex site at http://www.cinefex.com/. Note that only subscribers can gain access to data archives on the first of these sites.

less than satisfactory, but it is probably as close as it is possible to come to a definitive compilation at this point in time.

In the spring of 2002, these 780 firms were all sent questionnaire forms by mail and/or e-mail, with a second questionnaire being sent to nonrespondents in the summer of the same year. In total, 127 completed or partially completed questionnaires were returned, representing a response rate of 16.3%, which is fairly typical for postal surveys of this kind. It may be noted in passing that some of the firms that responded to the survey are among the most reputable in the industry. In the absence of other sources of data, it is not possible to check this (self-selected) sample for possible sources of bias, though a total of 66.1% of the returned questionnaires came from firms in Southern California, a figure that is not significantly different (on the basis of a z-test) from the 69.0% of the population of firms located in the same region. In spite of this equivalence, due caution is required in interpreting any statistical results based on the questionnaire data.

The Size and Employment Characteristics of Sample Firms

An initial view of the firms that responded to the questionnaire survey is provided by tables 6.1 and 6.2, giving frequency distributions of employment and gross revenue by respondent. Both tables show that small firms greatly predominate in numerical terms, with just a few large firms occupying the extreme upper tails of each distribution. The median firm in the sample has employment of six workers and gross annual revenues of $3 million.

Notice that employment in the present context refers to permanent employees only. Most firms also employ freelance workers whose numbers rise and fall depending on the flow of work, which tends to be rather erratic in this business. There is, however, a systematic relationship between these two forms of employment, in that the number of freelance workers in

TABLE 6.1
Frequency Distribution of Employment for Sample Digital Visual Effects Firms in the United States

Employment size class	Frequency	
	absolute	percent
0–4	48	38.7
5–9	22	17.7
10–19	25	20.2
20–49	23	19.4
50–99	24	19.4
100+	5	3.2
Total	124	100.0

TABLE 6.2
Frequency Distribution of Annual Gross Revenues for
Sample Digital Visual Effects Firms in the United States

| Revenue size class | Frequency | |
($millions)	absolute	percent
0–$1	57	48.3
$1–$5	44	37.3
$5–$10	10	8.5
$10–$25	3	2.5
$25–$50	0	0.0
$50–$100	1	0.8
$100–$250	1	0.8
> $250	2	1.6
Total:	118	100.0

any firm bears a decreasing-returns relationship to the number of permanent employees in the same firm. For the 92 firms in the sample with at least one freelance worker, this relationship can be expressed as the regression equation $F/P = 3.12P^{-0.73}$ (adjusted $R^2 = 0.41$), where F is the number of freelance workers in the firm and P is the number of permanent employees. The coefficient attached to the variable P is significant at well beyond the 0.01 level. This equation indicates that small firms tend to employ proportionately more freelance workers than large, which in turn signifies—since freelance workers can be hired and laid off at short notice—that small firms are more flexible in their employment practices, presumably because they face higher levels of risk than larger, more established firms. A very similar relationship has been shown to obtain for multimedia firms generally in Southern California.[2] There is also a numerically small but highly significant positive correlation between the use of freelance workers in any firm and the proportion of female workers in its cadre of permanent workers.

The digital visual effects labor force can be broadly characterized by reference to four principal occupational categories, namely, creative (or artistic), technical, administrative, and other workers (receptionists, office staff, cleaners, and so on). It should be noted that these four categories are far from being watertight, and some overlap between them inevitably occurs. Table 6.3 provides a tally of the distribution of workers over the four categories for questionnaire respondents, where the information is presented in terms of both simple and weighted averages. Weighted averages, of course, bring the influence of large firms into full evidence. Creative workers clearly

[2] In this earlier study (Scott 1998a), the equation $F/P = 1.97P^{-0.54}$ ($R^2 = 0.33$) was computed for 108 multimedia firms in Southern California.

TABLE 6.3
Main Types of Workers Employed by Sample Digital
Visual Effects Firms in the United States (weighting is
performed in relation to firm revenues)

	Average percentage	
	simple	weighted
Creative	52.2	62.9
Technical	25.1	15.9
Administrative	18.8	20.2
Other	3.5	0.5
Number of cases	125	108

preponderate over the other categories, especially when weighted average values are considered, and this result conforms well to general opinions expressed by firm representatives to the effect that the industry as a whole seems to be evolving from its former preoccupation with raw technology toward a much more resolute focus on matters of content. Technical workers come in second place when measured by simple average percentage of employment. However, when we weight individual percentages by firm size, administrative workers occupy second place, reflecting, no doubt, disproportionate increases in managerial and commercial tasks as firms grow larger. An echo of the preponderance of creative workers over technical workers in the employment structure of the industry can be found in the fact that 41.9% of firms that responded to the questionnaire indicated that they owned one or more image copyrights, as compared with a much more modest 24.8% owning software copyrights.

Production Processes

The production activities of digital visual effects firms revolve primarily around computer graphics operations carried out within project-oriented work groups (Grabher 2001). Each such group usually consists of a tightly knit team of creative and technical workers led by a digital effects supervisor who is responsible for day-to-day production activities. In larger firms, the *digital* effects supervisor in turn reports to a *visual* effects supervisor who is responsible for the overall creative effort and for ensuring that the client's aesthetic vision is fully captured in the final product (Goulekas 2001). A complex array of other tasks complement these core operations (see below), sometimes in vertically integrated relationship, sometimes breaking off to form the nuclei of more specialized vertically disintegrated firms.

In order to shed more light on the nature of production processes in the industry, firms responding to the questionnaire survey were asked to specify which of twelve main tasks, ranging across the gamut of digital visual effects operations, they were able to perform in-house. A full list of these tasks, together with a brief definition of each, is presented in table 6.4. The most commonly occurring tasks are three-dimensional animation, compositing, and scanning. The least common are film development/printing, film recording, and motion capture. Between these two extremes comes a miscellaneous group of activities made up by matte painting, model making, physical/analog effects, software programming, texture mapping, and video transfer. The entire set of raw data on in-house operations was then subject to factor analysis. The detailed technical results of this procedure are laid out in the appendix to this chapter. What now follows is a nontechnical description of the general substantive findings.

The factor analysis reveals that production processes in the digital visual effects industry collapse into four main categories or factors. The first and largest of these can be identified as *General graphics work*, as represented by compositing and matte painting, which are actually rather nontechnical operations. The second is focused on the *processing of film*, such as scanning or developing and printing. The third involves *advanced graphics capabilities*, most notably three-dimensional animation, which involves extremely high-skill work. The fourth concerns *technical backup operations*, notably software programming and motion capture, which are also highly skilled tasks. These four factors, or basic dimensions of variation, come forth with unusual statistical clarity (see appendix). They inform us that internal structures of production in the digital visual effects industry are by no means monolithic, but are rather differentiable into distinctive classes of activities. Inspection of the questionnaire returns suggests that individual firms occasionally specialize in just one class of activities, but that most firms are made up of some combination of the four. The most highly specialized firms in regard to production processes are those that score heavily on the second category (film processing activities), but even here the absolute level of specialization is quite modest. When firms do lack the capacity to perform certain functions in-house—or when their installed capacity is overloaded—they readily subcontract out work. Firms in the sample indicated that on average 17.5% of their total costs are accounted for by subcontracting. This finding is consistent with a system of production in which firms are reasonably self-sufficient in regard to their most critical operations, but where they must occasionally look to other firms to make up for deficiencies that exist in their own operating capacities.

Outputs and Markets

Digital visual effects are used in six main kinds of end products: commercials, computer games, feature films, music videos, television programs,

TABLE 6.4
Selected Tasks in the Digital Visual Effects Industry and Brief Definitions

	Definition
Compositing	A process in which multiple images are combined into one
Film development/printing	Processing of an exposed film to make the images visible
Film recording	The transfer of digital images onto the negative of a film
Matte painting	Production of painted images by hand
Model making	Construction of three-dimensional analog models whose coordinates are then used as the basis of digital images
Motion capture	Translation of live action movement into digital images
Physical/analog effects	Non-digital mechanical or material contrivances used for producing special effects (smoke, thunderclaps, prosthetics, background paintings, etc.)
Scanning	Transfer of visual images from a physical base into a computer by means of an electronic beam
Software programming	Development of computer code for processing information, visual and otherwise
Texture mapping	Manipulation of surface colors and forms so as to make three-dimensional objects appear realistic in a two-dimensional space
Three-dimensional animation	Computerization of images such that all information about them from all perspectives is in storage and can be brought into use as the images shift position
Video transfer	Transfer of digital images into video format

Note: *The glossary of visual effects terms compiled by Goulekas (2001) was used to verify the definitions set forth in this table.

TABLE 6.5
Average Percentages (Simple and Weighted) of Firms'
Output Used in Final Product Categories (Weighting is
performed in relation to firm revenues.)

Final product categories	Average percentage	
	simple	weighted
Commercials	15.3	37.6
Computer games	7.0	2.5
Feature films	23.6	41.7
Music videos	3.2	2.2
Television programs	15.4	8.5
Web design	13.1	3.6
Other	22.5	3.6
Number of cases	126	118

and web design. The questionnaire survey also included a residual "other" products category.

Firms were asked to indicate on the questionnaire how much of their digital visual effects work goes into these different end products, whether directly or indirectly. Table 6.5 presents a summary of responses expressed in terms of simple and weighted averages. Feature films stand out as being overwhelmingly the main end product for digital visual effects service providers. Commercials and television programs also represent significant final product categories. The residual "other" category accounts for a high 22.5% of end-product destinations when measured on a simple average scale, but falls dramatically to 3.6% on a weighted scale, implying that this category is most characteristic of small firms serving rather limited markets. Further inquiry into the substantive meaning of the "other" products category elicited a great diversity of responses, among which theme parks, corporate videos, training films, kiosks, and print media figured with some prominence.

In order to clarify something of the broad structure of the market affinities of digital visual effects firms, a further factor analysis was performed, this time in a search for order in the data underlying table 6.5. The results of this exercise are rather straightforward and are not reported here in any detail.[3] Suffice it to say that three factors were extracted each of which

[3] For the purposes of this exercise, the raw percentage data were translated into binary quantities, with 0 indicating no activity with respect to a given end market, and 1 designating activity at some positive level. This was done because the percentage data represent a closed number system which results in artificially high negative correlations between the individual variables.

is identified here in terms of basic end products: (a) feature films and television programs, (b) commercials and music videos, and (c) computer games. These three factors can be taken as representing the main kinds of markets to which digital visual effects firms are oriented. Curiously, perhaps, there is little relationship between these three factors on the one hand and the four factors extracted from the data regarding production processes on the other, except for the high positive correlation between the level of technical backup operations on the production side and the incidence of computer games on the end-market side.

Firms rarely specialize entirely in serving just one main end market. More often than not, they straddle a number of different markets, thereby securing a reduction in the risks they face and enlarging the opportunities for the exploitation of intellectual property created for one market segment in other market segments (Hozic 2001). Many firms, for example, seek out synergies between feature films and computer games, a trend that is dramatically illustrated by the interactive games divisions that have been established by a number of Hollywood majors such as Disney and Universal (LARTA 2001). Others combine services for television with the production of commercials and music videos. The point can be made more succinctly by computing Herfindahl indexes of firm specialization across the seven market segments designated in table 6.5. A firm with an index of 1 is completely specialized, whereas a firm with an index of 0 (more accurately, 0.14, given that there are only seven options in this case) is equally ensconced in all seven market segments.[4] The average value of the Herfindahl indexes over 126 valid sets of questionnaire responses is 0.59, so that firms are ranged for the most part in an intermediate position between complete specialization and complete diversification. Visual effects firms that have at least some sales to motion picture producers tend to be the most highly specialized. However, even in this instance (and excluding any firms that have no sales whatever to the motion picture industry), the simple average percentage of output dedicated to this end use is just 41.0% (or, in weighted average terms, 45.3%).

PATTERNS OF LOCATION: AN OVERVIEW

I have shown that within the bounds of their peculiar sectoral niche, digital visual effects firms in the United States exhibit much variety in their internal production organization and in the external markets to which they are linked. The motion picture industry represents the main outlet for effects producers, though this is far from being an overwhelmingly dominant relationship. Most firms in the sector are small in size and flexible in their operating characteristics. There is also a limited set of large and successful firms

---

[4] The Herfindahl index (H) for any given array of data, $x_1, x_2, \ldots, x_n$, can be found by first converting the array to proportional values, $p_1, p_2, \ldots, p_n$, and then computing $H = \Sigma p_i^2$.

that enjoy comparatively stable relations with their main clients as a consequence of their superior product quality and acquired reputations. Employment is mostly accounted for by creative workers, but there are significant numbers of technical and administrative workers in the industry as well. These observations all provide useful insights into the nature of the digital visual effects industry, but their import can also be greatly extended by means of a more searching analysis of the locational proclivities of the industry. This proposition is a laconic allusion to the uneven geographic pattern of the industry in the United States and the ways in which this pattern is structured by and in turn structures important aspects of its economic performance.

The geographical distribution of the 780 digital visual effects firms included in this study is depicted in figure 6.1. The most remarkable feature of the figure is the concentration of firms in Southern California, where as many as 69% of the U.S. total are located. (As large as this percentage is, it is actually somewhat less than the 77% concentration of firms in Southern California that is revealed by examination of the Cinefex database referred to in note 1 of this chapter. The Cinefex data, however, refer mainly to firms that have worked on major motion pictures, and are hence to that degree biased.) The Bay Area occupies distant second place

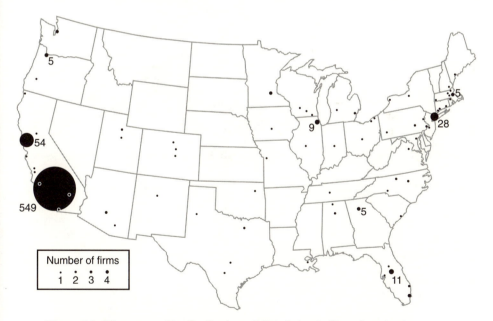

Figure 6.1. The geographic distribution of digital visual effects firms in the United States. Numbers attached to circles indicate total firms in the local area. Source of address data: Various directories, trade journals, and internet sites (see text for details).

after Southern California with 6.9% of the total number of digital visual effects firms, and New York is in third place with 3.6%. There are also small clusters of firms in Atlanta, Boston, Chicago, Orlando, and Seattle. Only a thin scattering of firms occurs elsewhere in the United States.

The locations of individual firms *within* Southern California are displayed in figure 6.2, which reveals at once their gravitation to the northwest quadrant of Los Angeles County. The pattern traced in figure 6.2 coincides with that of the entertainment industry generally in Southern California. From this observation we may surmise that the patterns of co-location between the two sets of firms have much to do with their functional interrelations. Confirmation of this point will be offered at a later stage when we examine detailed questionnaire data on transacting behavior.

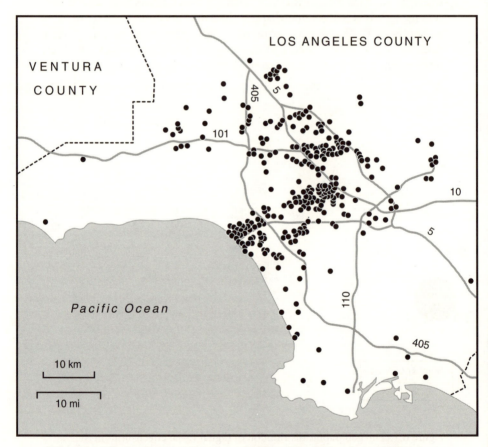

Figure 6.2. The locations of digital visual effects firms in Southern California. Source of address data: Various directories, trade journals, and internet sites (see text for details).

Meanwhile, I should stress that managers of digital visual effects firms interviewed for the purposes of this study confirmed that relations with their clients tend to be recurrent and tightly wrought. Managers also put much emphasis on the creative symbioses embodied in these transactions. Above all, managers referred repeatedly to the high incidence of face-to-face interaction with their clients, even though technologies for remote collaboration are coming into common usage in the industry (Palmer et al. 2001). Much of this interaction, moreover, is not simply about the technical specifications of this or that digital image, but is also centrally concerned with the overall creative thrust of any given project. Accordingly, interaction usually begins at an early stage, and is an occasion of substantial mutual learning (cf. Feldman 2000; Russo 1985). In motion picture work, relations between the two sides are almost always established even before film shooting begins so that critical creative decisions can be closely coordinated. Intense interaction persists all the way through to the postproduction phase.[5]

STATISTICAL EXPLORATIONS OF THE INDUSTRY'S LOCATIONAL LOGIC

In light of this overview of the digital visual effects industry in the United States and Southern California, we may ask what if any impacts do its locational characteristics have on various performance criteria (and vice versa), and in particular, how are its spatial relationships to the motion picture industry structured in practice? The method by which we broach the tasks raised by this question involves many-layered statistical comparisons between (relatively agglomerated) producers in Southern California and (relatively dispersed) producers in the rest of the United States.

Market Outlets and Location

Sample firms were divided into two groups: those located in Southern California, and those located in the rest of the United States. Data on the final product categories served by firms in the two groups were then processed statistically[6] as indicated in table 6.6. The main body of table 6.6 records mean rank information on the two groups in regard to the different markets that they serve, where the rank of any individual firm is defined as its position in an ordered data series (here, percentage of output tied to a given final product). Mean rank is thus an index of the scores of firms in each group on the criterion variable (commercials, computer games, feature films, etc.).

---

[5] In spite of this tendency to early initiation of relations between digital visual effects firms and film production companies, digital visual effects are widely but imprecisely referred to as a postproduction activity.

[6] A Mann-Whitney U test was used for this purpose.

TABLE 6.6
Mean Rank Comparison of Firms in Southern California and the Rest of the United States According to the Final Product Categories for Which They Provide Inputs

	Mean rank of firms located in	
Final product categories	Southern California	rest of the United States
Commercials	57.7	67.3
Computer games	60.3	62.4
Feature films	71.0**	42.3**
Music videos	59.1	64.6
Television programs	63.0	57.2
Web design	57.4	67.9
Other	52.5**	76.9**
Number of firms:	79	42

** = significant at the 0.01 level by means of a Mann-Whitney U test.

The most significant piece of information yielded by table 6.6, as may be expected, is the very much more marked engagement of firms in Southern California in activities related to feature films compared to firms in the rest of the country. In simple average terms, 32.6% of the output of Southern Californian firms—and 42.6% in weighted average terms—is destined for use in cinematic products. The corresponding statistics for firms in the rest of the country are 7.7% and 17.1%,[7] a circumstance that points indirectly to an inverse relationship between firm size and the distance over which transacting tends to occur. Thus, the relatively low value of the simple average and the notably higher value of the weighted average for firms located outside Southern California (and given that cinematic products are made overwhelmingly in Hollywood) suggests that the outputs of small firms travel less easily than the outputs of large. More specifically, as we observed in chapter 4, smaller firms tend to be more closely tied to local markets because they cannot achieve economies of scale in long-distance transacting, whereas larger firms can operate successfully at a greater distance because of their command of transactional economies of scale. We shall return to this point later.

The second most significant finding presented in table 6.6 is the relative concentration of firms in the rest of the United States on the "other" end markets category. Sales from Southern Californian firms going to this category represent 15.9% of the total when measured as a simple average and

[7] Firms in Southern California also tend to be more strongly tied to television programming markets than firms in the rest of the country, though the difference is not statistically important.

3.3% when measured as a weighted average. But equivalent sales from firms in the rest of the United States are 37.3% and 16.7%. The indications here are that the rest of the United States has a relatively large representation of rather small digital visual effects firms tied in finely grained transactional relations to miscellaneous clients. In addition, the data in table 6.6 inform us that firms in the rest of the country are more highly connected (but not significantly so) to end markets in commercials, computer games, music videos, and web design than firms in Southern California.

It turns out, despite the distinctive character of Southern Californian digital visual effects firms, that some significant spatial differentiation of the industry *within* the region can be observed. For present purposes, the region as a whole may be divided into three spatial units: (a) a central core represented by Hollywood, Burbank, and Studio City, (b) a sub-agglomeration comprising Santa Monica, Venice, and Culver City in the west, and (c) the rest of Southern California. The data show quite plainly that digital visual effects firms in the core area are relatively specialized in serving the feature film and television program sectors. The western sub-agglomeration has an unusually high representation of computer games providers, which is consistent with the findings of an earlier study of the multimedia industry generally in this part of Southern California (Scott 1998b). Firms in the rest of the region tend to be more involved in web design activities. Notwithstanding these intra-regional differences, it is to be stressed that diverse types of digital visual effects production are inter-mingled across the entire set of locations shown in figure 6.2.

The Spatial Organization of Transactions

Table 6.7 provides a summary overview of the flow of outputs between digital visual effects producers in two origin regions (Southern California and the rest of the United States), and markets in three destination regions (Southern California, the rest of the United States, and the rest of the world). The data in the table highlight the dominant tendency of digital visual effects firms to sell their products intra-regionally, no matter whether they are located in Southern California or in the rest of the country. Conversely, cross-regional sales are much less well developed, and sales to foreign markets are notably modest. Table 6.7 also shows that the incidence of intra-regional sales decreases when measured on a weighted average scale as compared with simple averages. Conversely, weighted averages magnify the measured incidence of *inter*-regional sales, both from the rest of the country to Southern California and in the inverse direction. Again, then, the conclusion is that small firms transact over significantly shorter distances than large firms do.

Further evidence on the same point may be adduced by examining the detailed pattern of digital visual effects sales to the seven Hollywood

TABLE 6.7

Simple and Weighted Average Percentages of Firms' Output Sold on Different Markets (Weighting is performed in relation to firm revenues.)

	To markets in			
	Southern California	Rest of the U.S.	Rest of the world	Number of cases
From firms in				
Southern California				
Simple average	70.0	23.2	6.5	80
Weighted average	55.0	42.4	2.5	75
Rest of the U.S.				
Simple average	11.2	82.8	4.8	41
Weighted average	32.2	63.1	3.1	38

majors, MGM, Paramount, Sony-Columbia, Twentieth Century Fox, Universal, Walt Disney, and Warner Brothers. The data laid out in table 6.8 show, not unexpectedly, that the majors figure very strongly in the overall sales activities of digital visual effects firms. More important for the present investigation is the way in which this relationship is structured by location, with Southern Californian firms far outstripping firms in the rest of the country as suppliers of digital visual effects services to the majors. In simple average percentage terms, the majors absorb 32.8% of the sales of Southern Californian digital visual effects firms, but just 7.7% of the sales of firms in the rest of the country. In weighted average terms, the figures are 47.1% and 24.7%, respectively. Again, the distinction between large and small producers in the matter of interlinkage makes its appearance, with larger firms clearly transacting more actively over longer distances than smaller. When the survey was taken, Warner Brothers was by a large margin ahead of all the other majors in the dollar value of purchases of digital visual effects services from external sources.

Of all the large firms outside Southern California that furnish the majors with digital visual effects services, a select group in the Bay Area is unquestionably the most successful and influential overall. Among this group are Industrial Light and Magic, Pixar, and Tippett Studio, all of which have been involved in numerous large-scale feature films. Firms like these typically enjoy a high level of stability relative to the industry as a whole, and—of special significance—are connected in various kinds of long-term relational contracts to the majors and other large motion picture production companies in Southern California. Indeed, Industrial Light and Magic has a long-standing and absolutely dominating position in the supply of digital visual effects to the Hollywood majors, with over 75 big-budget feature films to its credit.

TABLE 6.8
Simple and Weighted Average Percentages of Firms' Outputs Sold to Individual Hollywood Majors

	MGM	Paramount	Sony-Columbia	Twentieth Century Fox	Universal	Walt Disney	Warner Brothers	All majors	Number of cases
				To the Hollywood majors					
From firms in									
Southern California									
Simple average	1.1	5.3	5.8	3.5	5.0	4.6	7.5	32.8	68
Weighted average	0.5	4.7	12.3	9.6	1.5	3.8	14.7	47.1	62
Rest of the U.S.									
Simple average	0.0	0.0	0.0	0.9	0.9	3.0	3.0	7.7	35
Weighted average	0.0	0.0	0.0	2.6	2.4	8.4	11.3	24.7	33

Circumstances of this sort, combined with strong internal economies of scale and scope, make it feasible for these firms to sustain spatially extended external relations. As a corollary, they are able to operate successfully from a wider circle of production locations than many of their competitors. The Bay Area, moreover, is an attractive location for technical inputs and skilled labor. However, the Bay Area is not the budding alternative to Hollywood that Clough (2002) has claimed it be, so much as a sort of specialized outlier. A number of large and highly regarded firms located in Australia, Britain, Canada, France, and other countries are also among the providers of digital visual effects services to the Hollywood majors, but large foreign suppliers almost always set up subsidiary operations in Southern California whenever they are working on a contract with one of the larger production companies.

The Agglomeration in Perspective

The Southern Californian agglomeration of digital visual effects firms is thus held together in large degree by a taut network of transactional relations whose locationally polarizing influence is made yet more pronounced by reason of the status of the agglomeration as an intensely competitive, high-performance business environment.

One index of this polarizing influence is the degree of competitive open bidding that digital visual effects firms engage in when they are hunting for work. On average, 61.0% of questionnaire respondents located in Southern California stated that they are typically caught up in competitive bidding for contracts, in contrast to a significantly lower (at the 0.01 level) 45.1% for firms in the rest of the country. By this measure, firms in Southern California are considerably more active on the external relations front than firms in the rest of the country. Moreover, competitive bidding in Southern California is just as characteristic of large firms as it is of small. At the same time, firms in Southern California are more likely than firms elsewhere to engage in joint venture activities, and when they do so they tend to prefer partnerships with local firms. Firms in the region are also generally more specialized than firms elsewhere, which in turn can possibly be interpreted as a symptom of greater levels of vertical disintegration and transactions-intensive interaction. Thus, again using Herfindahl indexes, it was found (with a level of significance greater than 0.05) that digital visual effects producers in Southern California operate in much more specialized market niches than firms elsewhere in the country.

The more pronounced incidence of specialized technology-intensive production among Southern Californian firms relative to firms in the rest of the country is echoed by other measures of performance. Reexamination of the factor analysis results presented in the appendix is helpful here. When firms are arrayed along an axis defined by factor 1 (general graphics work), those located in Southern California score low values, whereas those elsewhere score high positive values, with the difference between the two groups being significant at the 0.05 level. In concrete terms, this suggests that Southern Californian digital visual effects firms tend, on average, to be somewhat more specialized and more technically advanced than firms in the rest of the country. Additionally, Southern Californian firms score toward the top end of factors 2, 3, and 4 compared with firms in the rest of the country, but in this instance, although the direction of difference points again to higher levels of specialization and skill for Southern Californian firms, the two groups are not significantly distinguishable from one another. At the same time, Southern Californian firms are tightly bound to the dense local labor market, which functions not only as a repository of the requisite highly trained and experienced employees but also as a mechanism through which workers become more effectively socialized into appropriate norms of on-the-job activity. A related point concerns the unusually large percentage of foreign-born workers in the local labor market for digital visual effects workers. In all, 17.8% of the employees of sample firms in Southern California are foreign-born, compared with a very significantly lower (at the 0.01 level) 6.2% in firms in the rest of the country. This peculiar structure of employment can be traced back to the 1990s, when digital visual effects firms in Southern California were facing acute skills shortages due to their rapid expansion, a situation to which they responded by importing large numbers of highly skilled workers from other countries; these workers now constitute a major fraction of the local labor force.

A FORWARD GLANCE

The digital visual effects sector is of quite recent origin, dating back no more than a decade or two; in the sample of firms under scrutiny here, the median date of founding is 1995. Over the brief span of time in which it has been in existence, however, the sector has grown apace and has developed rapidly in terms of its basic technological and creative capacities. It is now an indispensable element of the audiovisual and media industries generally, and it is, above all, increasingly critical to contemporary motion picture production. The sector is chiefly located in Southern California, where, as the present analysis has shown, it is rooted in a complex web of transactional linkages and other relational assets. Southern California is also the site of a dense pool of labor that is the source of multiple skills and creative sensibilities. The whole productive system forms a vast interconnected field in which firms and workers are caught up in fluid relations of interchange.

In view of its youth and the dynamism of the technologies on which it is based, the digital visual effects industry will doubtless continue to evolve substantially over the coming decades, one possible direction of change being a shift toward a wider social division of labor and higher levels of firm specialization than have prevailed hitherto. Whether or not the continued evolution of relevant technologies will have disruptive consequences for the structure of production and locational outcomes in the entertainment industry as a whole remains be seen. There is much evidence to suggest that the motion picture industry proper and the digital visual effects sector have been converging of late, as digital visual effects firms move more resolutely into cinematograhic products and as a number of motion picture production companies acquire internal capacity for the production of digital visual effects, including computer games. Increasingly, too, major changes are occurring in audiovisual production processes generally, as digital visual effects displace live action in favor of computer-generated images and sounds. As it has grown and developed, the industry has steadily proven its ability to move beyond the rapid-fire but aesthetically and semiotically limited pyrotechnics that have characterized a high proportion of its most commercially successful achievements thus far, and of building much more subtle and emotive nuances into its products. By the same token, digital visual effects have increasingly become the subject of intellectual property disputes as more and more copyrighted material assumes the form of the digitized symbols that are the industry's stock in trade.

As noted earlier, some observers have suggested that the digital visual effects industry is likely eventually to shift away from Southern California into other parts of the country and especially into the Bay Area, where much of the basic hardware and software powering its production processes originates. This claim is not unpersuasive at first sight, above all since there is already a secondary concentration of successful digital visual effects producers in the latter area (see figure 6.1). Once this point has been admitted, the data and analysis presented in this chapter still suggest that the Southern Californian agglomeration is very firmly ensconced in its current location as an operating, competitive, multifaceted industrial cluster. There are few signs of long-term internal decay within this cluster, even if selected decentralization has been one of its endemic features (as it is of virtually all industrial agglomerations). For the present, continued intensification of the Southern Californian agglomeration would seem to represent the most plausible prognostication, especially as the region remains the privileged locus of multiple small-scale entrepreneurial efforts within the digital visual effects industry. Over the longer run, depending on many imponderables, the outlook is considerably more opaque. One thing is evident in this respect. Several European and Asian Pacific countries are now aggressively seeking to establish globally competitive digital visual effects industries as part of wider programs to build up their domestic audiovisual production capabilities, sometimes in association with investors from Hollywood.

As these competitor industries come on line, they could conceivably make further inroads into markets for digital visual effects in Southern California, with ensuing shifts in the basic geography of production, though it seems unlikely that they could entirely supplant Southern Californian producers.

APPENDIX TO CHAPTER 6
FACTOR ANALYSIS OF PRODUCTION ACTIVITIES IN THE
   DIGITAL VISUAL EFFECTS INDUSTRY OF LOS ANGELES

Data were collected in the questionnaire survey on which of twelve main tasks digital effects firms in Los Angeles could perform in-house (see table 6.4). The data were coded as either 1 or 0, signifying, respectively, presence or absence of any given activity in a given firm. These data were then subject to factor analysis in order to uncover their basic dimensions of variation.

Factor analysis is a tool for reducing one set of variables to a computed set of proxy variables, or factors, where the latter express the basic structures of intercorrelation in the initial variables. The specific mechanics of factor analysis need not detain us here, except to note that the meaning of any computed factor is determined by reference to the loadings of the original variables on that factor. A specific loading can be directly interpreted as the simple correlation between a given factor and a given variable in the original data set. Loadings on all twelve original variables are recorded in table A6.1. Four factors were identified in this instance.

   Factor 1: The first factor extracted can be construed as representing basic graphics operations. The tasks of compositing, matte painting, physical/ analog effects, and texture mapping are the main constituents of the factor. As such, factor 1 captures the relatively low-technology (even pre-digital) spectrum of visual effects activities.
   Factor 2: The loadings on factor 2 are highest for scanning, film recording, and film development/printing. The evident interpretation is that factor 2 stands in for specialized film processing functions.
   Factor 3: The variable that loads most heavily on this factor is three-dimensional animation, followed by model making and texture mapping. Factor 3 can be identified as a measure of advanced graphics capability in the digital visual effects industry.
   Factor 4: For the most part, factor 4 picks up on two highly specialized but often inter-associated activities in the digital visual effects industry, i.e. software programming and motion capture, both of which have high positive loadings. Factor 4 can be defined as an index of basic technical operations that underpin actual computer graphics operations.

TABLE A6.1
Factor Analysis Results: Rotated Component Matrix

| Activity | Sampled firms able to carry out this activity | | Loadings | | | |
	Number	Percent	Factor 1	Factor 2	Factor 3	Factor 4
Compositing	84	70.6	0.60	0.09	0.03	−0.34
Film development/printing	28	23.5	0.29	0.57	−0.01	0.29
Film recording	28	23.5	0.05	0.79	−0.07	−0.09
Matte painting	62	52.1	0.70	0.05	0.40	−0.07
Model making	42	35.3	0.06	0.02	0.61	0.00
Motion capture	34	28.6	0.23	0.29	−0.22	0.57
Physical/analog effects	57	47.9	0.71	0.01	−0.05	0.24
Scanning	68	57.1	0.03	0.80	0.20	0.02
Software programming	56	47.1	−0.13	−0.09	0.23	0.78
Texture mapping	61	51.3	0.68	0.02	0.51	0.03
Three-dimensional animation	92	77.3	0.08	0.04	0.81	0.07
Video transfer	52	43.7	0.38	0.19	−0.03	0.04

Note: Factor loadings with absolute values greater than 5.0 are italicized.

Local Labor Markets in Hollywood

Setting the Scene

Hidden behind the flickering images that are the average consumer's dominant sense of Hollywood, there lies another and very different world of production and employment, the greater part of it quite humdrum. Thus far in this book, we have focused our attention on productive organization and the interrelations between firms. But Hollywood is also the center of a complex local labor market (or, more properly, a series of overlapping labor markets), whose form and functions contribute significantly to its status as a durable agglomeration of high-performance firms.

For our purposes, the history of this local labor market can be divided into two main episodes. The first of these corresponds to the classical studio system of production that developed over the 1920s and 1930s, when workers functioned for the most part as permanent company employees with a regular wage or salary (Ross 1941, 1947). This state of affairs obtained, moreover, for workers of all gradations, from the blue-collar manual workers at the bottom of the job ladder to the stars at the pinnacle. The second episode coincides with the so-called new Hollywood that came into existence after the 1950s as the old studio system broke down, and when the employment relation was largely externalized for all but selected groups of workers providing managerial and administrative continuity within the firm. In this new order of things, perhaps the majority of workers now assumed temporary or freelance status, being taken on by production companies as limited-term employees or operating on a commission basis, and moving irregularly from job to job depending on the fluctuations of productive activity.

Thus, as the new Hollywood consolidated its productive and competitive capacities over the second half of the twentieth century, the local labor market also became increasingly flexible and volatile, so that workers caught up in it today are subject to extremely high levels of risk in regard to remuneration, benefits, job prospects, and so on. Labor markets like this are nowadays a common feature in many segments of the American and European economies, and their modes of operation present a number of puzzling questions (cf. Blair et al. 2001; Menger 1991; Peck 1996; Scott 2000a). In Hollywood, the problem is posed with particular force because the local labor market is made up not so much of a mass of low-skill, low-wage workers, but of some of the most creative and most highly paid workers in the world. What strategies, we may ask, do different groups of workers deploy in pursuit of their careers when faced with labor-market conditions of this sort? How do these strategies intersect with and restructure wider labor-market dynamics? What kinds of organizational/institutional responses occur in the labor market, and what effects do these responses have on the operation of the local economy generally? A further important set of questions intersecting with all of these points concerns the geography of the local labor market, and more specifically, the emergent effects that are set in motion by its function as a bridge between the residential and production spaces of the city.

HISTORICAL EMERGENCE OF THE EMPLOYMENT RELATION IN HOLLYWOOD

The Classical Studio System

The main features of the Hollywood production system in the golden age of the 1920s and 1930s can be succinctly captured by direct reference to the large vertically integrated studios or majors that dominated the motion picture industry at that time (Bordwell et al. 1985). Vertical integration in the majors involved, in the first instance, single units of ownership spanning the whole chain of business activities from production through distribution to exhibition. In the second instance, production itself was organized as a vast in-house operation bringing together in one establishment the tasks of writers, directors, producers, actors, composers, musicians, costume designers, cinematographers, and so on, and a supporting army of manual, crafts, and technical workers (Lovell and Carter 1955). As we saw in chapter 3, several analysts have erroneously referred to this system as a form of mass production, whereas it is more accurately describable as a curious combination of craft and bureaucratic production models *à la* Stinchcombe (1959), in which the commercial exigencies of product differentiation ran permanently counter to the efforts of studio managers to streamline production. While integrated studio production was based on craft labor entailing highly personalized skills and much dedication on the part of workers to teamwork as well as to their individual specialized tasks, the system was also overlain by large internal bureaucracies seeking wherever possible to deskill work through divisions of labor and to standardize the final product.

The classical studio system was certainly not optimized for flexibility in its external relationships, but it enjoyed the countervailing advantage of always having full complements of essential skills and talents on hand to keep production going at a rapid pace. A further advantage, from the studios'

perspective, was that the stars they created served under long-term salary agreements (usually of seven years' duration), and thus could not—even given their exceptionally high levels of remuneration—appropriate the full value of the rents that they generated as their celebrity expanded (Kindem 1982). This captive or semi-captive labor force meant, too, that each studio's films tended to be stylistically distinct. It would be an error, however, to presume that there was *no* temporary or short-term employment (or, in modern parlance, numerical flexibility) in Hollywood in the prewar years. Even at the height of the classical era, the studios as well as independent production companies sought to fine-tune their use of labor by frequent hiring and lay-off at the margins, most especially of workers on the lower rungs of the job ladder. Great throngs of extras added to the pool of floating short-term labor in Hollywood at this time. The problems created by the expansion of this body of day workers—exacerbated as they were by continual new influxes into Southern California of aspiring actors and actresses—became so pressing that the studios joined together as early as 1926 to set up the Central Casting Corporation to serve as a clearinghouse for casual acting jobs (Ross 1947).

Numerous attempts were made in Hollywood during the classical era to unionize the workers, a daunting task under any circumstances, but exceptionally difficult in Los Angeles at this period when the local elite was resolutely committed to the maintenance of the region as a citadel of the open shop (Davis 1997; Ross 1941). Throughout the 1920s and 1930s, political clashes between the studios and the nascent unions were rampant. In an attempt to forestall labor-organizing activities, the studios went so far as to set up the Academy of Motion Picture Arts and Sciences in 1927 to function as a company union (Nielson and Mailes 1995). The Academy, as initially constituted, had five branches representing producers, writers, directors, actors, and technicians. For a time, the Academy worked reasonably well, but it lost all credibility in the eyes of its members in the depression years when it supported the majors in their efforts to induce workers to agree to voluntary reductions in their wages and salaries. Accordingly, it steadily gave ground to independent unionization movements over the 1930s. The Academy, which still exists, has long since abandoned its original goals, and is now mainly known for its patronage of the annual Oscar awards.

The rise of an independent union movement in Hollywood in the prewar years is a complicated story that has been treated at length elsewhere (e.g., Amman 1996; Horne 2001; Prindle 1988; Ross 1941). For present purposes, we need only note that the urge to unionization of the Hollywood labor force was greatly energized by the passage of the Wagner Act in 1935, and that by the time of the outbreak of World War II, most of the workers in the large studios had been successfully incorporated into either blue-collar unions or professional guilds.

The New Hollywood

Immediately after the Second World War, as already indicated, the studios were subject to severe destabilization of their final markets. Industrial sectors that are subject to stresses and strains of this sort commonly respond by some degree of vertical disintegration, particularly where, as in the case of the Hollywood studios, their operation incurs high fixed costs (Carlton 1979; Scott 1986). The push to vertical disintegration was all the stronger because of the large numbers of workers that the studios were carrying on their permanent payrolls, workers could no longer be efficiently employed on a full-time basis in a context where the flow of production was becoming increasingly irregular. The studios thus went through a period of disintegration and downsizing from the late 1940s to the early 1960s, leading eventually to the entirely new pattern of production in Hollywood described in chapter 3. This new pattern was associated with a shift away from permanent employment in favor of limited-term contracts covering the duration of particular projects. Thus, there were 804 professional actors under contract to the Hollywood studios in 1945, whereas by 1960, the number had dwindled to just 139 (Cantor and Peters 1980). The search for numerical flexibility has intensified over succeeding decades, and today most workers in the industry act as temporary employees or freelance agents, so that they constantly circulate through the job system in spasmodic bouts of employment and unemployment.

As the 1960s came and went, the stripped-down majors found themselves well positioned to deal with the new market realities of the motion picture business, and this turn of events sparked further adjustments in the local labor market that are still in many ways working themselves out. One conspicuous outcome was that the stars at the top of the job ladder, freed from long-term contractual obligations to individual production companies, were now fully able to appropriate the rents due to their celebrity. But the mass of workers in the industry, no matter what their standing in terms of skill or talent, were faced with the greatly increased risks of an unstable project-oriented employment system, and were obliged to find ways, socially and individually, of adapting to it. The human resource management functions of the firm now gave way to the self-management of workers. Equally, traditional forms of advancement based on the building up of firm-specific human capital and seniority were supplanted (for all but a cadre of managers and administrative workers) by the establishment of reputation as the main currency of worker evaluation. Workers adopted as far as possible the strategic imperative of planning their credits and experiences across the entire entertainment industry in the quest to mold their reputations (cf. Menger 1999). Along with these changes came a distinctive manner of classifying workers according to their labor-market power.

Workers were now either "above the line" (signifying individuals whose salaries are individually negotiated and who are named explicitly as line item entries in any project budget), or "below the line" (with remuneration being set impersonally according to wage schedules defined in collective-bargaining agreements). As a general, though by no means absolute, rule, professional guilds became the collective representatives of above-the-line workers, and various manual, crafts, and technical employees' unions of below-the-line workers.

These changes in the structure of the local labor market consequent upon the advent of the new Hollywood represent a dramatic vanguard case of the flexibilization of work arrangements that was later to spread much more widely throughout the United States. In the 1950s and 1960s, when flexible labor markets were seen largely as throwbacks to nineteenth-century forms of industrialization, Hollywood was already pioneering on a large scale the contingent model of employment that is now more or less taken for granted across a large portion of the contemporary American economy.

EMPLOYMENT, LOCAL LABOR MARKET DYNAMICS, AND THE METROPOLIS

Agglomeration Economies and the Local Labor Market

Industrial districts are a geographic expression of the agglomeration economies, or localized increasing returns effects, that almost always spring forth when different participants in any industrial system locate in close proximity to one another. They are thus a source of multiple benefits that boost the competitive advantages of firms and the welfare of workers. Agglomeration economies have many different points of origin, but local labor markets are certainly one of the more important of them, and not least because of their character as concentrated pools of workers living in residential neighborhoods in and around the clusters of jobs on which they depend for their livelihoods (Kim 1987; Scott 1981). The high levels of accessibility that invariably characterize the spatial relations between these neighborhoods and employment locations ensure that commuting costs will be relatively low and that upward pressures on wages will be to that degree contained. Local labor markets in this sense are also repositories of diverse skills and aptitudes more or less corresponding to the array of specialized tasks that make up the entire production system. The mutual propinquity of home-places and workplaces hence also facilitates effective matching of workers and jobs. In addition, local labor markets are almost always shot through with overlapping networks of interpersonal contacts through which large quantities of useful information (about employers, job opportunities, conditions of work, and so on) constantly circulate. Lastly, local labor markets are sites of socialization and habituation such that individuals are in various subtle ways—even in their social lives—pre-adapted to the experience of work in the local production system.

In this fashion, the production system of Hollywood together with its surrounding residential communities constitute mutually reinforcing elements of a territorial system whose viability over time depends critically on the place-specific agglomeration economies that it generates. The force of these economies resides both in the close proximity of many different firms and workers to one another, and in the specific institutional frameworks that invariably spring up in order to manage market failures in these kinds of spatial complexes. Hollywood is notably rich in regard to the institutional arrangements that have appeared over the course of its development in response to local labor market dilemmas, and, as will be made evident, these make important contributions to the total stock of agglomeration economies in and around the area.

The Local Labor Market in Time and Space

Aggregate employment in the motion picture industry of Hollywood has expanded rapidly since the early 1980s. Figure 7.1 shows employment in SIC 78 (Motion Pictures)[1] in Los Angeles County on a month-by-month basis from January 1983 to December 2002. At the start of this period, employment stood at about 65,000. It subsequently grew to a peak of 158,300 in October 1998. Since then employment has declined somewhat, so that in December 2002 it was just slightly above 130,000. The reasons for the fall in employment over the last few years are not well understood but are probably related to a combination of deteriorating conditions in the larger U.S. economy and locational decentralization from Hollywood (runaway production). Employment patterns over time also exhibit strong short-term fluctuations, reflecting both random instabilities in the labor market and a persistent seasonal effect. Employment in television program production, in particular, has a tendency to turn downward in spring and upward again in autumn as work expands in preparation for the winter season. The prominent decline in employment in SIC 78 over the summer of 1988, as indicated in figure 7.1, is a consequence of the strike by members of the Writers Guild between March and August of that year.

---

[1] SIC 78 includes motion picture production in the narrow sense as well as television program production, video production, services allied to motion pictures, and distribution, all of which are relevant to the present investigation. SIC 78 also includes motion picture exhibition, which is not particularly relevant here, but which represents only a small proportion of total employment in SIC 78 in Los Angeles County.

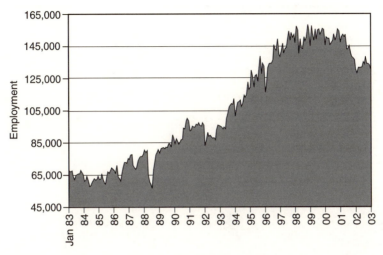

Figure 7.1. Monthly employment in SIC 78 (Motion Pictures), Los Angeles County, January 1983 to December 2002. Source: California Employment Development Department, http://www.edd.ca.gov/.

In geographic terms, the local labor market of Hollywood ramifies across both residential and employment locations in the city, with both sets of locations being linked together by the daily journey to and from work. This relation finds explicit spatial expression in a relatively centralized system of job locations, and a relatively dispersed pattern of residences, but where the outward extension of the latter is constrained by rising costs of commutation as a function of rising distance from workplaces. Something of this state of affairs is captured in figures 7.2 and 7.3, where the residential locations of members of two representative Hollywood labor organizations are mapped out. Figure 7.2 shows the locations of the 2,934 members of IATSE (International Alliance of Theatrical and Stage Employees) Local 80, or Studio Grips and Craft Service. Local 80 represents a low- to medium-skilled group of workers whose jobs are mostly concerned with arranging production sets, props, and lighting. The local also includes a small "crafts service" element of catering and cleaning personnel. Figure 7.3 shows residential locations of members of the Writers Guild West. The guild's total membership is 7,727, though in contrast to Local 80, a significant proportion (16.5%) lives outside Southern California. Screenwriters are, of course, highly skilled professionals, but with widely varying job prospects and incomes depending on ability, experience, and reputation (Bielby and Bielby 1993).

Figures 7.2 and 7.3 are quite representative of the spatial distribution of the residences of workers in the Hollywood motion picture industry

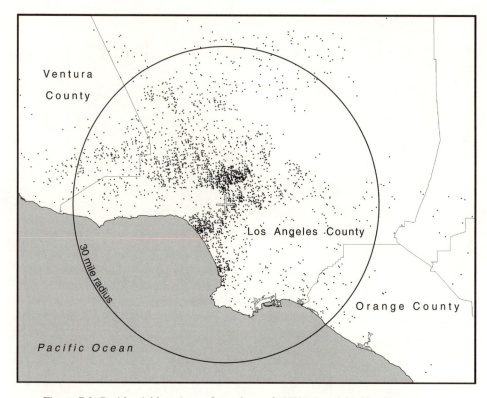

Figure 7.2. Residential locations of members of IATSE Local 80 (Studio Grips and Crafts Service) in Southern California. The center of the Hollywood labor market (as defined in union and guild contracts) is represented by a cross marking the intersection of Beverly and La Cienega Boulevards, and the thirty-mile circle around this point is shown. The map is based on zip code data provided by Local 80.

generally.[2] For example, they both bear a striking resemblance to a map of the residences of animated-film workers in Los Angeles in the mid-1980s (Scott 1984). Figures 7.2 and 7.3 show that members of both Local 80 and the Writers Guild are densely concentrated in the west side of Los Angeles, in the San Fernando Valley, and in the Pasadena/San Gabriel Valley area, though members of Local 80 are more prone to fan out into areas of suburban tract housing, just as they avoid the upscale Hollywood Hills, where writers' residences are more commonly found. A strong geographic symbiosis obviously exists between residential and employment lo-

---

[2] Data were obtained on the residential locations of the members of a number of other labor organizations besides IATSE Local 80 and the Writers Guild. Maps based on these data essentially replicate the patterns shown in figures 7.2 and 7.3.

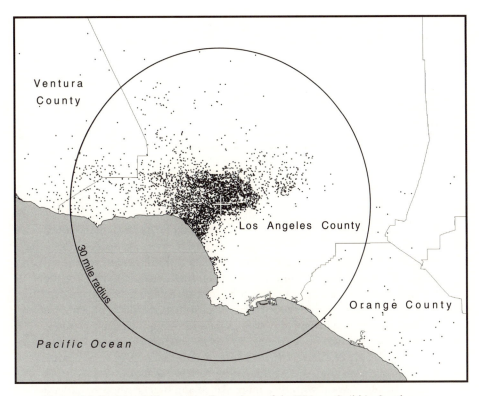

Figure 7.3. Residential locations of members of the Writers Guild in Southern California. The center of the Hollywood labor market (as defined in union and guild contracts) is represented by a cross marking the intersection of Beverly and La Cienega Boulevards, and the thirty-mile circle around this point is shown. The map is based on zip code data provided by the Guild.

cations, where the latter are represented symbolically in figures 7.2 and 7.3 by a cross showing the intersection of Beverly and La Cienega Boulevards. This point marks the center of the thirty-mile circle conventionally used in union and guild collective-bargaining agreements to differentiate work locations where normal contract provisions prevail from locations where special allowances for travel need to be made. Almost all workers in the two groups live within this circle; indeed, 49.6% of them live within 7.5 miles, and 93.3% live within 15 miles. Not surprisingly, given the difficulties that African-Americans and other minorities face in obtaining jobs in the motion picture industry, figures 7.2 and 7.3, but especially the latter, are largely blank in and around south central Los Angeles. The actual center of gravity of the residences of members of IATSE 80 and the Writers Guild

Table 7.1

Residential Density as a Function of Distance from Central Hollywood for Members of IATSE 80 (Studio Grips and Craft Service) and the Writers Guild

	Constant term (α)	Parameter of distance (β)	Adjusted R^2	Number of observations (zip-code areas)
IATSE 80	56.27	−1.4493	0.62	234
Writers Guild	115.73	−1.6532	0.63	273

The terms α and β represent parameters in a regression equation of the form $D_i = \alpha e^{\beta d_i}$ where D_i is equal to the residential density per square mile of the ith zip-code area, and d_i is the distance in miles of the ith zip-code area from the overall center of gravity. All parameters are significant at well beyond the 0.01 level of confidence.

lies just a short distance northward of the central point indicated in figures 7.2 and 7.3.

Table 7.1 reveals the precise statistical relationship between residential density (by zip-code area) and distance from this center of gravity for the two case-study organizations. The table shows in more explicit terms than do the maps the negative exponential relation that prevails between density and distance. This specific type of relation recurs virtually without exception in studies of local labor market geography, going back to the original work of Clark (1951) on population densities in various metropolitan areas around the world. Unexpectedly, as figures 7.2 and 7.3 reveal, the Hollywood writers (a more skilled and higher-wage group) are subject to a more powerful distance-decay effect than the grips (who are less skilled and less well paid); this is due no doubt to the peculiar layout of the different socioeconomic neighborhoods in Los Angeles relative to central Hollywood, and in particular, to the proximity of the Hollywood Hills and adjoining upscale communities which are particularly attractive to writers.

The entire local labor market is thus deeply but differentially inserted into the urban milieu of Southern California, which serves not only as a reservoir of labor but also as a sort of social buffer, with its many casual employment opportunities helping to keep new entrants to the labor market going until they are able to establish themselves in their preferred careers. This aspect of the urban milieu is especially important for neophytes who migrate into the region from other areas in search of work. The milieu also sustains the functions of socialization and habituation referred to earlier by reason of its embedded assets in the form of traditions, memories, cultures, visual cues, and so on, that filter into the consciousness of workers, and then feed in various ways into the whole creative thrust of Hollywood's dream factories.

CAREERS AND COLLECTIVE ORDER

Occupational Structures and Worker Interaction

The Hollywood labor market can be described as a pyramid, with a bloated mass of workers at the bottom, and a few lavishly paid writers, producers, directors, actors, and other highly skilled professionals at the top. In practice (and always excepting permanent managerial and administrative workers), there are really two overlapping pyramids, one representing the manual, crafts, and technical workers in the industry, the other—which has many more tiers in the upper ranges—representing the creative or talent workers. In the latter case, much of the base of the pyramid is made up of individuals whose eventual goal is to move into the above-the-line category, and who, in a statistical sense and in their as-yet-undifferentiated labor-market performance, might be said to have equal *a priori* chances of success. Then, as the competitive sorting process works itself out, with some individuals making their exit from the labor market altogether, and others rising into higher tiers, differentiation in terms of revealed ability and acquired reputation becomes more and more evident. In the limit, this upward mobility progresses into stardom, with both its extraordinary financial rewards and the fetishization of personality that is one of its essential attributes.

The labor market as a whole is structured by an elaborate system of occupational categories, much of it formally codified in collective bargaining arrangements. These categories reflect the extended divisions of labor that exist within the motion picture industry, as represented, for example, by such job categories as gaffers, grips, set painters, costume designers, camera technicians, sound engineers, composers, actors, and so on. Different levels of skill within the same trade are also subject to contractual definition, as illustrated by the Directors Guild, which specifically recognizes the following occupational distinctions: director, unit production manager, first assistant director, second assistant director (graded into key, second, and additional second assistant director), and technical coordinator. IATSE 700 (the Editors Guild) makes reference to 26 different job categories in its contract. This formalization of occupational categories, and the rather rigid demarcation of job assignments that is one of its effects, helps to impose some order on a production process whose extremely fluid character might otherwise induce it to veer frequently out of control (Sydow and Staber 2002). But it can also engender frustration among workers as they contrast the tasks they are actually called upon to perform with their ultimate creative aspirations. The experience of certain kinds of writers on television shows, and their reduction to the status of, say, dialogue technicians, is a case in point, even in the probably less extreme instance of French television, as Pasquier and Chalvon-Demersay (1993) point out.

Occupations on the manual, crafts, and technical side of the industry are differentiated from one another across an enormous range of characteristics and skills. Most of these occupations are hourly rated, but some of the more professionalized workers, such as costume designers, cinematographers, or film editors, are paid on a salary or commission basis. Even for the least skilled occupations, wages are high in comparison with wage rates generally in Southern California, and the sweatshop conditions that prevail in other industries of the region, such as clothing and furniture, are virtually nowhere to be found in the motion picture industry, though occasional cases can be observed of firms on the far fringes of the production system that employ low-wage immigrant labor (see chapter 5). The generally favorable wage conditions in the Hollywood labor market can no doubt be ascribed both to its tradition of craft skill and to the relatively high rates of unionization that prevail. The long-run success of Hollywood entertainment products on international markets and the absence until very recently of serious competition from other production locales has also certainly played a part in maintaining wages at a high level. That said, the rising tide of runaway production to Canada and other parts of the world may yet begin to exert serious downward pressure on labor market conditions in Hollywood.

Creative or talent occupations in the motion picture industry are primarily (but not exclusively) represented by actors, directors, and writers, with producers forming an ambiguously situated group somewhere between the creative and management sides. It is above all in the creative segment of the employment system that persistent labor oversupply at the base of the job pyramid occurs. This phenomenon stems predominantly from the large numbers of aspirants willing to make significant sacrifices in the short term for the sake of potentially massive monetary and psychological gains in the long term. Hollywood, too, is a magnet for migrants from all over the country and from all over the world with burning ambitions to work in the motion picture industry. In this respect, Los Angeles functions much like other creative cultural centers, such as Paris or New York, in that it exerts a virtually irresistible attraction on budding talent workers seeking fulfillment in their chosen field (Kraft 1994; Menger 1993; Montgomery and Robinson 1993). As Menger (1991) suggests, the supply of creative workers at the low end of the labor market is yet more inflated by the subjective overevaluations that aspirants tend to make of their prospects and talents. Still, from this starting position some individuals filter up into higher ranges of the pyramid as they accumulate job credits, as their reputation expands, and as they become enculturated into the norms of the industry, including the interpersonal skills that sustain effective teamwork (Batt et al. 2001; Faulkner 1983; Jones 1996; Menger 1999). Success at one moment in time, however, is no guarantee of continued upward mobility. Weiss and

Faulkner (1983) have demonstrated for the case of directors, screenwriters, and producers that one screen credit is actually more often followed by anonymity than by yet more credits. The top echelons of the industry are controlled by a remarkably small number of super-productive individuals who account for the vast majority of successful projects (Jones 1996).

Each of these two main fractions of the labor force is preeminently given to temporary and freelance forms of work. Workers at every level of skill and experience move periodically from employer to employer as projects come and go, and this creates vicissitudes that workers seek in part to manage with the aid of informal social organizations (cf. Ekinsmyth 2002). These in turn rely heavily on what Ursell (2000) has called an "economy of favors," a process in which workers throughout the job hierarchy build relationships of reciprocity and mutual aid. The most obvious instance of this phenomenon can be found in the tangled interpersonal networks through which much of the information in the local market circulates (Batt et al. 2001; Blair et al. 2001; Scott 1998b). In many segments of the industry, too, workers team together in small multivalent groups that move from project to project, gaining and losing members as they do so (Blair 2001). Certain combinations of skilled workers (e.g., producer-composer or director-actor pairs) recur with some frequency in these groups. Moreover, the individuals in any given group are almost always equally matched in terms of experience and accomplishments (Faulkner 1983; Faulkner and Anderson 1987). Relations of reciprocity in the local labor market are further consolidated by the sharing out of assignments that sometimes occurs when individuals have more work than they can personally handle at any given time. Faulkner (1985) has noted the particular prevalence of this practice among composers of music for films and television.

The local labor market in Hollywood, then, is a field of turbulent but structured social activity in which large numbers of individual workers constantly confront the need for strategic planning of their careers. Once committed to a particular project, workers are mobilized in cooperative and often rather freely flowing teamwork efforts, and in this manner, each individual's creative labor makes an essential contribution to the texture of the final output (Elliott 1972). Even in a personalized *film d'auteur*, teamwork is a necessary element of the labor process, but in the more industrialized and modular world of Hollywood it is the very foundation of the entire system of production (cf. Darré 1986; Scott 2000b). The concomitant diffusion of creative responsibilities, together with the socialization of workers into industry-wide norms, is almost certainly one of the main factors sustaining the ability of Hollywood production companies to make films pitched right to the cultural and ideological core of mainstream American society.

Coordinating Mechanisms of the Local Labor Market

I have referred already to the informal networks that represent a first collective response to uncertainty and potential disorder in the local labor market of Hollywood. These networks are complemented by numerous other instruments of social coordination that serve, as well, to resolve industry-wide predicaments and to enhance the competitive advantages of the region as a whole. This proposition may be extended by means of three main observations.

First, the proclivity for serious information gaps to appear in local labor markets encourages the rise of intermediaries who trade on the consequent demand for contacts and referrals. Hollywood is rich in intermediaries of this sort not only because there are so many discontinuities throughout the system, but also because the short-term nature of many jobs means that both firms and workers are constantly searching out new relationships with one another. Three different categories of intermediaries play a special role here, namely, agents, casting directors (who specialize in finding appropriate actors for roles), and talent managers. Figure 7.4 displays their geographic locations and reveals their tendency to cluster at the spatial core of Hollywood—a locational trait that enhances their joint accessibility to prospective employees and employers and thereby facilitates their role as network brokers. While this spatial relationship is important for intermediaries of all sizes and varieties, it is probably of special advantage to the smaller and less successful ones attempting to build up their clientele. Scale and past performance are what count most among the more dynamic intermediaries, and only a small elite of these participates in the top deals that are executed in Hollywood (Bielby and Bielby 1999). Many talent agencies seek to extend their traditional functions by assembling composite entertainment packages (say, a concept, a writer, a director, and a cast), which are then put on offer to production companies.

Second, the associations that proliferate in and around Hollywood provide workers with opportunities to pursue diverse collective interests and objectives. The Academy of Motion Picture Arts and Sciences, now a nonpartisan group with its members carefully selected on the basis of merit, occupies a central place in this associational environment. The Academy's annual Oscar awards ceremony is the single most important occasion in North America for recognizing the achievements of elite workers in the industry, and a public relations event with worldwide impact. There are, in addition, literally scores of other associations serving the collective needs of workers in the motion picture industry, ranging as far afield, for example, as the Production Assistants Association, the Society of Motion Picture and TV Art Directors, Women in Film, the Stuntmens' Association, and the Visual Effects Society. Associations like these constitute forums in which problems of common interest can be discussed and acted upon,

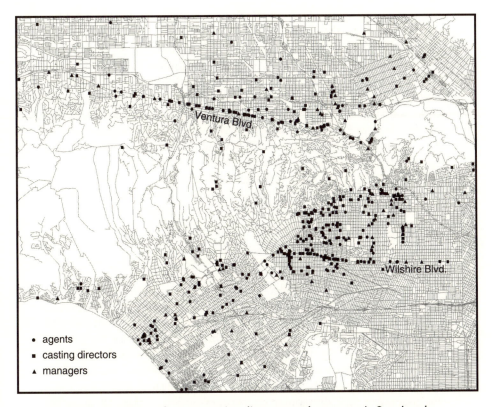

Figure 7.4. Locations of agents, casting directors, and managers in Los Angeles. Observe the clustering of firms in the central core of Hollywood, together with the alignment of firms along Ventura and Wilshire Boulevards. Source of address data: Hollywood Creative Directory, *Agents and Managers* (Los Angeles, 2002).

while providing useful information, contacts, mutual support, training programs, and so on. Workers on the creative side of the industry appear to be especially prone to participate in employment-related associations, and this again probably reflects the play of risk-reducing and opportunity-enhancing strategies in individual behavior as a way of countering the insecurities of the local labor market (cf. Scott 1998b).

Third, many different organizations and agencies throughout Southern California provide educational and job-training opportunities for workers (and would-be workers) in the motion picture industry. The region is home to numerous colleges and universities, which in their turn are an important element of the agglomeration economies of Hollywood. Several local branches of the California State University system have significant professional programs focused on film, television, and media (at Northridge, Long Beach, Fullerton, and Los Angeles). Other colleges and universities, such as Los Angeles City College, Chapman University, and Loyola Marymount University, offer diplomas in film-related activities, as do the more specialized Los Angeles Film School and the American Film Institute. At the head of the list of local educational institutions offering programs relevant to the industry are UCLA's School of Theater, Film and Television and the University of Southern California's School of Cinema-Television. Many of the alumni of these two programs have attained to the highest levels of accomplishment in acting, producing, directing, writing, and so forth. Also, a profusion of part-time training programs, workshops, and courses are constantly available throughout the region, on topics ranging across the gamut from studio management to costume design or lighting techniques.

Unions and Guilds

Of all the instruments of collective order in the Hollywood local labor market today, the unions and guilds are, without question, of the utmost significance. I argue here that these institutions are, in fact, an essential condition of the continued health and vibrancy of the labor market as a whole. Needless to say, this claim is far from being universally endorsed. The initial emergence of unions and guilds in Hollywood was accompanied by great controversy, and they have frequently faced difficult political challenges over their subsequent course of evolution, as they still do today.

To begin with, the political upheavals that attended the formation of the unions and guilds in the years before World War II continued virtually unabated once the war was over. A bitter rivalry existed at this time between IATSE and the CSU (Conference of Studio Unions), the former having had a rather sordid history of control by organized crime, the latter being a left-leaning amalgam of skilled trades. The majors were strongly inclined in favor of the less militant IATSE, and the CSU rapidly faded away after a mass lockout in 1946 that greatly undermined its influence. From the late 1940s on, then, IATSE locals came to function as the principal unions for the manual, crafts, and technical workers in Hollywood (Horne 2001). The immediate postwar years in Hollywood were also marked by red scares and black-lists, and—from 1947 to 1954—by the persistent scrutiny of the House Un-American Activities Committee, all of which had profound effects in disciplining the labor force as well as in regulating the political content of films (Ceplair and Englund 1983; Prindle 1988). In spite of (or perhaps because of) these clashes in the postwar period, a remarkably stable and resilient system of unions and guilds emerged over the 1950s and 1960s;

and even given the continuing propensity of some of these organizations to go out on strike, they have played a critical role in maintaining a smoothly operating system of labor relations and collective bargaining in Hollywood down to the present.

A comprehensive list of unions and guilds in Hollywood today is presented in table 7.2. The organizations identified in the table are all collective bargaining units certified by the National Labor Relations Board; professional associations lacking such certification (such as the Producers Guild) are not included in the table. Three guilds and twenty-three IATSE locals, as well as two other union locals with close ties to the motion picture industry, are recognized in table 7.2, and information on their total membership (as of March 2002) is provided. A number of other organizations, such as the American Federation of Television and Radio Artists, the National Association of Broadcast Employees and Technicians, and the American Federation of Musicians, are also *bona fide* collective bargaining agencies, but their membership spills over far beyond the motion picture industry, and for this reason, no reference is made to them in table 7.2. The organizations listed in the table have an aggregate membership of 162,955, which is suspiciously high compared to the 131,800 workers actually employed in SIC 78 in Los Angeles County according to the California Employment Development in early 2002. The discrepancy between the two figures can in part be accounted for by the fact that some of the organizations designated in table 7.2 represent workers all over the United States, and in part by the circumstance that only a fraction of union or guild members are employed at any one time. The largest organization designated in the table, the Screen Actors Guild, has 98,000 members, but in practice only about two-thirds of them live in Southern California, and most of the time only about 25% of these actually have jobs. Members of IATSE Local 80 occupy a more stable niche in the local labor market, but even they face an average unemployment rate of 30%. While the majority of talent workers in the industry are members of a guild, only about half of all manual, crafts, and technical workers belong to a union (Paul and Kleingartner 1996). Indeed, union (but not guild) density is widely thought to be decreasing at the present time, due in part to the great expansion of small independent production companies able to sidestep labor-organizing activities in manual, crafts, and technical occupations.

The main business of the unions and guilds is collective bargaining, especially, but not necessarily exclusively, with the AMPTP (Alliance of Motion Picture and Television Producers). The latter organization acts as the MPAA's instrument in all collective bargaining situations (Counter 1992; Gray and Seeber 1996; Wasko 1998). Contracts are negotiated by each union or guild separately with the AMPTP on a three-year cycle, with pattern bargaining commonly occurring as each contract falls due.

TABLE 7.2

A Comprehensive List of Union Locals and Guilds with Collective-Bargaining Authority in Contemporary Hollywood

	Total membership in 2002
Professional guilds	
Directors Guild	12,420
Screen Actors' Guild	98,000
Writers Guild West	7,727
IATSE locals	
44 Affiliated Property Craftspersons	6,755
78 Plumbers	109
80 Motion Picture Studio Grips and Crafts Service	2,934
600 International Cinematographers	4,643
683 Film Technicians	1,725
695 Production Sound Technicians, TV Engineers, and Video Assistant Technicians	2,224
700 Motion Picture Editors	4,859
705 Motion Picture Costumers	1,983
706 Makeup Artists and Hair Stylists	1,625
724 Studio Utility Employees	1,454
728 Studio Electrical Lighting Technicians	2,553
729 Motion Picture Set Painters	1,357
755 Plasterers, Modelers, and Sculptors	345
767 First Aid Employees	359
790 Studio Art Craftsmen	186
816 Scenic, Title, and Graphic Artists	227
818 Publicists	310
839 Motion Picture Screen Cartoonists and Affiliated Optical Electronic and Graphic Arts	1,800
847 Set Designers and Model Makers	233
871 Script Supervisors and Continuity Coordinators	1,738
876 Motion Picture and Television Art Directors	723
884 Studio Teachers and Welfare Workers	173
892 Costume Designers	352
Other locals	
International Brotherhood of Electrical Workers, Local 40	672
Teamsters Local 399, Studio Transportation Drivers	5,469
Total union and guild membership	162,995

Source: Individual guild and union records.

Depending on the union or guild at issue, independent production companies often join with the AMPTP as cosignatories on contracts. As a general
rule, contracts signed between the guilds and the AMPTP are cosigned by
large numbers of independents; but IATSE contracts, notably insofar as
less skilled IATSE locals are concerned, tend to attract fewer independent
signatories.

Contracts negotiated between the unions and guilds with the AMPTP
contain three critical clauses in regard to remuneration. These provide for
(a) minimum pay scales for specific occupational categories and levels of
experience, (b) personal services contracts, which is industry jargon for
individually negotiated above-scale wage or salary payments, and (c) the administration of residuals, a form of compensation based on secondary runs
or releases of any given entertainment product (Kleingartner 2001; Paul
and Kleingartner 1996). In the case of IATSE locals, any residuals that can
be identified are paid into union pension funds; in the case of the talent
guilds, residuals are appropriated by designated individuals. Union and
guild contracts also make stipulations about health and pension payments
and vacation benefits, and specify the rules governing conditions of work
performed beyond the thirty-mile circle (see figures 7.2 and 7.3). The
IATSE locals combine their welfare plans together in the centrally adminis-
tered Motion Picture Industry Pension and Health Plans, while the guilds
manage their own individual plans. In either case, the system that has
emerged in practice has the signal advantage that individuals' benefits packages are not tied to any single employer but are fully portable from firm to
firm. In this way, the Hollywood unions and guilds play a role somewhat
analogous to that played by the government-sponsored *Intermittence du
Spectacle* in France, which provides unemployment compensation and other
benefits to workers in the French entertainment industry (Rannou and Vari
1996; Scott 2000b). Additional important functions of the unions and
guilds are (a) the codification and regulation of professional categories,
(b) accreditation of members' work experiences, and (c) the provision of
educational, labor-training, and other qualification-enhancing services. The
roster system that operated in at least some IATSE locals in the 1950s according to Christopherson (1992) and Christopherson and Storper (1989)
now no longer exists, though the qualifications lists maintained by some
organizations have a somewhat similar sorting effect.

The unions and guilds, then, are a source of significant benefits, above all
by coordinating certain critical kinds of transactions, by correcting market
failures that would otherwise be likely to occur in the intricate operations
of the local labor market, and by reducing the potential for exacerbated
inter-worker competition over jobs and pay. They lower the labor-market
risks and raise the living standards of their members. The continuing
success of the talent guilds in holding and expanding their membership

reflects the real advantages that they offer, above all, through their capacity to negotiate attractive wage and salary scales and residuals payments. The manual, crafts, and technical workers' unions also continue to be a significant force in Hollywood, though the fact that union pay scales (unlike those of the guilds) do not seem to differ very much from nonunion wage rates[3] can perhaps be taken as a sign that their power may be waning somewhat. Additionally, the acceleration of runaway production now raises a major dilemma for the IATSE unions, for the potential long-run effects of this phenomenon could conceivably pose a threat to the very existence of the unions as they are currently constituted in Hollywood. By contrast, the strength and influence of the guilds (and the comparative immunity of their workers from the side effects of runaway production) remain largely undiminished, as is most especially evident in the circumstance that they are very much more apt to strike, or to threaten to strike, than the politically weaker IATSE locals.

Both the Screen Actors Guild and the Writers Guild have gone on strike with some frequency in the last few decades over basic issues of work conditions and financial rewards. However, the Directors Guild has struck only once in its existence (for a few hours in 1987), a circumstance that can probably be ascribed to the close association that usually prevails between directors and production managers on film projects. In recent years, strike activity in Hollywood has been largely confined to the Screen Actors Guild and the Writers Guild. The most recent strike of the former was from May to October 2000 as a result of a breakdown in negotiations over the guild's commercials contract. The Writers Guild for its part last struck in the period from March to August 1988, and threatened to go out on strike again in Spring 2001 over pay structures. This threatened strike was averted only by a last-minute agreement with the majors. The last major work stoppage by an IATSE local occurrred more than two decades ago in the late summer of 1982, when IATSE 839 called an unsuccessful strike over the subcontracting of animated-film work to firms in Asia (cf. Lent 1998; Scott 1984).

CONCLUSION

I have presented a sketch of the organization and dynamics of local labor market activities in the motion picture industry of Hollywood. I have tried to indicate how the local labor market operates both as a system of individual decision-making and action and as a composite structure through which individual behaviors are coordinated. The picture that emerges

---

[3] This judgment is based on extensive interviews with officials and individual members of different unions and guilds.

reveals a labor market that is highly flexible and that generates much insecurity, but that is at the same time regulated in ways that mitigate the uncertainties with which it is associated, and that on balance yields significant pecuniary returns to those who participate in it. I have tried, in addition, to emphasize how the local labor market generates agglomeration economies for the entire motion picture production system within the wider urban milieu of Southern California.

In view of the success and durability of its institutional arrangements hitherto, the local labor market of Hollywood may well be a source of important lessons for other places and other kinds of labor markets as flexible work programs continue to diffuse more widely through the American economy. Contrary to certain critics (e.g., Hyman 1991; Pollert 1991), flexibilization does not necessarily result in an endless downward spiral for workers, provided that appropriate social safeguards can be constructed to combat its most deleterious effects. And contrary to familiar criticisms from the other side of the politico-theoretical fence, strong labor organizations do not necessarily mean that business is destined to continual disruption. From all that has gone before, it is evident that the unions and guilds of Hollywood indeed perform numerous useful functions in bringing to the labor market forms of order that are ultimately beneficial to firms as well as workers. Not least among these is the part that unions and guilds play in regulating labor market insecurities, in promoting the long-term commitment of their members to a vocational or quasi-vocational sense of their work, and hence also to the maintenance of the industrial/cultural creativity and innovation that have always been one of the hallmarks of Hollywood.

All that being said, the phenomenon of runaway production has recently been responsible for a decided shift in the balance of forces in the local labor market (Kleingartner and Raymond 1988). This state of affairs unquestionably represents one of the greatest challenges facing Hollywood at the present time, and the tensions that it is generating will almost certainly be accompanied by major adjustments and restructuring over the next few years. Conversely, the very agglomeration economies built into the production system and its associated local labor market suggest that there are probably limits as to how much further this process can go, certainly insofar as more skilled employment in the industry is concerned. A measured conclusion, then, is that continued decentralization of jobs will probably not undermine the core functions of Hollywood in any irrevocable fashion, even if it does generate increasing employment at a number of satellite production locations, above all, as things now stand, in Toronto and Vancouver. Some continued loss of influence among the IATSE locals in Hollywood may well result, but the professional guilds will almost certainly continue to play a large and indeed expanding role as Hollywood moves into the next main phase of its development.

CHAPTER EIGHT

Hollywood in America and the World: Distribution and Markets

IN ONE SENSE, Hollywood is a very specific place in Southern California, and, more to the point, a particular locale-bound nexus of production relationships and local labor market activities. In another sense, Hollywood is everywhere, and in its realization as a disembodied assortment of images and narratives, its presence is felt broadly across the entire globe. These local and global manifestations of Hollywood are linked together by a complex machinery of distribution and marketing. In this manner, Hollywood's existence as a productive agglomeration is sustained, while the images and narratives it creates are dispersed to consumers far and wide. Indeed, much of Hollywood's success over the long term can be attributed to the dynamic interplay between its localized system of agglomeration economies and its aggressive conquest of markets. Hollywood producers enjoy the added benefit of huge domestic sales, a circumstance that right from the early decades of the twentieth century has provided them with a platform from which to attack international markets (cf. Porter 1990).

In the present chapter, I shall focus mainly on first-run distribution of feature films to theater audiences in the United States and the rest of the world. There are, to be sure, other important channels of diffusion for Hollywood films involving broadcast and cable television, VHS (video home system) and DVD (digital videodisc), and, more prospectively, the Internet. Television and in-flight entertainment represent additional market windows. At the same time, the actual exhibition of feature films is only one phase of a process of commercial exploitation that eventually fans out into extensive product franchises, including books, toys, games, CDs, clothing, and theme park attractions (Wasko et al. 1993; Wyatt 1994). All of these alternative outlets will be referred to from time to time as we proceed, but will remain largely in the background. Instead, the emphasis here is on issues surrounding the initial release, marketing, and distribution of films for theatrical exhibition. This emphasis is all the more appropriate because the first-run phase of the diffusion process has major impacts on the subsequent commercial performance of any film and its spin-off products.

DISTRIBUTION AND EXHIBITION

The Organization of Motion Picture Distribution

As in the case of production, the distribution of Hollywood motion pictures is organized within a predominantly bipartite structure of majors and independents.

All the majors are vertically integrated across production and distribution, and they typically distribute their own films in all their main markets. In less lucrative markets, the majors often license other companies to handle their distribution needs. In addition, the majors play an important role in distributing selected independently made films. Independents, for their part, are sometimes vertically integrated across production and distribution but are more commonly specialized on the one side or the other. However, when independents distribute films made by other companies, they often take equity positions in those films, thus acquiring a greatly intensified interest in their commercial success (Rosen and Hamilton 1987). Also, independents are more inclined than majors to confine their distribution activities to relatively narrowly circumscribed territories where they have special knowledge of market conditions, leaving it to others to assume responsibility for distribution in other regions and countries. Thus, production companies whose films are distributed by independents are often obliged to seek out multiple distribution deals in order to secure an adequate rate of return on their initial investment. Multiple deals of this sort are generally essential before any film in the independent sector can be successfully released today.

The business strategies of the majors—focused as they are on high-budget blockbuster films—call for an extensive and efficient infrastructure of distribution. In response to this need, the majors all possess vast networks for the circulation of their films across both domestic and international markets. Although the films themselves may be extremely variable in content, they flow through these networks in a more or less routinized fashion, thus making it possible for major distributors to achieve significant internal economies of scale. In this sense, motion picture distribution systems today are somewhat like the early railroad and telegraph companies described by Chandler (1990). The majors' domestic distributional infrastructure is primed above all to achieve saturation theatrical openings in domestic markets, and to maximize box-office returns from the first weekend of exhibition. Previously, by contrast, distribution strategies were geared to a staggered system of openings moving progressively from flagship theaters down the hierarchy of exhibition venues, and depending on word of mouth for publicity. The currently prevailing strategy is particularly important given that initial exhibition is the first stage in a chain of market windows for any given film, with big effects on the film's subsequent performance throughout the chain (Litman and Ahn 1998). At the present time, saturation openings are almost entirely confined to the United States, but there is some likelihood that the strategy will be extended to international markets in the not-too-distant future, not only as a commercial goal in its own right, but also as a way of preempting film piracy activities. Worldwide saturation openings will no doubt become increasingly practicable with the eventual shift from analog to digital film recording.

As we observed earlier in this book, there is a marked degree of business concentration on the distribution side of the motion picture industry (recall table 3.3). The current four-firm concentration ratio for NAICS 512120 (Motion Picture and Video Distribution) in the United States is an unusually high 81.9%. The elevated degree of concentration in distribution is a function of internal economies of scale in operational structures, and it points to the sector as the key organizational bottleneck in the industry as a whole. This state of affairs, of course, is entirely consonant with the domination of the industry by a small number of majors. The high level of business concentration in distribution is reinforced by the need to coordinate simultaneous placement of any one film in theaters across the country according to a tight schedule of release dates, and to maintain continuous contact with large numbers of different theater chains. Levels of concentration are further boosted by the need to back up distribution with massive marketing campaigns, and, above all, to generate sufficient publicity for each film so that the opening weekend brings in significant box-office returns. In order to achieve these objectives, the majors all maintain branch offices in critical regional markets across North America, thereby facilitating close and steady contact with theater operators. Figure 8.1 displays the locations of these branch offices in the United States and Canada, all of which coincide with metropolitan areas in states or provinces with large numbers of theater screens.

On the basis of information garnered in interviews with distribution companies, the interactions between these branch offices and the theater chains with which they deal can be generally described as a form of relational contracting. This means that the parties to any given transaction have long-term relations with one another built on strong personal familiarity, in contradistinction to purely arms'-length dealings. Relational contracting between distributors and exhibitors is almost certainly a partial substitute for vertical integration, for it permits both parties collaboratively to program their interdependent activities over some fairly extended time horizon. Indeed, the incentives to reintegrate exhibition back into the production-distribution chain remain so strong that most of the majors are now aggressively reacquiring large numbers of film theaters (Blackstone and Bowman 1999). The

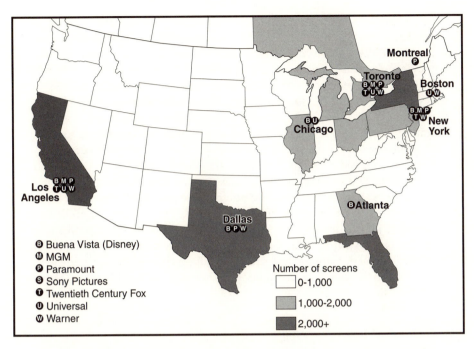

Figure 8.1. Offices of major Hollywood distribution companies in relation to the geographic incidence of theater screens in the United States and Canada. Based on information provided by the National Association of Theatre Owners and the Motion Picture Theatre Association of Canada.

most visible instance of this trend involves the Sony Corporation, which now owns Loew's Cineplex, one of the largest theater chains in the United States, with 264 sites and 2,323 screens. The same search for vertical synergy is apparent in the majors' continuing quest for ownership (both directly and through their corporate umbrellas) of broadcast and cable television networks (see chapter 4). Also, as home-video markets have expanded during the last decade, the majors have established specialized divisions to distribute films in both VHS and DVD formats.

Independent film distributors are mostly small in size and are subject to very high levels of market uncertainty. The largest independent distributor in the country currently, USA Films, released 15 films in the year 2000 and earned just one percent of gross box-office receipts nationwide. Artisan Entertainment, Lion's Gate Films, Shooting Gallery, and Winstar Cinema are a few of the many other independent distributors operating in the country today. According to data on motion picture credits published by AMPAS (2001), the vast majority of independent distributors in the United

States handle no more than two or three films a year, though the larger independents may take on from a dozen to a score of films a year. Independent distributors almost never deal with films produced by the majors; instead, they handle films made by their own production arms or more commonly by other independents, both American and foreign. In a questionnaire survey of independent production companies carried out in Los Angeles over the summer of 2001, it was found that fully 72.3% of firms that had made a feature film in the previous year relied on independent distributors to place their product on the market. Film festivals are also nowadays important venues in which independent producers and distributors come together to make deals with one another. On occasion, individual production companies dispense with distributors, and attempt to market their own films, especially where these films are aimed at very particular types of audiences and the company has an informed sense of how to publicize its product, as in the case, say, of films that appeal to gays or certain ethnic groups. An increasing practice among independent producers is to make direct-to-video films and to dispense with distribution to theatrical outlets altogether (Vogel 1998).

Domestic Motion Picture Markets

As table 8.1 indicates, gross domestic box-office returns in the U.S. motion picture industry as a whole grew from $5.7 billion in 1980 to $7.7 billion in 2000 (in constant dollar terms). By far the greatest share of these returns is accounted for by films released by the majors. In table 8.2, aggregate box-office returns are broken down to show the portion earned by each of the major distributors at five-year intervals from 1980 to 2000. Buena Vista (the distribution arm of Disney) has tended to dominate the

TABLE 8.1
Gross Domestic Box Office, 1980–2000

	Current $M	Constant $M	Majors' share
1980	2,749	5,745	91%
1985	3,749	6,000	77%
1990	5,022	6,617	80%
1995	5,494	6,208	86%
2000	7,661	7,661	83%

Sources: Motion Picture Association of America (http://www.mpaa.org/) and National Association of Theatre Owners, *Encyclopedia of Exhibition, 2001–2002.*

Note: Domestic box office includes receipts for both the United States and Canada.

TABLE 8.2
Domestic Theatrical Film Distribution, Market Shares of Hollywood Majors, 1980–2000

	Buena Vista/ Disney	Columbia/ Sony	Market share (%)		Twentieth Century Fox	Universal	Warner
			MGM	Paramount			
1980	4	14	7	16	16	20	14
1985	3	10	9	10	11	16	18
1990	16	5	3	15	14	14	13
1995	19	13	6	10	8	13	17
2000	15	9	1	11	10	15	12

Source: National Association of Theatre Owners, *Encyclopedia of Exhibition, 2001–2002.*

market over the last decade, but never by more than one or two percentage points. Actually, the data presented in table 8.2 conform to a pattern of revolving leadership in which no one major remains at the head of the league for very long. MGM has clearly been a laggard over the last two decades, a circumstance that in part reflects its turbulent recent history of reorganizations and corporate takeovers. As important as the theatrical box office may be, it is no longer the main source of the majors' revenues, though exhibition remains the key initial market for any film before it moves through subsequent windows. According to data published by Veronis Suhler (2001), home-video sales and rentals in the United States (both VHS and DVD) amounted to $22.5 billion in 2000, some three times larger than the total gross domestic box office for that same year.

The historical pattern of annual releases of films in the United States is presented in figure 8.2. The figure shows films released by the majors since 1945 and by independents since 1980. Over the crisis years in Hollywood, stretching from the 1950s to the 1970s, releases by the majors declined continually if erratically. These were years in which the majors were struggling to cope with shifting consumer tastes and market trends, and to work out a viable new economics and aesthetics of popular cinema, leading eventually to the development of the high-concept blockbuster film as the industry's competitive mainstay. The information presented in table 8.3 is symptomatic of the ever-intensifying competitive urge among the majors to put big-budget films on the market, a trend that essentially began in the years following the *Paramount* decision in 1948 (Sedgwick 2002). The data reveal a notable increase in the costs of producing and marketing films released by the majors between 1980 and 2000. In constant dollar terms, these costs rose approximately threefold over this two-decade period.

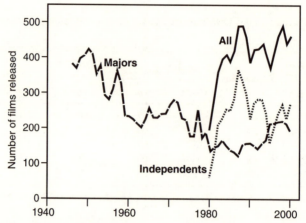

Figure 8.2. Number of new feature films released annually in the United States by major and independent distributors. Published data on releases by independent distribution companies are available only since 1980. Note that releases by majors also include films released by their subsidiaries. Source of data: Motion Picture Association of America (http://www.mpaa.org/).

Marketing costs have on average run at just below half of production costs (negative costs), though in the case of specific highly promoted films, marketing costs may even sometimes surpass production costs.

Figure 8.2 also shows that the 1980s was a period of dramatic growth in the number of films released by independent distributors, a growth that

TABLE 8.3
Average Negative and Marketing Costs, Hollywood Majors, 1980–2000

	Millions of current dollars		Millions of constant dollars		
	Negative costs[a]	Marketing costs[b]	Negative costs[a]	Marketing costs[b]	Marketing costs as % of negative costs
1980	9.4	4.3	19.6	9.0	45.7
1985	16.8	6.5	26.9	10.4	38.7
1990	26.8	12.0	35.3	15.8	44.8
1995	36.4	17.7	41.1	20.0	48.6
2000	54.8	27.3	54.8	27.3	49.8

Source: Motion Picture Association of America (http://www.mpaa.org/).
[a]Production costs, studio overhead, and capitalized interest.
[b]Prints and advertising.

occurred partly in response to the rise of diverse niche markets in exhibition, and partly as a function of the great expansion of ancillary markets in video and deregulated television broadcasting (Prince 2000). The enormous expansion of independent film festivals worldwide—in Chicago, New York, Park City (Sundance), Toronto, Edinburgh, Venice, Shanghai, and so on—has unquestionably helped to support this trend. The 1980s was a period in which the so-called mini-majors (such as Cannon, Carolco, Miramax, Orion, and New Line) rose to prominence by capitalizing on some of the same opportunities, though a number of these firms have since vanished. At this time, too, the majors began systematically to acquire or create smaller affiliated production and distribution companies in order to exploit and shape some of the same market niches. These shifts are reflected in the fact that whereas the number of theater sites in the United States has declined sharply over the last two decades, multiplex theaters (distinguished by their flexibility in accommodating films with widely variable audience appeal) have increased greatly in number, with a concomitant large expansion of the total number of screens available for exhibiting films. In 1980, there were 17,675 screens in the country as a whole; in 1990 there were 23,814; and in 2000, there were 36,264, concentrated at 6,979 sites, thus giving an average of 5.2 screens per theater.

MARKET STRUCTURES AND THE DYNAMICS OF FILM RELEASING

Economic systems are shaped by both the production strategies of firms and the demand patterns of consumers. Out of this tense force field of relations there emerges an architecture of the market, which, in the motion picture industry, is expressed in complex, shifting structures of releasing activity over time, space, and delivery format.

Some Determinants of Releasing Behavior

As stated earlier, the majors release films that they produce in-house, as well as films that are produced with varying degrees of participation by independents. A first question, then, revolves around the corporate origins of the films that flow through the majors' distribution systems. To answer this question, I constructed a data series for the period 1980–2000 from listings of individual film credits given in the *Annual Index to Motion Picture Credits* published by the Academy of Motion Picture Arts and Sciences. The *Annual Index* provides information on the production and distribution companies involved in all films released in Los Angeles every year. From this information we can identify which of the films released by any major are produced with independent participation and which are not.

Unfortunately, our source of information does not provide us with clues about the precise nature of any given instance of participation. In some cases, the major distributing the film exerts dominant control over the decisions of the designated independent producer(s). In others, the control is nominal. In yet other cases, as represented by negative pickups, the distributor only becomes involved with the film after it is completed.

Despite these ambiguities, a fairly robust series of statistical observations can be made on the basis of the data in hand. In particular, regression analysis (as described in the appendix to the present chapter) shows that a pronounced inverse association exists for any given major between the number of its own films and the number of independently made films that it distributes. This finding indicates that the majors consistently substitute between these two types of films in their production and distribution systems, so that when they deal with more of the latter, they deal with fewer of the former, and vice versa. This further suggests that the majors play on this form of substitution in an attempt to achieve an even flow of films through their installed distribution capacity and to ensure that this capacity operates as close to optimality as possible over time.[1]

The regression analyses presented in the appendix also point to some important differences in production-*cum*-releasing strategies among the majors. At the one extreme, Paramount Pictures is characterized by a greater tendency to substitute between its own and independently made films in distribution than any other major, implying that it has developed a very flexible organizational strategy across both production and distribution. At the other extreme, Disney and its distribution arm Buena Vista are characterized by a very small and statistically insignificant relation between their own and independently made films. This is because Disney relies to an unusually great extent on its own internal resources to fill its production and distribution quotas, a feature that is consistent with the fact that its films have retained a much more firm-specific look than those of any other major in the new Hollywood.

A related question concerns temporal patterns of releasing in relation to general market conditions. Here, in addition to majors and independents, a third group of distribution companies is explicitly brought into the analysis, namely, the subsidiaries of the majors. Statistical analysis (again reported in the appendix) reveals that the number of films released by

---

[1] These remarks offer a somewhat more complex view of the relations between large and small firms than the one defined by Berger and Piore (1980) in terms of "industrial duality." In their concept, large and small firms occupy distinctive market niches, the former serving a spectrum of stable demands, the latter being relegated to a more unstable market residuum. In the present instance, there is a zone of overlap between the two in which large firms use smaller firms as a means of ensuring synchronic stability of product flow.

majors, their subsidiaries, and independents in any given year is positively related to money spent at the box office in the previous year. Independents are most especially prone to this effect, which doubtless reflects in part a diminishing (if lagging) sense of risk as overall box-office revenues increase. All three types of distributors also tend to reduce the number of films that they release as interest rates rise. This tendency is particularly evident in the case of the majors, as we might expect in view of the enormous sums of money that they expend each year in producing and distributing films.

A Tripartite Model

In previous chapters I have referred from time to time to an essentially bipartite pattern of production relations in the motion picture industry, revolving around the split between the majors and independents. Only an occasional acknowledgment of a possibly distinctive role for the majors' subsidiaries has thus far been offered. In fact, since the early 1980s, and especially since the early 1990s, there has been a strong proclivity for this group of companies to emerge as an identifiable domain of business activity in its own right.

Today, every major has a larger or smaller stable of these subsidiaries, most of which possess a high degree of autonomy in their corporate decision-making, and act as quasi-independent production and distribution entities. In this regard, the majors are coming increasingly to resemble the music majors that pioneered this form of corporate organization (Negus 1998; Scott 1999). These subsidiaries function primarily in intermediate markets lying between those in which the majors themselves operate and those in which the independents are typically ensconced. They also act as scouts for their corporate owners by reason of their ability to identify market trends at an early stage, a capacity that in turn is based on their more experimental approaches to the motion picture business and their intermediate position between the world of the independents and the world of the majors. Among the more important subsidiaries with a substantial stake in distribution activity at the present time are Disney's Miramax, Sony Classics, Warner's New Line, MGM's Orion Pictures, Twentieth Century's Fox Searchlight, Universal Focus, and Paramount Classics.

Figure 8.3 provides some details as to how the conjectured tripartite structure of U.S. motion picture markets is actually delineated. The figure shows frequency distributions of percentage box-office returns for films distributed by independents, majors' subsidiaries, and majors (less subsidiaries) in the year 2000. These percentage figures sum to a hundred for each of the three types of distributor. (The x-axis of figure 8.3 is drawn on a logarithmic scale in order to facilitate visual comparison of the information presented.) What is immediately striking about the figure is the clear separation of the

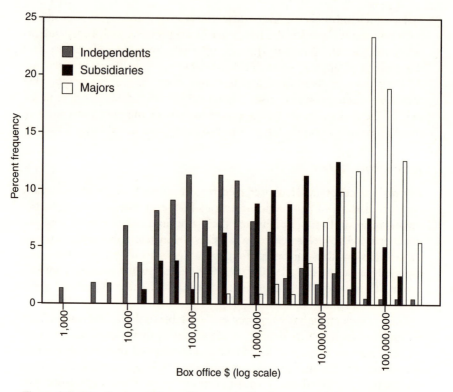

Figure 8.3. Distribution of box-office returns for domestic exhibition, 2000; releasing companies categorized by independents, subsidiaries of majors, and majors. Calculated from data contained in National Association of Theatre Owners, *Encyclopedia of Exhibition, 2001–2002.*

three frequency distributions into lower, middle, and upper segments, with the individual segments being sharply divided from one another in terms of their average box-office returns. Thus, average box office in the year 2000 for independents was $3.8 million, for subsidiaries it was $14.3 million, and for majors $55.6 million (see table 8.4). A t-test indicates that these values are all different from one another at well beyond the 0.01 level of statistical confidence. In the same year, the average number of films per firm distributed in each segment was 2.0, 8.6, and 14.3, respectively, though there is much variance around these values. From these data it is apparent that the majors' subsidiaries (together with a few selected independents) are carving out a very definite middle-range market niche for themselves. Concomitantly, when any independent begins to contest this same niche, it becomes a potential target for takeover by a major. Scrutiny of figure 8.3 suggests that there is a degree of competition *within* each of the

TABLE 8.4
Breakdown of Average Box-Office Returns by Types of Releasing Companies, 2000

	Number of films released	Average box office ($ millions)	Percent of total box office
Independents	221	3.752	10.2
Subsidiaries of majors	80	14.264	14.0
Majors	111	55.639	75.8

Source: Calculated from data in National Association of Theatre Owners, *Encyclopedia of Exhibition, 2001–2002.*

three niches, and more limited competition *between* them, and that the majors have a tight oligopolistic hold over the upper reaches of the market, strengthened by the strategic positioning of their subsidiaries in a sort of intermediate buffer zone. Given that the middle sector has only recently made its appearance as a distinctive segment of the production-distribution system, we cannot push the analysis very far back in time. However, the data appear to show that since 1991 a mainly bifurcated market (structured around majors and independents) has been gradually giving way to a trifurcated pattern in which the majors' subsidiaries expand in number and enlarge their lists of releases.

These remarks can be clarified and extended with the aid of a speculative model of hierarchical market relations in the motion picture industry. The model is based on two key assumptions. The first is that we can identify different types of film in terms of the different market segments to which they appeal (e.g., low-budget films for limited audiences, middle-range films for wider but still selective audiences, blockbusters for mass popular appeal, and so on). Wyatt (1991), for example, argues that high-concept blockbusters are a distinctive product deeply differentiated from other motion picture products by their content and packaging. The second assumption is that the expected gross box-office returns for films of any given type bear an average statistical relationship to the amount of money invested in production and marketing. Of course, other factors play a role in generating expected returns for any given film, such as the cast, the director, and press reviews, but production and marketing budgets represent a primary element on which many other of these other factors themselves depend (cf. Daly 1980; de Vany and Walls 1997; Litman and Ahn 1998; Robins 1993). For present purposes, we also need to recall that the commercial performance of any single film is extremely unpredictable. An industry rule of thumb is that seven or eight out of every 10 films show a net loss, so that overall profitability in the industry is dependent on the other two or three films out of the 10 that actually earn money above and beyond their costs. Thus expected returns are represented here by expected *average* returns.

For the sake of simplicity, let us consider the case where just two market segments exist, one dominated by films with dense production values and appealing to mass audiences, the other characterized by films made by independents for much narrower audiences. For each market segment, i, the expected box office per film will be some positive function of the total amount of money invested in producing and marketing the film. More specifically, the function can be identified as a logistic curve. This proposition follows from the strong likelihood that for any given film we will almost always observe low returns per dollar invested at high and low levels of investment, and relatively high returns per dollar at some intermediate point. As indicated in figure 8.4, the curves that typify different market

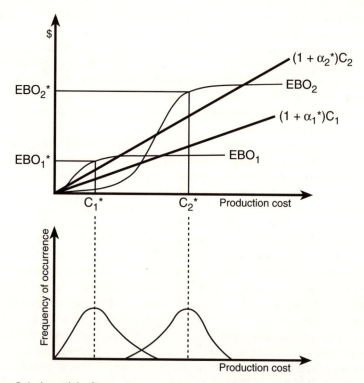

Figure 8.4. A model of investment, expected box-office returns, and frequency of occurrence for films of types 1 and 2. Optimal values of endogenous variables are indicated by an asterisk. Note that values of EBO_i are a function of both α_i and C_i. See text for explanation of symbols.

segments can be expected to have quite different shapes. Let us now define C_i as the total production cost of a film serving market segment i, and let the film's distribution and marketing cost be a simple proportion, α_i, of the same amount. Total investment in the film is thus $I_i = (1 + \alpha_i)C_i$ and its expected box-office earnings are $EBO_i = f_i(\alpha_i, C_i)$. The producer-distributor must now deal with two problems. The first is to determine to which market segment, i, any prospective film is to be allocated. Once this problem has been resolved, the second is to find values of α_i and C_i that maximize $EBO_i - I_i$. A typical solution for the latter problem is shown in figure 8.4, where for a film of type 1, a production cost of C_1^* yields a profit-maximizing value of EBO_1^*. The optimal solution for a film of type 2 is derived in exactly the same manner. The lower panel of figure 8.4 displays hypothetical frequency distributions of the occurrence of type 1 and type 2 films. Obviously, the number of different market segments that come into existence may vary from time, though it is likely to be small given finite markets; equally, frequent overlap between the segments will be apt to occur, as exemplified by crossover films that are programmed to serve one segment but whose box-office performance finally places them in another.

   This analysis proposes a mechanism whereby stable, differentiated market segments in the motion picture industry might emerge, at least for a given period of time. The model mirrors the earlier descriptive discussion of the layered structure of box-office returns in the motion picture industry. However, it represents only a first attempt at an explanatory schema, and its value is purely propaedeutic as things now stand. Considerable further refinement combined with rigorous empirical testing are essential before the model can be taken to be anything much more than a speculative gesture.

INTERNATIONAL TRADE ISSUES

Export Markets

From the very beginnings of Hollywood a century ago, American motion pictures have found ready markets in other countries. Since the Second World War, this outward flow has expanded dramatically, and today the presence of Hollywood is felt virtually around the globe (Hoskins et al. 1997; Miller et al. 2001; Wildman and Siwek 1988).

   Data on U.S. film and tape rental exports to other countries between the years 1986 and 2000 are laid out in table 8.5. The data refer to videotape rentals as well as motion picture distribution overseas, and they cover all U.S. exports in these services. These rentals have grown with notable vigor over the last two decades (almost doubling in dollar value every five years or so) and now exceed the domestic box office by a considerable margin. Whereas the gross domestic box office for motion pictures increased

TABLE 8.5
U.S. Exports in the Form of Film and Tape Rentals (percentage values by destination)

	1986	1991	1996	2001
France	10.2	8.6	8.6	6.7
Germany	7.5	9.6	10.5	12.4
Italy	10.0	7.3	4.7	4.9
Netherlands	15.2	17.5	17.4	9.0
Spain	—	5.1	5.9	6.2
Sweden	—	1.8	1.4	1.2
United Kingdom	10.6	11.0	9.8	15.3
Europe	60.3	66.5	64.9	62.8
Australia	10.3	3.4	4.8	3.6
Japan	8.3	11.5	8.7	8.9
Republic of Korea	—	0.8	1.8	1.2
Taiwan	—	0.5	0.7	1.0
Asia and Pacific	22.1	18.3	19.3	17.1
Brazil	—	0.8	2.2	2.5
Canada	10.4	8.7	6.8	8.0
Mexico	1.3	0.9	1.3	2.6
Americas	17.9	12.5	13.0	16.9
South Africa	—	—	1.1	1.0
Africa	—	1.0	1.2	1.0
Middle East	—	0.5	0.8	1.1
World ($ millions, current)	1,071	1,962	4,982	9,304
World ($ millions, constant)	1,628	2,400	5,290	9,304

Source: U.S. Bureau of Economic Analysis, Survey of Current Business.

(in constant dollar terms) by 40.9% from $5,970 million in 1986 to $8,413 million in 2001, exports of film and tape rentals over the same period increased by 452.8% from $1,683 million to $9,304 million. Table 8.5 informs us that by far the main importers of the products of Hollywood are European countries. The United Kingdom, Germany, and the Netherlands alone account for 36.7% of all rental exports from the United States. Outside of Europe, Japan and Canada are large importers, as are Australia, Brazil, and the Republic of Korea.

The majors maintain extensive distribution and marketing networks in all of the main countries mentioned in table 8.5. They also have direct control over distribution in many more secondary markets. For example, United International Pictures—a joint venture of Universal and Paramount—owns distribution facilities in 37 different countries, including Britain, France, Germany, the Netherlands, Australia, and Japan, as well as less lucrative countries like Hungary, Chile, Peru, the Philippines, and Thailand. Twentieth Century Fox owns 21 foreign distribution facilities in an equally diverse set of countries. In countries where the majors do not actually own a distribution network outright, they frequently enter into joint ventures or long-term agreements with local distribution companies. Films made in Hollywood usually capture a major portion of total box-office receipts in virtually all principal foreign markets. This phenomenon can be ascribed to the unequaled capacity of American multinational media corporations to disseminate the products of Hollywood across the globe, as well as to their ability to make big-budget films that appeal powerfully to popular tastes in many different cultures. In testimony to this remark, films that do well at the box office in the United States invariably also do well abroad. Hence, the simple correlation between gross domestic box-office and foreign box-office earnings of 121 Hollywood films released in the year 2000 is 0.81, which is significant at well beyond the 0.01 level.[2]

Strategic Trade in Hollywood Films

Strategic trade involves governmental support for export activities in pursuit of national interests (cf. Tyson 1992). One of its recurrent manifestations in the case of the United States is the exertion of political pressures on other countries to open their markets to freer trade. In some instances the motive behind strategic trade initiatives is political influence, in others it is economic gain. Governments will be particularly tempted to push for market-opening measures in other countries where expansion of their export flows generates rents based on increasing-returns effects in wider domestic production systems.

Exports of motion pictures from the United States have long been a classic instance of this phenomenon, with federal bureaucracies continually pressing in various forums of trade negotiation for foreign governments to open their doors more widely to Hollywood films. Indeed, Hollywood has always received abundant help from the U.S. State Department, the Commerce Department, and other agencies of federal government. At least since the Second World War, the interests of Hollywood and the aims of Washington have consistently coincided on the economic front, even when there has been less accordance on the ideological front (Segrave 1997). One particularly notable case of this convergence of interests occurred at the time of the Marshall Plan for Europe (1948–51), whose provisions linked levels of aid directly to recipients' willingness to accept imports of U.S. motion pictures (Guback 1969). This requirement was of course immediately and directly beneficial to Hollwood production companies and their cohorts of

---

[2] Data for this exercise were obtained from http://www.worldwideboxoffice.com/.

suppliers. In addition, it functioned as a means of stimulating American exports at large (by helping to reshape overall tastes and preferences among Western European consumers) and as an ideological weapon at a time when significant segments of the European working classes seemed disposed to adopt left-wing doctrines and to sympathize politically with the Soviet Union. More recently, as globalization has started to intensify, the United States government has been aggressively promoting free trade agendas generally and unhampered trade in cultural products in particular.

In the never-ending effort to advance the interests of Hollywood in various forums of national and international deliberation, the majors are jointly represented by the Motion Picture Association of America (MPAA), which plays a critical role as an industry mouthpiece and lobbying organization. Symptomatically, the association has offices in Washington, DC, as well as in Southern California. The MPAA preaches an aggressive doctrine of free trade, and it played a notably active role behind the scenes at the GATT negotiations in 1993 in the confrontation between the United States and Europe (led by France) over trade in audiovisual products. Although the European position prevailed at that time by the assertion of a "cultural exception" permitting each country to set up trade restrictions according to its own cultural preferences, there is every likelihood, in the newly constituted WTO that succeeded GATT, that the US/MPAA position will eventually prevail. The MPAA is also the parent organization of the MPA (Motion Picture Association), formerly known as the MPEA (Motion Picture Export Association), established in 1946 as a legal cartel under the provisions of the Webb-Pomerane Export Trade Act. The same piece of legislation permits block-booking by American motion picture distributors on foreign markets even though this practice is expressly forbidden on domestic markets by antitrust legislation. Outside the United States, the MPA has offices in Brussels, Rome, New Delhi, Rio de Janeiro, Singapore, Mexico City, Toronto, and Jakarta, and from these bases it carries out its mission of promoting exports of Hollywood motion pictures, policing intellectual property rights violations, and advancing the goals of the industry generally in foreign markets.

Independent motion picture distributors are represented by AFMA (the American Film Marketing Association), an active and influential organization founded in 1981. AFMA's membership roster of over 130 firms is composed primarily of independent distributors and allied firms based in Hollywood, but a large proportion is made up, as well, of firms from other parts of the country and from abroad. Like the MPAA, AFMA is concerned to advance the interests of its members in regard to trade and public relations, with a special emphasis on issues of arbitration, piracy, marketing, and tracking members' earnings from foreign sources. AFMA also organizes the American Film Market, an annual event in Santa

Monica representing the largest motion picture trade event in the world, attracting over 7,000 people from over 70 different countries. The American Film Market has come to play a major role in the promotion of independently made Hollywood films.

The Globalization of Hollywood

For almost a century, and especially since the Second World War, Hollywood has maintained an unparalleled ability to cater to popular audiences, and it has used this ability to dominate national and international motion picture markets. This record of success has been reinforced partly by the complex production machinery of Hollywood itself, and partly by the industry's early perfection of its capacity to distribute films to mass markets across the nation and across the world. The combined effect of these three factors—popular appeal, a powerful system of production, and mastery in distribution—has for decades made Hollywood virtually unassailable on the commercial front, both at home and abroad.

The steady globalization of Hollywood, has, of course, engendered numerous clashes and disputes. Some of these reflect purely commercial differences of interest; some are focused on cultural conflicts of one sort or another; and some, perhaps the majority, are a complex mixture of the two. The official line of the MPAA and the U.S. Department of Commerce is that international trade in cultural products should proceed in as open and as free a manner as possible, and should not be subject to any special restrictions. This line, however, overlooks the circumstance that unlike wheat or coal, cultural products are also intimately bound up with matters of selfhood, identity, and consciousness. Conflicts over these matters as a consequence of the flow of cultural products from one society to another are to be expected and need to be examined on their own terms. A rhetoric of market ideology inevitably misses the crucial point here. Even in the United States, governmental engagement with the social and political content of motion pictures has occurred at frequent intervals. One might plausibly argue, in fact, that such engagement has not been more intense only because of the preemptive self-regulation of the industry, dating from the promulgation of the Hays Code in 1930 and the notorious blacklist maintained by the studios in the postwar years.

These remarks raise difficult questions about the interplay between economic and cultural forces in the modern world. Nowadays, international trade increasingly functions as a form of cultural as well as economic exchange. Trade has certainly always been characterized by this dual role, but in recent decades, its cultural impacts have intensified greatly as a consequence of the enormous expansion of cultural-products industries in many different parts of the world, especially in the advanced capitalist countries. The outputs of these industries circulate with increasing ease through global circuits of commerce, bringing in their train a complex series of cultural and political collisions. Of all contemporary cultural products, none is more deeply implicated in these processes than motion pictures made in Hollywood, and in many countries, the frequent agitation set in motion by this state of affairs is all the more intense because of the unusually large share of these products in their domestic markets. To be sure, a number of other centers of production outside the United States are currently seeking to position themselves more effectively on global markets, but none has yet found either the economic or the cultural formulae that might allow it to contest Hollywood's market supremacy with decisive results.

In the next and last chapter of this book, I attempt to bring these issues further into focus by means of two critical arguments. One of these is concerned with a more extended examination of cultural globalization, with an emphasis on the pros and cons of the cultural imperialism thesis. The other represents an attempt to identify some incipient shifts in the economic geography of global motion picture production, and in this context to make some tentative assessments of Hollywood's future prospects.

APPENDIX TO CHAPTER 8
REGRESSION ANALYSIS OF DISTRIBUTION AND
    RELEASING ACTIVITIES

As indicated in the main body of chapter 8, a data set was constructed for the period 1980–2000 on the releasing behavior of the Hollywood majors. The data are derived from the listings of individual film credits in the *Annual Index to Motion Picture Credits* published by the Academy of Motion Picture Arts and Sciences. Specifically, data were collected on two categories of films released by each major each year: (a) films made with independent participation, and (b) films made by the major in-house. See the main text for comments on certain ambiguities in these data.

Let y_t be the number of films made with independent participation and distributed in year t by any given major; let x_t be the number of films made in-house and distributed in the same year by the same major. These variables are de-trended by taking first differences ($\Delta y_t = y_t - y_{t-1}$, $\Delta x_t = x_t - x_{t-1}$), and simple regressions of the relationship between them are computed for all majors individually and collectively, as laid out in table A8.1. A negative and (in all but two cases) significant relationship between Δy_t and Δx_t obtains across all regression equations.

A further and related question concerns temporal patterns of releasing in relation to general market conditions. A third group of distribution companies in addition to majors and independents is introduced into the

TABLE A8.1
Linear Regression Equations Showing the Relations between Δy_t and Δx_t, 1980–2000 (See text for definitions of variables.)

	Constant value	Regression coefficient	Adjusted R^2
Columbia/Sony	0.24	−0.8741**	0.52
Disney/Buena Vista	0.56	−0.2448	−0.02
MGM	−0.12	−0.5250	0.09
Paramount	−0.18	−1.4172**	0.52
Twentieth Century Fox	−0.09	−0.7292**	0.51
Universal	−0.07	−0.9216**	0.36
Warner	−0.07	−0.7481**	0.33
All majors	0.58	−0.8813**	0.50

**The double asterisk indicates significance level of 0.01 or better.

analysis here, namely, the subsidiaries of the majors. The variables of interest in the present phase of investigation are defined:

A_t Total money spent in the United States on film admissions in year t (in constant dollars)
I_t Number of films released by independent distributors in year t
M_t Number of films released by major distributors in year t
r_t the interest rate (federal funds, effective rate) in year t
S_t Number of films released by majors' subsidiaries in year t

A series of linear regression equations was then computed linking the number of films distributed by majors, majors' subsidiaries, and independents to money spent on admissions and interest rates for each year from 1980 to 2000 (see table A8.2). Notice that A_t enters these regressions with a time lag of one year in order to capture the follow-on effects of shifts up and down in the market. The signs on the coefficients of the independent variables in the regressions are all as expected. The number of films released by each of the three groups of distributors, and by all three in aggregate, is positively related to money spent at the box office in the previous year, and negatively related to interest rates in the current year. Independent distributors are particularly sensitive to the former variable, possibly because they ride on the coattails of majors' successes. The releasing patterns of majors' subsidiaries are not significantly related to either of the independent variables. The majors themselves (excluding their subsidiaries) are highly sensitive to interest rates in their releasing behavior. When we rerun the regression analysis using all categories of releases $(I_t+S_t+M_t)$ as the dependent variable, both A_{t-1} and r_t emerge as having

TABLE A8.2
Linear Regression Equations Showing the Effects of Box Office Returns and
Interest Rates on Temporal Variations in Films Released by Independents, Majors'
Subsidiaries, and Majors, 1980–2000 (See text for definitions of variables.)

Dependent variable	Constant value	Regression coefficients		Adjusted R^2
		A_{t-1}	r_t	
I_t	−168.05	0.0577**	−2.1198	0.49
S_t	−52.16	0.0188	−3.7797	0.23
M_t	125.58	0.0010	−3.0057**	0.40
$I_t + S_t + M_t$	−94.66	0.0775**	−8.9052**	0.74

Regressions based on data derived from the Academy of Motion Picture Arts and Sciences, *Annual Index to Motion Picture Credits*, and from the U.S. Department of Commerce, Bureau of the Census, *Statistical Abstract of the United States*.
**The double asterisk indicates significance level of 0.01 or better.

extremely significant effects, with an adjusted R^2 of 0.74. The regression coefficients in the latter model suggest, reasonably enough, that the composite pattern of releasing is rather more volatile than it is in the case of independents, subsidiaries, or majors taken in isolation from one another.

CHAPTER NINE

Cinema, Culture, Globalization

IN ALL OF THE ABOVE, I have tried to offer a description of Hollywood as a dense, multifaceted agglomeration of capital and labor whose organizational dynamics and socially constructed competitive advantages, in combination with massive capabilities in distribution and marketing, have enabled it to rise to virtually absolute mastery of global film and television markets. No motion picture or television program industry in any ot :r part of the world today comes anywhere near Hollywood in commerc.al prowess and geographic reach. By the same token, Hollywood has for long functioned as the premier center of commercialized culture generally across the entire contemporary world.

In the light of these remarks, we may ask:

1. What is the current status of national cinemas in the rest of world, and what are the prospects for Hollywood's continued ability to outstrip them on global markets?
2. Concomitantly, under what conditions might a resurgence of centers of motion picture production outside the United States be expected to occur?
3. What can we learn from the specific case of cinema about the wider problems of international trade in cultural products as globalization runs its course?
4. What is the general social and political significance of a cinema—whatever its geographic point of anchorage—that is deeply rooted in commercial and corporate imperatives?

These are troublesome questions. For one thing, opinions about them vary widely, and there is not much likelihood in the context of the present book that we shall be able to deal satisfactorily with all of the nuances of current debates, much less with their wider theoretical and ideological ramifications. For another, the paucity of relevant data on country-by-country production and trade in motion pictures imposes limits on the degree to which we can assess basic trends in most of the world. The standard warning also needs to be issued in any exercise of the sort proposed here, namely, that any attempt to assess future developments is apt to break down as the many imponderables that invariably come into play in real social contexts begin to make their influence felt in practice.

The discussion that follows, then, should be seen more as an attempt to refine the questions posed above than as a set of confident responses. The exercise is acutely important, however, not only because these are analytically interesting questions, but also because they intersect with important issues of policy, and the ways in which we seek to address them have direct implications for a variety of sensitive practical outcomes across the globe.

GLOBAL CINEMATIC PRODUCTION AND TRADE

The fact of Hollywood's domination of global trade in motion pictures is already well established. The data presented in table 9.1 add a brief further gloss on this issue by indicating the precise degree to which Hollywood motion pictures currently penetrate a number of important foreign markets. Table 9.1 shows, in particular, the share of total box-office receipts earned by domestic and U.S. producers in Australia, France, Germany, Italy, Japan, Spain, and the United Kingdom. A quick scrutiny of the table reveals that Hollywood films account for well over half, and, in some cases, well over two-thirds of total box-office receipts in the designated countries. Even in the case of France, which has sought more resolutely than any other European country to protect its film industry from American competition (Bonnell 1996; Scott 2000b), Hollywood's annual share of total box-office receipts averaged 57.3% over the 1990s (though there was a very noticeable drop to 46.4% in 2002). The global expansion of Hollywood's reach in the last few decades, moreover, has more often than not been associated with long-term declines in domestic motion picture

TABLE 9.1
Structure of Selected National Film Markets, 2000

	Number of films produced	Total theater entries (millions)	Total receipts ($ millions)	Domestic film industry share (%)	U.S. film industry share (%)
Australia	31	82.2	401.0	8.0	87.5
France	204	165.5	821.3	28.9	58.3
Germany	75	152.5	463.5	9.4	81.9
Italy	103	103.4	258.1	17.5	69.5
Japan	282	135.4	1,585.3	31.8	64.8
Spain	98	135.3	297.1	10.1	82.7
United Kingdom	90	142.5	941.2	19.6	75.3
United States	460	1,420.1	7,661.0	96.1	—

Source: CNC Info, no. 283, 2002 (Paris: Centre National de la Cinématographie).

production in importing countries. That being said, there are many centers of motion picture production around the world that still maintain high levels of output in terms of the number of films made per year. In certain cases (e.g., China-Hong Kong, India, Britain, and France), film production has actually expanded in recent years.

Data presented in the UNESCO *Statistical Yearbook* on motion picture import-export patterns sheds further light on the market power of Hollywood. Unfortunately, the data leave much to be desired in terms of accuracy and coverage, and the information for different countries is not all standardized as to the year of observation. We should also note that the UNESCO data are presented in terms of the number (not dollar value) of films imported by country. The United States again emerges as the major source of imported films all around the world. In 1995, 61.5% of all films that entered into world trade originated in the United States. France and Britain came in distant second and third places with 7.8% and 5.1%, respectively, of world markets in motion pictures. Once we strip away the dominating effects of U.S.-made films in trade, however, a number of secondary but conspicuous import-export clusters make their appearance as a reflection of various cultural and geographic biases in world markets. Sinclair (1996) has suggested the term "geo-linguistic regions" as a way of designating groups of countries that have distinctive motion picture trade profiles. French films, for example, have a relatively strong representation in the imports of European countries generally, as well as in francophone territories across the rest of the world. Indian productions make up a significant proportion of the film imports of Iran, Jordan, Kazakhstan, Kyrgyzstan, Morocco, and Romania, and they are imported in significant numbers into the countries of the Indian diaspora. The UNESCO data suggest that rather idiosyncratic import patterns also exist for films originating from China, Germany, and Russia.

Indeed, we have become so accustomed to thinking of Hollywood as the sole colossus of the international film industry that we frequently overlook the large production of motion pictures that occurs in the rest of the world. In monetary terms, certainly, production in other countries is at a low ebb when compared with Hollywood, but if we look at the number of films made, the situation becomes very much less tilted in Hollywood's favor. The point is driven home by a scrutiny of figure 9.1, which displays a map of film production activities across the globe in the 1990s. The map reveals the vigor of motion picture production, as such, in many different countries, especially in the Asia-Europe axis. India is by far the world's largest producer, with over 800 films a year to its credit, most of them originating in Mumbai/Bollywood. The Philippines occupies second place (just ahead of the United States), with 456 films in 1994. Other parts of Asia—Bangladesh, China, Hong Kong, Japan, Myanmar, Pakistan, and

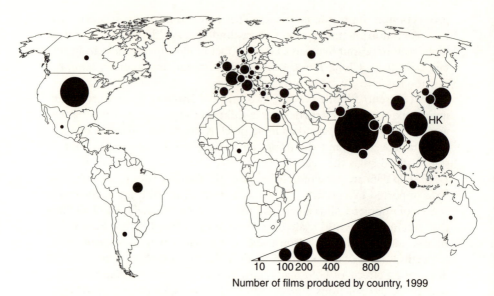

Figure 9.1. Number of feature-length films produced by country. Data are shown only for countries producing more than ten films a year. Source: UNESCO, *Statistical Yearbook*, 1999.

Thailand—also have substantial levels of production. In Europe there are long-standing traditions of cinematography and significant numbers of films continue to be produced there, above all in Britain, France, Germany, and Italy, as well as in Poland, Russia, Spain, and Sweden, among others. In the Middle East, Egypt is the dominant center of production, followed closely by Iran and Turkey. Latin American production is currently dominated by Brazil. The first impression conveyed by figure 9.1, then, is that world cinema is in a surprisingly robust state of health in terms of the sheer quantity of films produced and the diversity of countries from which they originate, though, again, Hollywood clearly reemerges in the lead position when we shift our point of observation from production back to export activity, and from number of films produced to revenues generated.

These remarks lead the discussion directly to two questions that are likely to become increasingly urgent as processes of globalization intensify further. What is the social and political significance of Hollywood's currently hegemonic position on world film markets, and to what extent is this state of affairs an expression of U.S. cultural imperialism? And to what extent will centers of production outside the United States be able to claim back domestic market share from Hollywood, and even to expand their presence on external markets?

A HEGEMONIC CULTURE?

The Cultural Imperialism Thesis

Hollywood's long-term ascendancy on world film markets flows in large degree from the advantages that derive from its large domestic base of consumers, its mastery of physical production, and its dominant control of distribution. Foreign producers have found it difficult to compete on any of these fronts. Above all, the Hollywood majors have perfected a competitive strategy that relies upon their massive productive assets to pump out enormously expensive blockbuster films with dense production values able to corner significant segments of the market. Simultaneously, the majors' unparalleled distribution and marketing capacities make it possible for them—on average—to recoup a large proportion of the costs of the same films in a matter of days from first release. The assimilation of the majors into multinational media conglomerates has endowed them with yet further competitive muscle. Among the world's top ten media conglomerates as measured in terms of annual sales (cf. table 9.2), as many as six incorporate Hollywood majors into their overall holdings. All of these giant corporate organizations are engaged in building synergistic bridges between their numerous internal divisions and operations, from computer software development, through the production of cultural outputs like film, television, and music, to the manufacture of hardware platforms. They represent overarching structures of ownership with significant internal synergies, including the ability to parlay intellectual property rights from one product line to another, with concomitant commercial benefits across the board. In addition to these potent advantages, exporters of Hollywood motion pictures, as I indicated at an earlier stage, have always received a boost from U.S. governmental agencies, which have worked hard over the decades to clear away impediments to the free flow of films across international borders.

Small wonder, then, that many countries on the receiving end of the Hollywood pipeline have attempted to resist in various ways, especially in view of the disproportionately narrow flow of films and other cultural products in the other direction (Mattelart 2000). In the light of this situation, a number of social theorists have sought to conceptualize the current situation as a form of outright American cultural domination or imperialism (Dorfman and Mattelart 1975). The basic thesis is succinctly expressed by Michalet (1987, pp. 205–6) in the following terms: "The laws of globalization are called homogenization, standardization of tastes, behavior, cultures. . . . The Hollywood model is inseparable from American imperialism."

There are certainly nuggets of truth in this statement, in that Hollywood films over the last several decades have had massive and not always

TABLE 9.2
The World's Top Ten Media Conglomerates as Measured in Terms of Annual Sales

	Country of origin	Primary SIC code	Explanation of SIC code	Most recent annual sales ($billion)
Sony Corporation	Japan	3651	Household audio and video equipment	57.9
Vivendi-Universal SA	France	7313	Radio, TV, publisher representatives	51.1
AOL Time-Warner	USA	7375	Information retrieval services	38.2
Walt Disney Company	USA	4841	Cable and other pay TV services	25.3
Viacom Inc.	USA	4833	Radio and television broadcasting	23.2
Bouygues	France	4833	Radio and television broadcasting	18.3
Bertelsmann AG	Germany	4833	Radio and television broadcasting	17.0
News Corporation	Australia	4833	Radio and television broadcasting	13.1
Lagardère	France	2713	Newspapers	11.9
Comcast	USA	4841	Cable and other pay TV services	9.7

Sources: Various databases and reports.

Note: Some interpretative discretion has been exercised as to which companies count as media conglomerates and which do not. National telecommunications companies such as AT&T, France Telecom, and Deutsche Telekom have been eliminated from consideration.

welcome impacts in many different parts of the world. The plaintive tone
of the statement is all the more compelling when we take into account not
only the steady erosion of local traditions and cultures as the spread of
American cultural products has accelerated, but also the insistent meretriciousness and philistinism of so much of the output of Hollywood, and the
sense many individuals in importing countries have that these products are
carriers of highly undesirable cultural effects. Certainly, whatever qualita-
tive judgments we may want to pass on the films of Hollywood, the natu-
ralization of American cinema has been going on in many countries for
a long time. The result has been a progressive, if contested, penetration
of American cultural norms and idioms into other social environments as
Hollywood's massive machinery of production, distribution, and marketing has gone about its work. This process has been especially forceful by
virtue of the much earlier development of large media conglomerates in
the United States as compared with other countries, and the lengthy
period of time over which they have held a quasi-monopoly on international commerce in entertainment products (cf. Mattelart 1976).

If the cultural imperialism thesis captures some aspects of a real problem
in the contemporary world, there are, on the other side of the coin, off-
setting circumstances suggesting that at least some nuances need to be
built into its main thrust. There is also merit to the view that the terms of
the thesis are a more accurate description of things as they were in the
recent past than as they are today, and that it fails to take adequate account
of several important new developments. For example, as I shall indicate
more fully later, powerful entertainment and media firms with global
influence are no longer uniquely or even mainly an American phenomenon, but are on the rise in Europe, Japan, and other places, and they are
becoming increasingly capable of offering products from their home bases
that can compete head-to-head with those of Hollywood. By the same
token, several major centers of audiovisual production around the world
are now clearly making efforts to contest and recontest global markets,
and with some success in a number of cases.

There is another reason why we might hesitate to endorse the all-out
version of the cultural imperialism thesis. Numerous culture theorists and
allied social scientists today hold that audiences, whatever their social identity, have highly developed critical sensors that help them filter out exogenous cultural influences (Hesmondhalgh 2002; Jaffe and Weimann 2000).
Recent work on the social reception of cultural messages suggests that
most consumers of media products are far from being consistently outwit-
ted by what they see or hear, no matter what the nature of the medium. In
particular, much recent work has suggested that as films and other audiovisual products pass from one society to another, active processes of rein-
terpretation and hybridization come into effect in the sense that consumers

habitually read their own cultural prepossessions into the messages they receive (Pietersee 1994). These claims are perhaps overoptimistic in their imputation of consistently high levels of autonomy and self-directedness to cultural consumers at large. They are doubtless on target, however, to the extent that they point to the existence of some sort of variable psychic buffer zone in which a degree of negotiation and hence diversion of incoming messages occurs.

National Interests and Market Imperatives

Even if the cultural imperialism thesis seems to offer much too blunt an instrument of critique, we must still acknowledge the tense and recurrent opposition that exists in many countries between national cultural interests on the one hand and incursions of external market forces into local life on the other.

Numerous countries (Canada, China, France, and South Korea, among others) have in fact made strenuous efforts on the policy front to counter the perceived commercial and cultural threats emanating from Hollywood. These efforts entail both defensive and offensive maneuvers, such as erecting tariff barriers on imports, placing restrictions on foreign content in television broadcasts, and the provision of subsidies or tax incentives in support of local film industries. This state of affairs is, of course, abhorrent to the Hollywood majors and to the various U.S. governmental agencies that from time to time speak and act on behalf of Hollywood. The arguments that these parties marshal against foreign restrictions on the unhindered flow of Hollywood films typically invoke, in one formulation or another, notions of consumer sovereignty, the efficiency and rationality of free markets, and the democratic virtues of the unhindered circulation of information. As such, these are arguments that need to be taken seriously, not just because they are appealing to large numbers of individuals, but also because they embody a number of genuinely meaningful and desirable norms. At the same time, a series of qualifying observations must be raised to the effect that the application of these norms in real social situations does not always lead on to unquestionably optimal results. I am referring here, above all, to certain aspects of the self-legitimating dynamics of the market, as well as to the sociopolitical significance of human culture above and beyond its functions in economic exchange.

At the outset, then, and in contradistinction to the assumptions of neoclassical economics, consumer tastes and preferences cannot be taken to be purely independent and exogenous variables. On the contrary, tastes and preferences are actively molded over the course of time in complex processes of socialization and the shaping of personal needs. In the modern world, the corporate champions of commercial culture command a disproportionate share of the instruments (production apparatuses, channels of distribution, marketing systems, celebrity icons, and so on) capable of acting on these processes and of maintaining a slow war of attrition where resistance occurs. I do not mean to insinuate that some sort of corporate conspiracy exists in this regard. But at least in some philosophical sense we must look critically at any argument proclaiming the universal equity and impartiality of market-driven exchange mechanisms, especially in the arena of cultural production and consumption, and especially where supply and demand have a tendency to lock into habituated patterns. An allied proposition is that structures of demand for cultural products are rife with externalities. To be more explicit, the consumption of culture is not only a matter of private choice, but is also, and inevitably, fraught with wider political meaning. This follows at once if we accept the idea that human consciousness is shaped in various ways by lengthy and repeated exposure to external cultural forces, and that forms of consciousness in turn are implicated in the manner in which social relationships play out in practice.

In the United States itself—the country that most vigorously promotes free-market principles in regard to trade in cultural products—recognition of the validity of this claim is implicit in national concerns about such matters as, for example, violence and pornography in film and television, certain kinds of public representation of certain social groups, open or covert advocacy of drugs in the media, and (in the not-too-distant past) messages with allegedly "un-American" meanings. Concerns of this sort, moreover, are not always confined to the domain of general public debate in the United States, but are sometimes taken up within the seat of government itself, in the form of congressional inquiries, or in the courts, and even in direct legislative action. We can hardly be surprised, then, that a number of other societies with other cultural sensibilities and traditions, and with a due sense of their own authentic forms of identity, consciousness, and ways of life are less enthusiastic about the idea of free trade in cultural products than the CEOs of the Hollywood majors and their allies in the federal government. Even if we are skeptical about theories of cultural imperialism, and even if we are passionately in favor of the free flow of information, we need to recognize that there is more to other countries' struggles to deal with cultural incursions from the outside than irrational opposition to the universal benevolence of the market.

Toward a Polycentric Audiovisual Landscape

While a global cultural system permanently dominated by an oligopoly of media corporations based in Los Angeles and New York still appears to many as the most likely scenario of the future; there are good reasons for thinking that this prospect is now actually beginning to blur in important respects. The deepening trend to globalization certainly makes any intimation of such domination a matter of profound concern. However, globalization also brings in its train a series of alternative outcomes whose effects tend to run in a contrary direction. One of the more important outcomes in this regard is the resurgence of motion picture production complexes in several different countries in Europe and Asia, and, more prospectively, in Latin America as well. Another is the increasing visibility and international competitiveness of non-American firms with interests in media and entertainment. Yet another is the great expansion of niche markets for cultural products in all of the main capitalist countries, and, more specifically, the recent growth in these countries of audiences for films and television programs made in places other than Hollywood. These developments suggest that increasing diversity rather than increasing uniformity is the prevailing— if still incipient—trend in the world's major markets for cultural products today.

The New Geography of Cultural Production

Basic concepts of the locational forces at work in cultural-products industries (as discussed in earlier chapters) suggest that a number of large global cities are particularly well positioned to play a major role as sites of production in the new cultural economy. Cities at the very top of the urban hierarchy of countries with well-developed cultural assets are in an especially favorable situation in this regard. The denizens of these cities are almost always more cosmopolitan in outlook than those of centers at lower levels in the urban hierarchy, and the same cities tend to be advanced foci of national cultural innovation and accomplishment. They also function as nodal articulations of the new global economy at large, and the widening framework of external relationships in which they are almost always embedded provides a grid through which complex processes of international cultural exchange and fusion can be mediated.

Large metropolitan regions like New York, Los Angeles, London, Paris, Tokyo, Beijing, Hong Kong, Seoul, and Mexico City display in varying degree the basic features of this syndrome. It is in metropolitan areas like these, above all, that the new cultural economy of global capitalism is taking shape. These are places where national motion picture and television program production tends to concentrate, and where many allied sectors, such as electronic games, recorded music, book and magazine publishing, advertising, the fashion industry, and design trades, are located. More often than not these sectors draw upon distinctive local traditions, crafts, and sensibilities, though the more internationally successful of them are typically adept at translating these cultural resources into products that can be readily decoded by nonlocal consumers. Cross-fertilization of ideas and other spillover effects between different sectors help to sustain the overall dynamism of cultural production within any given metropolitan region. In the wealthier countries of the world, some of these regions are sites of an emerging new symbiosis between work and social life that further enhances their cultural creativity. This phenomenon has sometimes been identified in terms of the city of spectacle (see Storper and Scott 1989), where, in architecturally dramatized environments, the workaday world of creative labor interpenetrates with shopping complexes, pedestrian walkways, outdoor cafés and restaurants, theaters, museums, and galleries (Brown et al. 2000; Florida 2002; Scott 2001; Storper and Scott 1989; Zukin 1995). The net effect is the formation of distinctive urban districts with high levels of consonance between economy, ambience, and community.

Cities with attributes of this sort are breeding grounds for dynamic cultural-products sectors, and magnets for the kinds of creative workers on which these sectors thrive. In Europe, for example, they are represented by places like London, Paris, Rome, Berlin, and Madrid, each of which is the site of a burgeoning cultural economy, and especially, of a sizable audio-visual industry. Indeed, these very cities produce, between them, considerably more films a year than Hollywood, and some of them were notably successful on the export front in the period from the 1950s to the 1970s. If they have since receded before the competitive onslaughts of American films, they are all now making serious efforts to regain a position on global markets. An important stimulus underlying these efforts is the current push by the European Union to promote film production and export activities in all the member countries. One of the main instruments of this push is the MEDIA Plus Program, initiated in January 2001, with its central goal being to enhance European capacities for film distribution. The Council of Europe, too, has been active in promoting European film industries via its Eurimages Program, which focuses on inter-country coproductions. The Eurimages Program has achieved a number of noteworthy successes since its initiation in 1989.

In Asia, as well, the film industry is concentrated in major metropolitan regions. The most outstanding of these are Mumbai/Bollywood, Manila, Tokyo, Beijing, Hong Kong, Seoul, and Bangkok. Between them, these cities produce by a wide margin the largest number of the world's motion pictures. However, most of the films made in these places play largely to local audiences, so that they are apt to exhibit rather intense national inflections and purely parochial points of reference (Dissanayake 2000). Yet, despite the generally restricted market appeal of Asian films hitherto, an increasing number of them are now starting to penetrate well beyond their usual range of trade. The Tokyo film industry has gained an important share of international markets with its *anime* productions of late years. Both Beijing and Hong Kong have produced large-budget films over the 1980s and 1990s that have attracted major international attention. Hong Kong cinema, in particular, with its emphasis on fast-paced action films, has acquired an extensive following in North America and Europe (Yau 2001). Even the Mumbai/Bollywood industry appears to be on the point of breaking out beyond its established market sphere, and gives every sign of connecting with a broader international audience.

Bottlenecks and Opportunities

These are promising trends, but a number of conditions will need to be satisfied before we can confidently assume the trends to have long-run durability in the face of continued competition from Hollywood.

Above all, the wider success of these alternative cinemas will depend on their ability to maintain and even intensify their distinctive differences from Hollywood while at the same time making films with high production values that appeal to global audiences. The general principle underlying this assertion is that monopolistic competition, not imitation, is the pathway to long-term viability for industrial agglomerations seeking to carve out a place for themselves in markets that are already swamped by the outputs of a dominant center of production. Dominant centers, by definition, have massive stocks of the competitive advantages that in the first instance have propelled their product lines into leading positions on world markets. Effective market contestation by subdominant centers, then, calls at least for some unique competitive asset that dominant centers cannot match. Additionally, and at the risk of some repetition, even if certain alternative production centers were able to accomplish the goal of making films with unique appeal on wider global markets, they would still not find it easy to achieve significant growth and repeated commercial success if they lacked the capacity to distribute and market their films on a large scale.

It has often been argued that films made in languages other than English encounter further barriers to the more extensive diffusion of their products, and that the English dialogue of Hollywood films endows them with broad accessibility to audiences by comparison with films made in non-English speaking countries. However, both of these arguments tend to overstate the case. Most audiences whose first language is not English are not much more capable of unaided comprehension of the dialogue in a Hollywood film than Americans are able to understand films in languages other than English. The point is that if significant habituation can work in one direction (meaning the relatively effortless reception of English-language films by non-English-language audiences), there is no reason in principle why it cannot work in the other. Foreign commentators sometimes assert that audiences in the United States simply cannot in any case be persuaded to see films that originate in other parts of the world, but once more, the argument is overstated. If the French can be induced to eat McDonald's hamburgers washed down with Coca-Cola, then Americans can be induced to watch French films. Or, at least, they can in principle be induced to do so on a larger scale than is currently the case given sufficient investment in effective distribution and long-term marketing campaigns.

The idea that the motion picture industry of the twenty-first century may be more polycentric and more polyglot than it has been in the recent past is supported by the fact that large multinational media conglomerates with home bases outside the United States are now coming to be a significant force on the world stage. As suggested by table 9.2, and contrary to what we might at first assume, a high proportion of the world's largest media corporations originate from countries other than the United States, and a similar pattern of diversity of national origins is more or less replicated down the scale of corporate size. To be sure, almost all of the firms mentioned in table 9.2, whether headquartered in the United States or not, have direct interests in Hollywood motion picture and television production activities, but all of them are increasingly involved in various kinds of production activities in other parts of the world as well. Thus, even as they promote the products of Hollywood on wider markets, they are engaged in efforts to valorize the assets that they hold in other countries. One example out of many of this phenomenon is the recent foray by Twentieth Century Fox into the Bollywood production system. No doubt producers in Hollywood and their corporate owners will continue to dominate global markets in audiovisual products, but they will almost certainly be faced with rising competition from other centers of production and other corporate entities in the not-too-distant future. Ironically, (at least from the perspective of proponents of the cultural imperialism thesis), if any wider process of polycentric development in the motion picture industry were to occur, it would almost certainly be at least in part ascribable to the enabling role of large multinational media corporations.

CULTURE AND ECONOMY IN THE TWENTY-FIRST CENTURY

The Commodification of Culture

Over the last couple of decades, the general pattern of cultural production and consumption referred to in these pages has increasingly consolidated its hold in major capitalist societies. A primary aspect of this turn of events is that the culture we consume has its origins to an ever and ever greater degree in commercial sources of supply. Noteworthy, too, is the increasing diversity and exoticism of commercially produced culture notwithstanding the important role that mass-appeal blockbuster products (almost all of them originating from Hollywood) continue to play in the global cultural economy. At the same time, the conventional categories of high (noncommercialized) culture and low (commercialized) culture are no longer accepted quite so readily as they once were, and skepticism about the theoretical meaning (as opposed to the social functions) of this cultural dichotomy is widespread and rising. Already, in the 1930s, Walter Benjamin had made a bold attempt to demystify the notion of the aura in aesthetic objects, and this effort has been succeeded more recently by insistent critiques of any claim to the effect that fundamental distinctions exist between art and non-art in the sphere of culture (Hesmondhalgh 2002; Jameson 1992; Lash 1990). The same critiques, in turn, have dealt a blow to assertions that commercialized cultural products—even when they are fabricated in extended divisions of labor regulated by specialized managerial cadres— are without exception or of necessity inferior to products that convey the more personalized visions of an individual *auteur*. The motion picture industry of Hollywood, for its part, has never been suspected of according pride of place to the principle of art for art's sake, but it has arguably managed to create some of the most stunning masterworks of world cinema over the decades. It must be added that if commercialized forms of cultural creation do not always result in inferior quality, they do in everyday practice give birth to enormous flows of shallow and mercenary ephemera. Indeed, all else being equal, the long-term effects of Say's Law, and the tendency of tastes and preferences to lock in through habituation, suggest that there are many potent downward pressures on cultural quality in commercialized systems of supply, and all the more so given the complex cost and price dynamics involved.

In any case, there *are*, in every instance, judgments to be made beyond the act of purchase about the intrinsic meanings of cultural products and about their social effects. As the earlier discussion has shown, these products are not inert and neutral objects; rather, they exert profound transformative influences on human consciousness and social life. Precisely because of these influences, an active politics of engagement with the outputs of the cultural economy in contemporary capitalism is an essential accessory of any meaningful democratic order. This remark is not a covert call for censorship of any sort. On the contrary, it proceeds from the simple recognition that culture is always in one way or another something that goes far beyond the purely personal, and is therefore a matter of direct public interest. In contemporary America, of course, there are fluctuating—and perfectly legitimate—waves of political concern from both the Right and the Left about specific aspects of the cultural economy. But systematic,

persistent, and informed public deliberation about the nature of commodi-
fied culture generally and its relation to wider normative social questions
(such as: what kind of culture for what kind of citizenry?) is conspicuously
lacking, and even those brave but essentially conservative efforts by theorists like Bloom (1987) to project the issues into a wider forum of debate
appear to be of interest only to a small minority.

Anticipation of Things to Come

As it happens, these concerns are also intimately bound up with a number
of contentious claims about likely future changes in the organization and
geography of cultural production. A commonly held view of the main evolutionary tendencies in modern capitalism suggests that the combined
effects of digital technologies and globalization are leading to a form of
entropy in which small firms steadily displace large, and in which spatial
dispersal eventually supersedes agglomeration. An alternative perspective
suggests that, on the contrary, the corporate domination of economic life
is likely to intensify, and that core production centers, such as Hollywood
(or Mumbai or Hong Kong), can be expected to extend their grasp on
international trade. We may ask, what does the analysis proposed in this
book suggest about these issues in regard to the economy in general and
the cultural economy in particular?

   Certainly, as digital technologies evolve further, they will begin to pose
challenges to the distributional oligopoly that the Hollywood majors have
enjoyed since the 1920s. Just as television in the 1940s and 1950s drew
audiences away from motion picture theaters, so the eventual supply of a
vastly expanded range of entertainment products via the World Wide Web
will presumably tend to work in the same direction. Nevertheless, we
should also recall that the Hollywood majors learned in the end to turn
television to their own advantage. More recently, they have also adopted
videocassette and DVD technologies as important weapons in their arse-
nal of commercial assets. In the same manner, the majors will predictably
make strenuous efforts to exploit Web-based forms of distribution and
marketing to serve their own interests. The majors' competitive advantages in this matter reside in their ability to bring forth immensely expensive films with dense production values, and in their capacity for mass
marketing of the same films so that audiences are induced to flock to them
in huge numbers, especially in the brief period following their first release.
The precise impacts of digitization and Internet delivery are therefore
not entirely clear-cut. The discussion of the deregulation of television
broadcasting presented in chapter 4 may offer an important clue here.
Deregulation resulted in a great expansion in the number of different television channels available to viewers, leading to significant reductions in the

audiences that the major networks could command. Even so, deregulation never eliminated the networks' continued domination of the market. In view of this observation, a rather plausible inference is that the expanding global output of cinematographic products (including films made by independent Hollywood producers), and the increasing access that consumers will have to them by means of the Internet, will lead to some reduction in the relative, but not absolute, supremacy of the Hollywood majors in final markets.

An important corollary concerns the ways in which the further development of digital network technologies will affect the general tendency of firms in cultural-products industries to cluster together in geographic space. There is some evidence, already hinted at in chapter 3, to suggest that the Internet may favor the more extensive development of satellite production locations in relation to major agglomerations like Hollywood. However, contrary to much received opinion (e.g., O'Brien 1992), there appears to be little likelihood for the time being that the Internet will undermine overall tendencies to agglomeration in the contemporary economy, cultural or otherwise (cf Leamer and Storper 2001; Scott 1998c). The reasons for this may be summarized in two brief remarks. First, the improvement of Internet delivery technologies will almost certainly encourage expansion of the market, leading in turn to extensions of the social division of labor in cultural production. The result of this development is likely to be ever more finely grained inter-firm transactional relations within existing production complexes, giving rise to forces that run strongly counter to de-agglomeration tendencies. Second, to the degree that decentralization of functions from primary agglomerations does occur, it will probably be most evident in the case of relatively standardized, less skilled activities. Higher-level activities of all kinds are more likely to resist decentralization because they typically involve intense and rapidly changing forms of personalized face-to-face contact. For these reasons, significant spatial clusters of producers in the modern cultural economy are unlikely to dissolve, at least for the foreseeable future. The extreme prediction of an overall dispersal of formerly agglomerated production activities to isolated locations scattered across the globe is certainly not anywhere close to realization.

With these remarks in mind, and notwithstanding the hazards of speculating about future outcomes, the evidence appears to suggest on balance that the modern cultural economy is evolving toward a locational pattern made up of multiple clusters of different sizes and market power rooted in a global mosaic of large metropolitan regions. No matter how limited or far-reaching this trend may turn out to be, it will almost certainly involve some incursions into Hollywood's market power and the growth of at least a small number of alternative sites of audiovisual production with global reach. For this and all the other reasons marshaled above, the old dystopic conception of a world moving progressively into a state of cultural uniformity, and more specifically, into a state of uniformly Americanized culture, seems rather unpersuasive. More troubling, perhaps, is the likely continued control by large media conglomerates over significant segments of cultural production for global markets, no matter what the national origins of the dominant firms may be or the geographic sources of their outputs. The burning questions of the future, then, are less likely to be about monopolization of the creative economy by a single agglomeration or country than about the nature of the commercial and corporate interests at the basis of the entire system. In particular, we desperately need more research on the corporate organization of cultural production and its long-run social effects, as well as on the consequences of the wholesale commodification of culture that is currently under way in global capitalism.

Hollywood, at its best and at its worst, offers us a taste of things to come in this respect, just as it provides us with a glimpse of the types of cluster formation and cultural production that can be expected to appear in many other places over the coming decades. In parallel with the role that Silicon Valley plays in the computer and software industry, or the City of London in global business and finance, Hollywood is a central point of reference in the cultural economy of the modern world. Over the last century, Hollywood has displayed remarkable durability, and it will doubtless continue to do so on the basis of its accumulated sunk costs (both private and collective), its potent internal synergies, and its enormous creative energies. But as other cultural-products agglomerations continue their rise around the world, Hollywood is also likely to face intensifying competition whose net result may well be some erosion of the disproportionate dominance on international markets that it has enjoyed at least since the Second World War. Two imponderables, however, weigh heavily on this speculation. In the first place, we can by no means take it for granted that producers of motion pictures and policy makers in other parts of the world will seize the opportunities that now lie before them. In the second place, it is entirely within the bounds of the possible that producers in Hollywood will hit upon a fresh trump card—as they have done so often and so unexpectedly in the past—that carries them forward to new rounds of commercial and cultural supremacy over their actual and potential rivals in other places.

References

Acheson, K., and C. J. Maule (1994). Understanding Hollywood's organization and continuing success. *Journal of Cultural Economics*, 18, 271–300.

Adorno, T. W. (1991). *The Culture Industry: Selected Essays on Mass Culture*. London: Routledge.

Aksoy, A., and K. Robins (1992). Hollywood for the 21st century: Global competition for critical mass in image markets. *Cambridge Journal of Economics*, 16, 1–22.

Allen, J. T. (1976). The decay of the Motion-Picture Patents Company. In T. Balio, ed., *The American Film Industry*, 119–34. Madison: University of Wisconsin Press.

Amman, J. (1996). The transformation of industrial relations in the motion-picture and television industries: Craft and production. In L. S. Gray and R. L. Seeber, eds., *Under the Stars: Essays on Labor Relations in Arts and Entertainment*, 113–55. Ithaca: Cornell University Press.

AMPAS (2001). *Annual Index to Motion Picture Credits (2000 Edition)*. Beverly Hills, CA: The Academy of Motion Picture Arts and Sciences.

Anger, K. (1975). *Hollywood Babylon*. San Francisco: Straight Arrow Books.

Arthur, W. B., Y. M. Ermoliev and Y. M. Kaniovsky (1987). Path-dependent processes and the emergence of macrostructure. *European Journal of Operational Research*, 30, 294–303.

Balio, T. (1976a). A Mature Oligopoly, 1930–1948. In T. Balio, ed., *The American Film Industry*, 213–27. Madison: University of Wisconsin Press.

——— (1976b). Struggles for control, 1908–1930. In T. Balio, ed., *The American Film Industry*, 103–18. Madison: University of Wisconsin Press.

——— (1998). A major presence in all the world's major markets: The globalization of Hollywood in the 1990s. In S. Neale and M. Smith, eds., *Contemporary Hollywood Cinema*, 58–73. London: Routledge.

Barnatt, C. N., and K. Starkey (1994). The emergence of flexible networks in the UK television industry. *British Journal of Management*, 5, 251–60.

Batt, R., S. Christopherson, N. Rightor, and D. V. Jaarsveld (2001). *Net working: Work Patterns and Workforce Policies for the New Media Industry*. Washington, DC: Economic Policy Institute.

Becker, H. S. (1982). *Art Worlds*. Berkeley and Los Angeles: University of California Press.

Berger, S., and M. J. Piore (1980). *Dualism and Discontinuity in Industrial Societies*. Cambridge: Cambridge University Press.

Bernstein, I. (1957). *Hollywood at the Crossroads: An Economic Study of the Motion Picture Industry*. Los Angeles: Hollywood A. F. of L. Film Council.

Bielby, D. D., and W. T. Bielby (1993). The Hollywood graylist: Audience demographics and age stratification among television writers. In M. G. Cantor and

C. L. Zollars, eds., *Current Research on Occupations and Professions*. Vol. 8, *Creators of Culture: Occupations and Professions in Cultural Industries*, 141–72. Greenwich, CT: JAI Press.

Bielby, W. T., and D. D. Bielby (1999). Organizational mediation of project-based labor markets: Talent agencies and the careers of screenwriters. *American Sociological Review*, 64, 64–85.

Blackstone, E. A., and G. W. Bowman (1999). Vertical integration in motion pictures. *Journal of Communication*, 49, 123–39.

Blair, H. (2001). You're only as good as your last job: The labor process and labor market in the British film industry. *Work, Employment, Society*, 15, 149–69.

Blair, H., Grey, S., and K. Randle (2001). Working in film: Employment in a project-based industry. *Personnel Review*, 30, 170–85.

Blair, H., and A. Rainnie (2000). Flexible films? *Media, Culture and Society*, 22, 187–204.

Bloch, S. (2003). Prop house geography: Looking at one aspect of the film industrial complex. Unpublished seminar paper, Department of Geography, UCLA.

Bloom, A. (1987). *The Closing of the American Mind*. New York: Simon & Schuster.

Bonnell, R. (1996). *La Vingt-Cinquième Image: Une Economie de l'Audiovisuel*. Paris: Gallimard.

Bordwell, D., J. Staiger, and K. Thompson (1985). *The Classical Hollywood Cinema: Film Style and Mode of Production to 1960*. New York: Columbia University Press.

Bourdieu, P. (1971). Le marché des biens symboliques. *L' Année Sociologique*, 22, 49–126.

———— (1996). *Sur la Télévision*. Paris: Liber.

Bowser, E. (1990). *The Transformation of Cinema, 1907–1915*. New York: Charles Scribner's Sons.

Branston, G. (2000). *Cinema and Cultural Modernity*. Buckingham: Open University Press.

Braverman, H. (1974). *Labor and Monopoly Capitalism: The Degradation of Work in the Twentieth Century*. New York: Monthly Review Press.

Brown, A., J. O'Connor, and S. Cohen (2000). Local music policies within a global music industry: Cultural quarters in Manchester and Shefield. *Geoforum*, 31, 437–51.

Brownlow, K. (1979). *Hollywood: The Pioneers*. London: Collins.

Cantor, M. G., and J. M. Cantor (1992). *Prime-Time Television: Content and Control*. Newbury Park: Sage.

Cantor, M. G., and A. K. Peters (1980). The employment and unemployment of screen actors in the United States. In W. S. Hendon, J. L. Shanahan, and A. J. MacDonald, eds., *Economic Policy for the Arts*, 210–18. Cambridge, MA: Abt Books.

Carlton, D. W. (1979). Vertical integration in competitive markets under uncertainty. *Journal of Industrial Economics*, 27, 189–209.

Cassady, R. (1958). Impact of the Paramount decision on motion-picture distribution and price making. *Southern California Law Review*, 31, 150–80.

———— (1982). Monopoly in motion-picture production and distribution, 1908–1915. In G. Kindem, ed., *The American Movie Industry: The Business of Motion Pictures*. Carbondale: Southern Illinois University Press.

Caves, R. E. (2000). *Creative Industries: Contacts between Art and Commerce*. Cambridge, MA: Harvard University Press.

Ceplair, L., and S. Englund (1983). *The Inquisition in Hollywood: Politics in the Film Community, 1930–1960*. Berkeley and Los Angeles: University of California Press.

CFTPA (2001). *Profile 2001: Canadian Independent Production: Growth Opportunities in a Period of Consolidation*. Ottawa: Canadian Film and Television Production Association.

Chandler, A. D. (1990). *Scale and Scope: The Dynamics of Industrial Capitalism*. Cambridge, MA: Harvard University Press, Belknap Press.

Chipty, T. (2001). Vertical integration, market foreclosure, and consumer welfare in the cable television industry. *American Economic Review*, 91, 428–53.

Christopherson, S. (1992). The origins of fragmented bargaining power in entertainment media industries. *Industrial Relations Research Association: Proceedings of the Forty-Fourth Annual Meeting*, 10–31.

Christopherson, S., and M. Storper (1986). The city as studio, the world as backlot: The impact of vertical disintegration on the location of the motion-picture industry. *Environment and Planning D: Society and Space*, 4, 305–20.

——— (1989). The effects of flexible specialization on industrial politics and the labor market: the motion-picture industry. *Industrial and Labor Relations Review*, 42, 331–47.

Clark, B., and S. J. Spohr (1998). *Guide to Postproduction for TV and Film*. Boston: Focal Press.

Clark, C. (1951). Urban population densities. *Journal of the Royal Statistical Society, A*, 114, 490–96.

Clarke, C. G. (1976). *Early Film Making in Los Angeles*. Los Angeles: Dawson's Book Shop.

Clough, M. (2000). *Can Hollywood Remain the Capital of the Entertainment Industry?* Los Angeles: Pacific Council on International Policy.

——— (2002). Globalization, digitalization, and Hollywood. In E. J. Heikkela and R. Pizarro, eds., *Southern California and the World*, 17–47. Westport, CT: Praeger.

Coe, N. M. (2000). On location: American capital and the local labor market in the Vancouver film industry. *International Journal of Urban and Regional Research*, 24, 79–91.

——— (2001). A hybrid agglomeration? The development of a satellite-marshallian industrial district in Vancouver's film industry. *Urban Studies*, 38, 1753–75.

Collins, R. (1993). The internationalization of the television program market: Media imperialism or international division of labor? The case of the United Kingdom. In E. M. Noam and J. C. Millonzi, eds., *The International Market in Film and Television Programs*, 125–46. Norwood, NJ: Ablex Publishing.

Cones, J. W. (1997). *The Feature Film Distribution Deal*. Carbondale: Southern Illinois University Press.

Cooke, P., and K. Morgan (1998). *The associational economy: Firms, regions, and innovation*. Oxford: Oxford University Press.

Counter, N. (1992). New collective bargaining strategies for the 1990s: Lessons from the motion-picture industry. *Industrial Relations Research Association: Proceedings of the Forty-Fourth Annual Meeting*, 32–38.

Crane, D. (1992). *The Production of Culture: Media and the Urban Arts*. Newbury Park, CA: Sage.

Creton, L. (1994). *Economie du Cinéma: Perspectives Stratégiques*. Paris: Nathan.

———— (1997). *Cinéma et Marché*. Paris: Armand Colin.

Dale, M. (1997). *The Movie Game: The Film Business in Britain, Europe, and America*. London: Cassell.

Daly, D. A. (1980). *A Comparison of Exhibition and Distribution Patterns in Three Recent Feature Motion Pictures*. New York: Arno Press.

Darré, Y. (1986). Les créateurs dans la division du travail: Le cas du cinéma d'auteur. In R. Moulin, ed., *Sociologie de l'Art*. Paris: La Documentation Française.

David, P. (1985). Clio and the economics of QWERTY. *American Economic Review*, 75, 332–37.

Davis, M. (1990). *City of Quartz: Excavating the Future in Los Angeles*. London: Verso.

———— (1997). Sunshine and the open shop: Ford and Darwin in 1920s Los Angeles. *Antipode*, 29, 356–82.

Davis, R. L. (1993). *The Glamour Factory: Inside Hollywood's Big Studio System*. Dallas: Southern Methodist University Press.

de Vany, A., and W. D. Walls (1997). The market for motion pictures: Rank, revenue, and survival. *Economic Inquiry*, 35, 783–97.

Deakin, S., and S. Pratten (2000). Quasi-markets, transactions costs, and trust: The uncertain effects of market reforms in British television production. *Television and New Media*, 1, 312–54.

DeFillippi, R. J., and M. B. Arthur (1998). Paradox in project-based enterprise: The case of film-making. *California Management Review*, 40, 125–39.

Dissanayake, W. (2000). Issues in world cinema. In J. Hill and P. C. Gibson, eds., *World Cinema: Critical Approaches*, 143–50. Oxford: Oxford University Press.

Donahue, S. M. (1987). *American Film Distribution: The Changing Marketplace*. Ann Arbor: UMI Research Press.

Dorfman, A., and A. Mattelart (1975). *How to Read Donald Duck: Imperialist Ideology in the Disney Comic*. New York: International General.

EIDC (2001). *MOWs—A Three-Year Study: An Analysis of Television Movies of the Week, 1997–1998, 1998–1999, and 1999–2000*. Los Angeles: Entertainment Industry Development Corporation.

Ekinsmyth, C. (2002). Project organization, embeddedness and risk in magazine publishing. *Regional Studies*, 36, 229–43.

Elliott, P. (1972). *The Making of a Television Series: A Case Study in the Sociology of Culture*. London: Constable.

Englander, E. J. (1987). The inside contracting system of production and organization: A neglected aspect of the history of the firm. *Labor History*, 28, 429–46.

Faulkner, R. R. (1983). *Music on Demand: Composers and Careers in the Hollywood Film Industry*. New Brunswick, NJ: Transaction Books.

———— (1985). *Hollywood Studio Musicians: Their Work and Careers in the Recording Industry*. Lanham, MD: University Press of America.

Faulkner, R. R., and A. B. Anderson (1987). Short-term projects and emergent careers: Evidence from Hollywood. *American Journal of Sociology*, 92, 879–909.

FCC (1980). *An Analysis of Television Program Production, Acquisition, and Distribution*. Washington, DC: Federal Communication Commission, Network Inquiry Special Staff.

Feldman, M. P. (2000). Location and innovation: the new economic geography of innovation, spillovers, and agglomeration. In G. L. Clark, M. P. Feldman, and M. S. Gertler, eds., *The Oxford Handbook of Economic Geography*, 373–94. Oxford: Oxford University Press.

Fernett, G. (1973). *Poverty Row*. Satellite Beach, FL: Reef Publications.

——— (1988). *American Film Studios: An Historical Encyclopedia*. Jefferson, NC: McFarland and Co.

Firey, W. I. (1945). Sentiment and symbolism as ecological variables. *American Sociological Review*, 10, 1400–1408.

Florey, R. (1923). *Filmland: Los Angeles et Hollywood, les Capitales du Cinéma*. Paris: Editions de Cinémagazine.

——— (1948). *Hollywood d'Hier et d'Aujourd'hui*. Paris: Editions Prisma.

Florida, R. (2002). *The Rise of the Creative Class*. New York: Basic Books.

Garvin, D. A. (1981). Blockbusters: The economics of mass entertainment. *Journal of Cultural Economics*, 5, 1–20.

Gitlin, T. (1994). *Inside Prime Time*. Berkeley and Los Angeles: University of California Press.

Globerman, S., and A. Vining (1987). *Foreign Ownership and Canada's Feature Film Distribution Sector: An Economic Analysis*. Vancouver, BC: The Fraser Institute.

Gomery, D. (1994). Failed opportunities: The integration of the US motion-picture and television industries. In N. Browne, ed., *American Television: New Directions in History and Theory*. Chur, Switzerland: Harwood Academic Publishers.

——— (1998). Hollywood corporate business practice and periodizing contemporary film history. In S. Neale and M. Smith, eds., *Contemporary Hollywood Cinema*, 47–57. London: Routledge.

Gomery, J. (1976). The coming of the talkies: Invention, innovation, and diffusion. In T. Balio, ed., *The American Film Industry*, 193–211. Madison: University of Wisconsin Press.

Goulekas, K. E. (2001). *Visual Effects in a Digital World: A Comprehensive Glossary of over 7,000 Visual Effects Terms*. San Diego: Morgan Kaufmann.

Grabher, G. (2001). Locating economic action: Projects, networks, localities, institutions. *Environment and Planning A*, 33, 1329–31.

Gray, L. S., and R. L. Seeber (1996). The industry and the unions: An overview. In L. S. Gray and R. L. Seeber, eds., *Under the Stars: Essays on Labor Relations in Arts and Entertainment*, 15–49. Ithaca: Cornell University Press.

Grey, E. (1966). *Behind the Scenes in a Film Studio*. London: Phoenix House.

Guback, T. H. (1969). *The International Film Industry: Western Europe and America since 1945*. Bloomington: Indiana University Press.

Guelke, L. (1974). An idealist alternative in human geography. *Annals of the Association of American Geographers*, 64, 193–202.

Hampton, B. B. (1931). *A History of the Movies*. New York: Covici, Friede.

Hanson, P. K. (1988). *The American Film Institute Catalog of Motion Pictures Produced in the United States*. Berkeley and Los Angeles: University of California Press.

Hesmondhalgh, D. (2002). *The Cultural Industries*. London: Sage.

Hirsch, P. M. (2000). Cultural industries revisited. *Organization Science*, 11, 356–61.

Hirst, P., and J. Zeitlin (1992). Flexible specialization versus post-fordism: Theory, evidence and policy implications. In M. Storper and A. J. Scott, eds., *Pathways to Industrialization and Regional Development*, 70–115. London: Routledge.

Horkheimer, M., and T. W. Adorno (1972). *Dialectic of Enlightenment*. New York: Herder and Herder.

Horne, G. (2001). *Class Struggle in Hollywood, 1930–1950*. Austin: University of Texas Press.

Hoskins, C., S. McFadyen and A. Finn (1997). *Global Television and Film: An Introduction to the Economics of the Business*. Oxford: Clarendon Press.

Hozic, A. A. (2001). *Hollyworld: Space, Power and Fantasy in the American Economy*. Ithaca: Cornell University Press.

Huettig, M. (1944). *Economic Control of the Motion Picture Industry*. Philadelphia: University of Pennsylvania Press.

Hyman, R. (1991). Plus ça change? The theory of production and the production of theory. In A. Pollert, ed., *Farewell to Flexibility?* 259–83. Oxford: Blackwell.

ITA (2001). *Impact of the Migration of US Film and Television Production*. Washington, DC: U.S. Department of Commerce, International Trade Administration.

Izod, J. (1988). *Hollywood and the Box Office, 1895–1986*. London: Macmillan.

Jacobs, L. (1939). *The Rise of the American Film: A Critical History*. New York: Harcourt, Brace and Co.

Jaffe, J. M., and G. Weimann (2000). New lords of the global village? Theories of media domination in the internet era. In R. Wagnleitner and E. T. May, eds., *Here, There and Everywhere: The Foreign Politics of American Popular Culture*, 287–308. Hanover, NH: University Press of New England.

Jameson, F. (1992). *Postmodernism, or, the Cultural Logic of Late Capitalism*. Durhan, NC: Duke University Press.

Jarvie, I. (1992). *Hollywood's Overseas Campaign: The North Atlantic Movie Trade, 1920–1950*. Cambridge: Cambridge University Press.

Jessen, C. (1915). California is world's photoplay stage. *Motion Picture News*, April 3, West Coast section, 127–28.

Jones, C. (1996). Careers in project networks: the case of the film industry. In M. B. Arthur and D. M. Rousseau, eds., *The Boundaryless Career*, 58–75. Oxford: Oxford University Press.

——— (2001). Co-evolution of entrepreneurial careers, institutional rules and competitive dynamics in American film, 1895–1920. *Organization Studies*, 22, 911–44.

Kessler, J. A. (1999). The North American Free Trade Agreement, emerging apparel production networks and industrial upgrading: The Southern California/Mexico connection. *Review of International Political Economy*, 6, 565–608.

Kim, S. (1987). Diversity in urban labor markets and agglomeration economies. *Papers of the Regional Science Association*, 62, 57–70.

Kindem, G. (1982). Hollywood's movie star system: An historical overview. In G. Kindem, ed., *The American Movie Industry: The Business of Motion Pictures*, 79–93. Carbondale: University of Southern Illinois Press.

Kleingartner, A. (2001). Collective bargaining: Hollywood style. *New Labor Forum*, Fall/Winter, 113–21.

Kleingartner, A., and A. Raymond (1988). *Hollywood Goes International: Implications for Labor Relations*. Los Angeles: University of California, Institute of Industrial Relations, Working Paper no. 156.

Koszarski, R. (1990). *An Evening's Entertainment: The Age of the Silent Feature Picture, 1915–1928*. New York: Charles Scribners' Sons.

Kraft, J. P. (1994). Musicians in Hollywood: Work and technological change in entertainment industries. *Technology and Culture*, 35, 289–314.

Kranton, R. E., and D. F. Minehart (2000). Networks versus vertical integration. *RAND Journal of Economics*, 31, 570–601.

Krätke, S. (2002). Network analysis of production clusters: The Potsdam/Babelsberg film industry as an example. *European Planning Studies*, 10, 27–54.

Krugman, P. (1991). *Geography and Trade*. Leuven, Belgium: Leuven University Press.

LARTA (2001). *Hollywood Unstrung, 2*. Los Angeles: Los Angeles Regional Technology Alliance.

Lash, S. (1990). *Sociology of Postmodernism*. London: Routledge.

Lash, S., and J. Urry (1994). *Economies of Signs and Space*. London: Sage.

Latour, B., and S. Woolgar (1979). *Laboratory Life: The Social Construction of Scientific Facts*. Beverly Hills, CA: Sage.

Leamer, E. E., and M. Storper (2001). The geography of the internet age. *Journal of International Business Studies*, 32, 641–65.

Leborgne, D., and A. Lipietz (1988). L'après fordisme et son espace. *Les Temps Modernes*, 501, 75–114.

Lent, J. A. (1998). The animation industry and its offshore factories. In G. Sussman and J. A. Lent, eds., *Global Productions: Labor in the Making of the Information Society*, 239–54. Cresskill, NJ: Hampton Press.

Litman, B. R. (1979). *The Vertical Structure of the Television Broadcasting Industry: The Coalescence of Power*. East Lansing: Michigan State University Business Studies.

——— (1998). *The Motion Picture Mega-Industry*. Boston: Allyn and Bacon.

——— (2001). Motion picture entertainment. In W. Adams and J. Brock, eds., *The Structure of American Industry*, 171–98. 10th ed. Upper Saddle River, NJ: Prentice Hall.

Litman, B. R., and H. Ahn (1998). Predicting financial success of motion pictures: The early 90s experience. In B. Litman, ed., *The Motion-Picture Mega Industry*, 172–97. Boston: Allyn and Bacon.

Litwak, M. (1986). *Reel Power: The Struggle for Influence and Success in the New Hollywood*. New York: Morrow.

Lovell, H., and T. Carter (1955). *Collective Bargaining in the Motion-Picture Industry*. Berkeley: University of California, Institute of Industrial Relations.

Maltby, R. (1998). Nobody knows everything: Post-classical historiographies and consolidated entertainment. In S. Neale and M. Smith, eds., *Contemporary Hollywood Cinema*, 21–44. London: Routledge.

Mattelart, A. (1976). *Multinationales et Systèmes de Communication: Les Appareils Idéologiques de l'Impérialisme*. Paris: Editions Anthropos.

——— (2000). European film policy and the response to Hollywood. In J. Hill and P. C. Gibson, eds., *World Cinema: Critical Approaches*, 94–101. Oxford: Oxford University Press.

Menger, P. M. (1991). Marché du travail artistique et socialisation du risque: Le cas du spectacle. *Revue Française de Sociologie*, 32, 61–74.

——— (1993). L'hégémonie parisienne: Économie et politique de la gravitation artistique. *Annales: Economies, Sociétés, Civilisations*, no. 6, 1565–1600.

——— (1999). Artistic labor markets and careers. *Annual Review of Sociology*, 25, 541–74.

Mezias, J. M., and S. J. Mezias (2000). Resource partitioning, the founding of specialist firms, and innovation: The American feature film industry, 1912–1929. *Organization Science*, 11, 306–22.

Mezias, S. J., and J. C. Kuperman (2000). The community dynamics of entrepreneurship: The birth of the American film industry, 1895–1929. *Journal of Business Venturing*, 16, 209–33.

Michalet, C.-A. (1987). *Le Drôle de Drame du Cinéma Mondial*. Paris: Editions de la Découverte.

Miller, T., N. Govil, J. McMurria, and R. Maxwell (2001). *Global Hollywood*. London: British Film Institute.

Molotch, H. (1996). LA as design product: How art works in a regional economy. In A. J. Scott and E. W. Soja, eds., *The City: Los Angeles and Urban Theory at the End of the Twentieth Century*, 225–75. Berkeley and Los Angeles: University of California Press.

Monitor (1999). *US Runaway Film and Television Production Study Report*. Santa Monica: Monitor Company.

Montgomery, S. S., and M. D. Robinson (1993). Visual artists in New York: What's special about person and place? *Journal of Cultural Economics*, 17, 17–39.

Musser, C. (1994). *The emergence of Cinema: The American Screen to 1907*. Berkeley and Los Angeles: University of California Press.

Negus, K. (1998). Cultural production and the corporation: Musical genres and the strategic management of creativity in the US recording industry. *Media, Culture, and Society*, 20, 359–79.

Nielson, M., and G. Mailes (1995). *Hollywood's Other Blacklist: Union Struggles in the Studio System*. London: British Film Institute.

North, C. J. (1926). Our foreign trade in motion pictures. *Annals of the American Academy of Political and Social Science*, 128, 100–108.

O'Brien, R. O. (1992). *Global Financial Integration: The End of Geography*. London: Royal Institute of International Affairs.

O'Dell, P. (1970). *Griffith and the Rise of Hollywood*. New York: A. S. Barnes.

Palmer, E. O. (1937). *History of Hollywood*. Hollywood: Edwin O. Palmer Publisher.

Palmer, I., R. Dunford, T. Rura-Polley, and E. Baker (2001). Changing forms of organizing: Dualities in using remote collaboration technologies in film production. *Journal of Organizational Change Management*, 14, 190–212.

Pasquier, D., and S. Chalvon-Demersay (1993). Les mines de sel: Auteurs et scénaristes de télévision. *Sociologie du Travail*, no. 4, 409–30.

Paul, A., and A. Kleingartner (1996). The transformation of industrial relations in the motion-picture and television industries. In L. S. Gray and R. L. Seeber, eds.,

Under the Stars: Essays on Labor Relations in Arts and Entertainment, 156–80. Ithaca: Cornell University Press.

Peck, J. (1996). *Work-place: The social regulation of labor markets*. New York: Guilford Press.

Pietersee, J. (1994). Globalization as hybridization. *International Sociology*, 9, 161–84.

Piore, M., and C. Sabel (1984). *The Second Industrial Divide: Possibilities for Prosperity*. New York: Basic Books.

Pitts, M. R. (1997). *Poverty Row Studios, 1929–1940*. Jefferson, NC: McFarland and Co.

Pollert, A. (1991). The orthodoxy of flexibility. In A. Pollert, ed., *Farewell to Flexibility?* 3–31. Oxford: Blackwell.

Ponti, J. (1992). *Hollywood East*. Orlando, FL: Tribune Publishing.

Porter, M. E. (1990). *The Competitive Advantage of Nations*. New York: Free Press.

———— (2001). Regions and the new economics of competition. In A. J. Scott, ed., *Global City-Regions: Trends, Theory, Policy*, 139–57. Oxford: Oxford University Press.

Prince, S. (2000). *A New Pot of Gold: Hollywood under the Electronic Rainbow, 1980–1989*. New York: Charles Scribner's Sons.

Prindle, D. F. (1988). *The Politics of Glamour: Ideology and Democracy in the Screen Actors Guild*. Madison: University of Wisconsin Press.

Puttnam, D., and N. Watson (1998). *Movies and Money*. New York: Knopf.

Ramsaye, T. (1926). *A Million and One Nights: A History of the Motion Picture*. New York: Simon and Schuster.

Rannou, J., and S. Vari (1996). *Les Itinéraires d'Emploi des Cadres, Techniciens, et Ouvriers Intermittents de l'Audiovisuel et des Spectacles*. Paris: Ministère de la Culture, Direction de l'Administration Générale, Département des Etudes et de la Prospective (Observatoire de l'Emploi Culturelle).

Robins, J. A. (1993). Organization as strategy: Restructuring production in the film industry. *Strategic Management Journal*, 14, 103–18.

Robinson, D. (1968). *Hollywood in the Twenties*. New York: A. S. Barnes.

———— (1977). The twenties. In P. Cowie, ed., *Hollywood, 1920–1970*, 9–66. New York: A. S. Barnes.

Rosen, D., and P. Hamilton (1987). *Off-Hollywood: The Making and Marketing of Independent Films*. New York: Grove Weidenfeld.

Ross, M. (1941). *Stars and Strikes: Unionization of Hollywood*. New York: Columbia University Press.

———— (1947). Labor relations in Hollywood. *Annals of the American Academy of Political and Social Science*, no. 254, 58–64.

Russo, M. (1985). Technical change and the industrial district: The role of interfirm relations in the growth and transformation of ceramic tile production in Italy. *Research Policy*, 14, 329–43.

Schatz, T. (1983). *Old Hollywood/New Hollywood Ritual, Art and Industry*. Ann Arbor: UMI Research Press.

———— (1988). *The Genius of the System: Hollywood Film-Making in the Studio Era*. New York: Pantheon.

——— (1997). The return of the Hollywood system. In P. Aufderheide, ed., *Conglomerates and the Media*, 73–106. New York: The New Press.

Scott, A. J. (1981). The spatial structure of metropolitan labor markets and the theory of intra-urban plant location. *Urban Geography*, 2, 1–31.

——— (1984). Territorial reproduction and transformation in a local labor market: The animated film workers of Los Angeles. *Environment and Planning D: Society and Space*, 2, 277–307.

——— (1986). Industrial organization and location: Division of labor, the firm and spatial process. *Economic Geography*, 62, 215–31.

——— (1988a). *Metropolis: From the Division of Labor to Urban Form*. Berkeley and Los Angeles: University of California Press.

——— (1988b). *New Industrial Spaces: Flexible Production Organization and Regional Development in North America and Western Europe*. London: Pion.

——— (1993a). Inter-regional subcontracting patterns in the aerospace industry: The Southern California nexus. *Economic Geography*, 69, 142–56.

——— (1993b). *Technopolis: High-technology Industry and Regional Development in Southern California*. Berkeley and Los Angeles: University of California Press.

——— (1996). Economic decline and regeneration in a regional manufacturing complex: Southern California's household furniture industry. *Entrepreneurship and Regional Development*, 8, 75–95.

——— (1998a). From Silicon Valley to Hollywood: Growth and development of the multimedia industry in California. In H. Braczyk, P. Cooke, and M. Heidenreich, eds., *Regional Innovation Systems*, 136–62. London: UCL Press.

——— (1998b). Multimedia and digital visual effects: An emerging local labor market. *Monthly Labor Review*, 121, 30–38.

——— (1998c). *Regions and the World Economy: The Coming Shape of Global Production, Competition, and Political Order*. Oxford: Oxford University Press.

——— (1999). The US recorded music industry: on the relations between organization, location, and creativity in the cultural economy. *Environment and Planning A*, 31, 1965–84.

——— (2000a). *The Cultural Economy of Cities: Essays on the Geography of Image-Producing Industries*. London: Sage.

——— (2000b). French cinema: Economy, policy and place in the making of a cultural products industry. *Theory, Culture and Society*, 17, 1–38.

——— (2001). Capitalism, cities and the production of symbolic forms. *Transactions of the Institute of British Geographers*, 26, 11–23.

——— (2002). Competitive dynamics of Southern California's clothing industry: The widening global connection and its local ramifications. *Urban Studies*, 39, 1287–1306.

Scott, A. J., and M. Storper (1987). High technology industry and regional development: A theoretical critique and reconstruction. *International Social Science Journal*, 39, 215–32.

Sedgwick, J. (2002). Product differentiation at the movies: Hollywood, 1946 to 1965. *Journal of Economic History*, 62, 676–705.

Segrave, K. (1997). *American Films Abroad: Hollywood's Domination of the World's Movie Screens*. Jefferson, NC: McFarland.

——— (1998). *American Television Abroad: Hollywood's Attempt to Dominate World Television.* Jefferson, NC: McFarland.

Shindler, C. (1996). *Hollywood in Crisis: Cinema and American Society, 1929–1939.* London: Routledge.

Sinclair, J. (1996). Culture and trade: Some theoretical and practical considerations. In E. G. McAnany and K. T. Wilkinson, eds., *Mass Media and Free Trade: NAFTA and the Cultural Industries,* 30–60. Austin: University of Texas Press.

Sklar, R. (1975). *Movie-Made America: A Social History of American Movies.* New York: Random House.

Slide, A. (1994). *Early American Cinema.* Metuchen, NJ: Scarecrow Press.

Smith, M. (1998). Theses on the philosophy of Hollywood history. In S. Neale and S. Smith, eds., *Contemporary Hollywood Cinema,* 3–20. London: Routledge.

Spencer, R. V. (1911). Los Angeles as a producing center. *Moving Picture World,* 8, no. 14, 768.

Staiger, J. (1982). Dividing labor for production control: Thomas Ince and the rise of the studio system. In G. Kindem, ed., *The American Movie Industry: The Business of Motion Pictures.* Carbondale: University of Southern Illinois Press.

——— (2000). *Blockbuster TV: Must-See Sitcoms in the Network Era.* New York: New York University Press.

Stern, S. (1945). *Birth of a Nation.* London: British Film Institute (special supplement to Sight and Sound, Index Series, no. 4).

Stinchcombe, A. L. (1959). Bureaucratic and craft administration of production. *Administrative Science Quarterly,* 4, 168–87.

Storper, M. (1989). The transition to flexible specialization in the US film industry: External economies, the division of labor, and the crossing of industrial divides. *Cambridge Journal of Economics,* 3, 273–305.

——— (1993). Flexible specialization in Hollywood: A reply to Aksoy and Robins. *Cambridge Journal of Economics,* 17, 479–84.

——— (1997). *The Regional World: Territorial Development in a Global Economy.* New York: Guilford Press.

Storper, M., and S. Christopherson (1987). Flexible specialization and regional industrial agglomerations: The case of the US motion-picture industry. *Annals of the Association of American Geographers,* 77, 260–82.

Storper, M., and A. J. Scott (1989). The geographic foundations and social regulation of flexible production complexes. In J. Wolch and M. Dear, eds., *The Power of Geography: How Territory Shapes Social Life,* 21–40. Boston: Unwin Hyman.

——— (1995). The wealth of regions: Market forces and policy imperatives in local and global context. *Futures,* 27, 505–26.

Sturgeon, T. J. (2000). How Silicon Valley came to be. In M. Kenney, ed., *Understanding Silicon Valley: The Anatomy of an Entrepreneurial Region,* 15–47. Stanford, CA: Stanford University Press.

Sydow, J., and U. Staber (2002). The institutional embeddedness of project networks: The case of content production in German television. *Regional Studies,* 36, 215–27.

Thompson, K. (1985). *Exporting Entertainment: America in the World Film Market, 1907–34.* London: British Film Institute.

Torrence, B. T. (1982). *Hollywood: The First Hundred Years.* New York: Zoetrope.

Tyson, L. D. (1992). *Who's Bashing Whom? Trade Conflict in High-Technology Industries*. Washington, DC: Institute for International Economics.

Ursell, G. (2000). Television production: Issues of exploitation, commodification and subjectivity in UK television markets. *Media, Culture and Society*, 22, 805–25.

U.S. Department of Commerce (2001). Migration of US Film and Television Production. Washington, DC.

Varis, T. (1993). Trends in the global traffic of television programs. In E. M. Noam and J. C. Millonzi, eds., *The International Market in Film and Television Programs*, 1–11. Norwood, NJ: Ablex Publishing.

Véron, L. (1999). The competitive advantage of Hollywood industry. *Columbia International Affairs on Line*, https://www.cc.columbia.edu/sec/dlc/ciao/wps/ve101.

Veronis Suhler (2001). *Communications Industry Forecast*. New York: Veronis Suhler Media Merchant Bank, 15th edition.

Vianello, R. (1994). The rise of the telefilm and the networks' hegemony over the motion-picture industry. In N. Browne, ed., *American Television: New Directions in History and Theory*. Chur, Switzerland: Harwood Academic Publishers.

Vogel, H. L. (1998). *Entertainment Industry Economics: A Guide for Financial Analysis*. Cambridge: Cambridge University Press.

Walker, J., and D. Ferguson (1998). *The Broadcast Television Industry*. Boston: Allyn and Bacon.

Wasko, J. (1994). *Hollywood in the Information Age: Beyond the Silver Screen*. Oxford, UK: Polity Press.

——— (1998). Challenges to Hollywood's labor force in the 1980s. In G. Sussman and J. A. Lent, eds., *Global Productions: Labor in the Making of the Information Society*, 173–90. Cresskill, NJ: Hampton Press.

Wasko, J., M. Phillips, and C. Purdie (1993). Hollywood meets Madison Avenue: The commercialization of US films. *Media, Culture and Society*, 15, 271–93.

Weiss, P. R., and R. R. Faulkner (1983). Credits and craft production: Freelance social organization in the Hollywood film industry. *Symbolic Interaction*, 6, 111–23.

Wildman, S. S., and S. E. Siwek (1988). *International Trade in Films and Television*. Cambridge, MA: Ballinger.

Wollen, P. (2002). *Paris Hollywood: Writings on Film*. London: Verso.

Wyatt, J. (1991). High-concept, product differentiation, and the contemporary US film industry. In B. Austen, ed., *Current Research in Film: Audiences, Economics and Law*, 86–105. Norwood, NJ: Ablex.

——— (1994). *High Concept: Movies and Marketing in Hollywood*. Austin: University of Texas Press.

Yau, E. C. M. (2001). Hong Kong cinema in a borderless world. In E. C. M. Yau, ed., *At Full Speed: Hong Kong Cinema in a Borderless World*, 1–28. Minneapolis: University of Minnesota Press.

Zierer, C. M. (1947). Hollywood—world center of motion-picture production. *Annals of the American Academy of Political and Social Science*, 254, 12–17.

Zukin, S. (1995). *The Cultures of Cities*. Oxford: Blackwell.

Index